Coming Out of Feminism?

Coming Out of Feminism?

Edited by
Mandy Merck, Naomi Segal and
Elizabeth Wright

First published 1998

2 4 6 8 10 9 7 5 3 1

Blackwell Publishers Ltd
108 Cowley Road
Oxford OX4 1JF
UK

Blackwell Publishers Inc.
350 Main Street
Malden, Massachusetts 02148
USA

British Library Cataloguing in Publication Data

A CIP catalogue record for this book is available from the British Library.

Library of Congress Cataloging-in-Publication Data

Coming out of feminism? / edited by Mandy
  Merck, Naomi Segal, and Elizabeth Wright.
      p.   cm.
  Includes bibliographical references and index.
  ISBN 1–55786–701–1. — ISBN 1–55786–702–X
  1. Gay and lesbian studies — History.   I. Merck, Mandy.
II. Segal, Naomi.   III. Wright, Elizabeth, 1926– .
HQ75.15.L45   1998
305.9′0664′09 — dc21   98–4889
                                                                  CIP

Typeset in 10 on 12 pt Stempel Garamond
by Best-set Typesetter Ltd., Hong Kong
Printed in Great Britain by TJ Press International, Padstow, Cornwall

This book is printed on acid-free paper

Contents

Contributors

Emily Apter is Professor of Comparative Literature and French at UCLA. Her books include *Feminizing the Fetish: Psychoanalysis and Narrative Obsession in Turn-of-the-century France* (1991), *Fetishism as Cultural Discourse* (1993) coedited with William Pietz, and *André Gide and the Codes of Homotextuality* (1987). *Continental Drift: From National Characters to Virtual Subjects* is forthcoming from Chicago University Press (Fall, 1998) and she is currently working on two projects, one entitled 'Spaces of the Demimonde/Subcultural Identifications: 1890s–1990s', the other on 'Transnational Aesthetics: Translation and the Global Market'.

Judith Butler is Chancellor's Professor of Rhetoric and Comparative Literature at the University of California, Berkeley. She is the author of *Gender Trouble: Feminism and the Subversion of Identity* (1990) and *Bodies That Matter: On the Discursive Limits of Sex* (1993). Her most recent publications are *Excitable Speech: A Politics of the Performative* (1997) and *The Psychic Life of Power: Theories in Subjection* (1997).

Trevor Hope teaches Comparative Literature in the Department of Modern Languages and Cultures at the University of Rochester. He is the author of 'Melancholic modernity: the hom(m)osexual symptom and the homosocial corpse' in *differences* 6, 2/3 (1994) and of 'Sexual indifference and the male homosexual imaginary' in *diacritics* 24, 2/3 (1994). He is currently working on a book tentatively entitled *Radclyffe Hall and the Social Body*.

Biddy Martin is Associate Professor of German Studies and Women's Studies at Cornell University. She is currently serving a five-year term as Associate Dean of the College of Arts and Sciences. Her publications include *Woman and Modernity: The (Life)Styles of Lou Andreas-Salomé* (1991) and *Femininity Played Straight: The Significance of Being Lesbian* (1996).

Mandy Merck teaches on the Sexual Dissidence MA programme at the University of Sussex. The former series editor of Channel Four

Television's 'Out on Tuesday', she is the author of *Perversions: Deviant Readings* (1993) and editor of *After Diana* (1998). Her next book is *In Your Face: Essays on the Representation of Sex* (forthcoming).

Gayle Rubin has been involved as a scholar and activist in feminism and gay politics for nearly thirty years. A collection of her essays is being published by the University of California Press, and she is working to finish a book on the gay male leather community of San Francisco. She currently teaches Women's Studies at the University of California, Santa Cruz.

Naomi Segal is Professor of French Studies at the University of Reading. She is the author of *The Banal Object* (1981), *The Unintended Reader* (1986), *Narcissus and Echo* (1988) and *The Adulteress's Child* (1992) and the co-editor of *Freud in Exile* (1988) and *Scarlet Letters* (1996). Her next book, *André Gide: Pederasty and Pedagogy*, will appear in 1998.

William J. Spurlin is Visiting Scholar at Columbia University. He co-edited *Reclaiming the Heartland: Lesbian and Gay Voices from the Midwest* (1996) and *The New Criticism and Contemporary Literary Theory: Connections and Continuities* (1995). His essays on lesbian and gay studies and queer theory have appeared in numerous journals and in collections such as *Literature and Psychology*. Most recently he has published on cultural rhetoric and the politics of sexual and racial identity in the critical reception of James Baldwin in the early 1960s.

Carole-Anne Tyler is Associate Professor of English at the University of California, Riverside, where she teaches courses in film and visual culture and sexuality, literary and cultural theory, and modern fiction. She is the author of a book forthcoming from Routledge, *Female Impersonation*, portions of which have appeared in *differences, Inside/Out: Lesbian Theories, Gay Theories* and *Theory Between the Disciplines*.

Elizabeth Wright is a Fellow of Girton College, Cambridge. She is the author of *Psychoanalytic Criticism: Theory in Practice* (1984), *Postmodern Brecht: A Re-Presentation* (1989), and the editor of *Feminism and Psychoanalysis: A Critical Dictionary* (1992). Her forthcoming books are *Psychoanalytic Criticism: A Reappraisal* (second edition, 1998), *Speaking Desires can be Dangerous: Psychoanalysis, Language and Literary Theory* (1999), and *The Žižek Reader*, co-edited with Edmond Wright (1999).

Acknowledgements

The editors and publishers gratefully acknowledge the following for permission to reproduce copyright material:

Gayle Rubin for 'Sexual Traffic' which first appeared in *differences*, vol. 6, nos 2 and 3, Summer–Fall, 1994.

The Johns Hopkins University Press for Biddy Martin's 'Sexualities without Genders and Other Queer Utopias', which first appeared in *Diacritics*, vol. 24, no. 2–3 (Summer–Fall 1994), pp. 104–21.

Jason Aronson Publishers Inc. for the tables in chapter 3, taken from Irving Bieber et al., *Homosexuality: A Psychoanalytic Study*, Jason Aronson Inc. 1988.

The publishers apologize for any errors or omissions in the above list and would be grateful to be notified of any corrections that should be incorporated in the next edition on reprint of this book.

Introduction

Profound and intuitable as the bonds between feminism and
antihomophobia often are in society, the two are not the same.
As the alliance between them is not automatic or
transhistorical, it will be most fruitful if it is analytic and
unpresuming.

Eve Kosofsky Sedgwick, 1985[1]

'Gay studies' as an intellectual event was able to begin at a
highly sophisticated, theoretical level precisely because of the
informing influence of feminism.

Joseph Boone, 1992[2]

Queer theory, particularly in its more academic manifestation,
is often posed as a reponse to a certain kind of feminist and
lesbian theorizing that is now deemed hopelessly retro, boring,
realist, modernist, about shoring up identity rather than its
deconstruction.

Suzanne Danuta Walters, 1996[3]

The title of this collection questions the relation of what are now widely
understood to be two fields of study,[4] although, as the epigraphs
above suggest, the actual purview of their respective projects is much less
certain. Is it, as Eve Sedgwick suggests, a question of 'feminism and
antihomophobia'? Or, in the terms of Joseph Boone, 'gay studies' and
'feminism'? Or is it a matter of 'queer theory' counterposed to 'feminist
and lesbian theorizing'? Taken chronologically, these descriptions can be
organized into a disciplinary history, in which the antihomophobic
project espoused by Sedgwick in regard to 'the entire spectrum of male
relations'[5] develops into a (still male?) field of endeavour described by
Boone as 'gay studies' (despite his own citation of the 1987 conference at
Yale's Center for Lesbian and Gay Studies), and then becomes, as 'queer
theory', distinguished by its opposition, if not to feminist and lesbian
theory in general, then to that 'of a certain kind'.

If this is one genealogy of an academic division of labour, it is not by
any means the only one. In his 1992 reflections in 'Inventing a Lesbian and

Gay Studies', Ken Plummer recommends that the 'future problem to consider is not so much homophobia, which will continue to exist in pockets, but heterosexism. I think feminists have been much clearer about this than gay men in the past'[6] – a clarity which he then attributes to two theorists who would identify as both feminists and lesbians, Gayle Rubin and Adrienne Rich. Two points might be raised in reply to Plummer's history – first, the continued marginalization of lesbianism as a specific sexual and political practice by its equation with feminism; and second, the uncertain distinction drawn between 'homophobia' and 'heterosexism'. Certainly Rubin's critique of 'obligatory' and Rich's of 'compulsory' heterosexuality[7] indict a systematic regulation of sexual object and identification which sustains gender inequality. But Sedgwick also argues that homophobia is 'an immensely potent tool [. . .] for the manipulation of every form of power that [is] refracted through the gender system', notably the male exchange of women which is Rubin's central consideration. Moreover, other histories trace a critical discussion of heterosexuality, if not 'heterosexism' or 'heteronormativity', back to the founding texts of the modern women's movement. In a recent introduction to their reader, *Feminism and Sexuality*, Stevi Jackson and Sue Scott cite Anna Koedt's 1972 article, 'The Myth of the Vaginal Orgasm', to assert that an 'incipient critique of heterosexuality was evident in discussions among feminists from the earliest years', although Koedt's suggestion 'that men might not be necessary to women's sexual pleasure [. . .] did not extend this to advocacy of lesbianism'.[8]

Conversely, the editors of *GLQ: A Journal of Lesbian and Gay Studies* insist on the pioneering role of lesbians and gay men in the analysis of sexuality. Succumbing to what seems a virtually irresistible temptation to write their own version of this history, they introduce the first issue of their journal with an explanation of its title. Arguing for 'work that will bring a queer perspective to bear on any and all topics touching on sex, and sexuality', they continue:

> We have used the terms 'lesbian' and 'gay' in order to
> foreground what is specifically sexual about the subject matter
> of GLQ. With these words we want to combat the perennial
> dangers of sexual despecification, that ultimately hostile process
> whereby 'lesbian and gay studies' gets redescribed as 'gender
> studies', for example, in order to domesticate it or to make it
> more academically palatable. We consider these denominations
> – 'lesbian' and 'gay' – indispensable; by invoking them in our
> subtitle we intend to acknowledge the political and scholarly
> work that has historically been done under the banner of

lesbians and gay men, to acknowledge the fact that ideological critique on the basis of sexuality really began with lesbians and gay men.[9]

We counterpose these rival accounts to question the possibility of establishing where 'ideological critique on the basis of sexuality [. . .] really began'. Informed by a characteristically queer scepticism about all such originary claims, this collection is intended to interrogate the prevailing divisions of priority and project in sexual politics and its studies. Nevertheless, the contents of this fantasy demand consideration. Often, the presumption of feminism's seniority constructs it as the matrix, womb or closet from which lesbian/gay and then queer consciousness is said to have emerged: older, but not necessarily wiser in a political moment which prizes 'post'eriority. If this is so, have contemporary sexual politics (including what is often called 'post-feminism') not just 'come out' but also 'grown out' (in both senses) of their presumed predecessor? Does this explain the widespread rumours of the decline of women's studies in the academy, replaced by a more contemporary consideration of sexuality? Should feminism accept that it has done its work and productively led, like all good ideas, to ways of thinking that supersede it? Or is the relation less one of precedence and supersession than of continuing confrontation, positive and negative, between two bodies of thought more similar than different? In the present-continuous tense of our title – and our cover illustration – is there the suggestion of a motion-from or a motion-with?

Whether the chicken or the egg came first, all radical movements are about emergence, intellectual and political. The US Civil Rights movement and the European confluence of 1968 provided a surge of confidence in the possibilities of liberation, and it is not insignificant that second-wave feminism in both continents grew from and against those revolts. Feminism is the theory of a political practice which exposes as arbitrary the most taken-for-granted difference, that of two supposedly biological sexes extrapolated into two genders. Among the terms of the feminist argument, the sexual relation with a male other was always central to the identification of the personal with the political, and women's right to desire was implicit in this. What was not at first clearly faced was the complexity of desire and pleasure, its complicity with power and danger and its anti-political reliance on unconscious wishes for uncontrol. Such an inkling that sexual desire has no heroes or villains belongs to the early 1980s moment of the debates between feminists. When Adrienne Rich argued for a lesbian continuum across the range of women's loyalties and support for one another, she asserted a version of desire that would not distinguish between solidarity and sexuality. But if to be feminist was de facto to be in some vague sense lesbian, what became of the specificity of lesbian desire, of sexuality as a practice and an experience? The eighties became the era of internal differences between feminists, increasingly acrimonious as they multiplied logically across boundaries of race, class, ethnicity, age, and sexuality.

The gay liberation movement follows a similar trajectory during the same period, with identity politics and the claim to pride initially masking internal differences of sex, class, ethnicity or practice. Shaking off the inversion theory was one important way of loosening the traditional (post-Greek) 'right-sex-wrong-gender' knot which had survived into the writing of such as Proust and Hall. Gay masculinity was a kind of man-identification similar to the woman-identification of the feminist lesbian. AIDS is the wild card that brought an altogether new politics of solidarity, vulnerability and affirmation. Within the body's active strengths and weaknesses, desire may just be one function among many.

As difference becomes itself the object of desire and analysis, and every body the living site of differences, the straight lines of all the binaries begin to unravel. In the 1990s 'queer' emerges from the closet of insult, but also from the egg of 'lesbian and gay' as well as the womb of feminism. It replaces passing with crossing, and goes its own unpredictable way. So far it is still in the first stages of animation; but has that urge to name as you proclaim already started the process of solidification, and will the twin impulses to solidarity and intellection inevitably stop its free flight along the borderlines?

In 'Sexualities without Genders and Other Queer Utopias' (reprinted in this volume),[10] **Biddy Martin** criticizes much lesbian and gay scholarship for implicitly conceiving 'gender in negative terms, in the terms of fixity, miring or subjection to the indicatively female body, with the consequence that escape from gender [...] becomes the goal and putative achievement.'

Such scholarship's claim is one of 'coming out of feminism' in the sense of an erotic emergence from a de-sexualized theory that pertained only to gender and specifically only to one gender. Joseph Bristow, on the other hand, noting the coincidence of Millett's *Sexual Politics* with Stonewall, argues that feminism actually helped to bring the ideal of homosexual equality 'proudly out of the closet'.[11] More typically, however, Joseph Boone represents this history as one of generation, with feminism as a parent-figure to 'a discipline and an agenda that claim to be neither superior to nor the same as feminism, but rather in an ever-present relation of contiguity with the originating politics of feminism'.[12] If this originary role is added to the implicitly female gendering of the feminist project, the result is maternity, or in Eve Sedgwick's axiomatic definition of the object of gender struggle, 'control of women's (biologically) distinctive reproductive capability'.[13]

Distinguishing the women's movement from queer politics on this basis, Sedgwick, as Martin elucidates, makes the former into the body of thought from which the latter must be born. Where the remit of feminism is narrowly physical, the 'drag or limit' of an interest premised on anatomy, those politics which purport to address sexual practices defy the fixity which is ascribed, however minimally, to gender. Read retrospectively from this position, Boone and Bristow's genealogies seem rather more troubling, with Gay Studies' 'ever-present relation of contiguity' to feminism coming to resemble infantile separation anxiety, with Kate Millett – if not the mother of Gay Liberation, at least its midwife – proudly delivering it from the closet.

Perhaps the most influential articulation of this division of disciplines is that of **Gayle Rubin**, whose original theory of a 'sex-gender system' in which both gender identity and sexual desire derive from the organization of kinship, was crucially reformulated in her subsequent 'Thinking Sex'. There, citing Foucault's claim that modern societies superimpose a new apparatus of pleasure ('sexuality') on the older regulation of partners ('kinship'), Rubin revised her previous position to argue 'that it is essential to separate gender and sexuality analytically to more accurately reflect their separate social existence'.[14] Drawing a comparison with the failure of Marxism to address the non-economic structures of gender, Rubin warned against rival feminist attempts at theoretical totalization, to call for an explanatory pluralism which could acknowledge both the autonomy of, and the relations between, gender hierarchy and the social organization of sexuality. Subsequently, **Judith Butler** has commented on Rubin's revised position to argue that

> Politically, the costs are too great to choose between feminism,
> on the one hand, and radical sexual theory, on the other.
> Indeed, it may be precisely the time to take part in what Rubin
> in 1984 foresaw as the necessity, 'in the long run', for feminism
> to offer a critique of gender hierarchy that might be
> incorporated into a radical theory of sex, and for radical sexual
> theory to challenge and enrich feminism.[15]

In a conversation with Butler (reprinted from the journal, *differences*),[16] Rubin looks back at the circumstances which prompted both essays and forward to descriptive research which will recognize the specificity of contemporary sexual subcultures.

Such an impulse towards reasoned cooperation informs the essay by **William Spurlin**, whose personal debt to a generation of feminist teachers has made him particularly aware of the need for 'new alliances focusing on interarticulations of power'. Such coalitions would be dedicated to asking how the historical–political position of women (lesbian or not) and gay men 'converge by virtue of being situated in (ef)feminized positions in relation to patriarchal power'. In examining how the technologies of gender operate to insert subjects into an arbitrary gender system, he argues that we must resist any simple split between gender and sexuality. How else can we understand the pathologizing of 'Gender Identity Disorder' in male children within the current classifications of American psychiatry?

The fraught relation to a femininity conceived as aberrant and repulsive is the subject also of **Emily Apter's** essay on 'Gynophobia', a preoccupation she finds in what seems the least likely site, among feminists. In the 1920s flowering of lesbian-feminist creativity in the Paris of Natalie Barney, Djuna Barnes and Gertrude Stein, 'the fictitious value of woman' was stringently attacked, and the female condition judged a 'catastrophe'. Similarly, in today's feminism, women may still be marginalizing their own sex by a deep-seated dread of femininity which leads us paradoxically to trust the male drag-artist sooner than the femme.

In 'Mother, Don't You See I'm Burning?', **Trevor Hope** stays in the 1920s generation to reconsider the frequently noted opposition in Radclyffe Hall's fiction between a female homosociality represented, in *The Unlit Lamp*, by woman-identification and romantic friendship, and the female homosexuality of *The Well of Loneliness*, represented by congenital inversion and sexual desire. As he observes, this opposition is often characterized as one of feminism versus lesbianism, a polarity which his own reading of both novels rejects in order to propose female homosexuality as neither a relation of simple gendered semblance nor one of converse disidentification with women, but rather a historically specific complex of contradictory filiations. In Hope's account, Hall's fiction cannot reconcile feminism and lesbianism in a single utopian vision, but nor does it pit the two politics against each other in a static antinomy of identity and difference.

One crucial difficulty in articulating the current relation of feminist theory to lesbian and gay studies is the challenge posed to the latter in the 1990s by 'queer theory'. Variously defined against a politics of assimilation or the pursuit of toleration, against presumptive identities conferred by gender or sexual preference, or indeed against any 'certain political agenda', 'queerness', in Alexander Doty's admirably open attempt at a functional definition, 'is a quality related to any expression that can be marked as contra-, non-, or anti-straight'.[17] As for a definition of 'straight', Michael Warner supplies 'regime of the normal . . . and normal includes normal business in the academy'. This makes queer theory the anti-discipline discipline, not only sexualizing the academy's 'desexualized spaces',[18] but also subverting the norms of curricular division and research specialization, queering all theory.

Or so its advocates would argue. Examining their claims, **Carole-Anne Tyler** considers the queer theorization of cinema spectatorship, particularly its claims to challenge the heterosexism and general normativity of the feminist film studies which it would supersede. In a discussion of Laura Mulvey's influential reconsideration of the 'apparatus theory' developed by psychoanalytic critics of the cinema, she argues that no such 're-visions' have resisted the narcissistic urge to match the spectacle to its spectator. (Thus Mulvey's counter-cinema becomes the modernist mirror of its disintegrated subject.) Rereading a much discussed lesbian film, Sheila MacLaughlin's *She Must Be Seeing Things*, Tyler maintains that its own heterogeneous elements are themselves repressed by 'queer' readings, which seek the cinematic recognition of an identifiable homosexuality, rather than the differences which defy identity.

'The job of feminism', **Naomi Segal** observes in her contribution to this collection, 'is to continue asking after the place of the feminine'. But if the feminist critic of straight male-authored fiction can no longer ignore the ambiguities of her own engagement with the power structures she delights in exposing, how much more acute are the implications of her relation to gay men's writing. André Gide offers a particularly complex case in point, for Gidean pederasty is predicated on relations which are familial but not oedipal, and a sexuality which is skin-deep rather than penetrative; moreover, femininity in his writing is the object of both an oblique desire and of a certain identification. While Gide's authorial voice operates the mastery of his sex, class and race, and his homosexuality champions the chaste virility of the Greeks, his argument also carries a strain of erotic disembodiment that turns masculine excess into its obverse. The pleasure of the feminist critic then becomes something more perversely voyeuristic as she finds her own ambiguities reflected or pre-rempted.

Another version of 'de-masculinization' seems to be at work in the asceticism which Leo Bersani ascribes to male homosexual desire. In an argument derived from Foucault's claim for an 'isomorphism' between the subordinate status of women and male homosexuals in ancient Greece, Bersani reads the homophobia of contemporary discourses on AIDS as the denigration of all forms of sexual submission. Citing radical feminist critiques of penile penetration as personal violation, Bersani goes on to claim that in such invited violation lies the merit of gay men's sexuality – its challenge to the masculine pride in social and sexual dominance. But, as **Mandy Merck** points out in her reading of texts by gay authors and feminists alike, the agonistic representation of penetrative intercourse tends to restore the penis to the phallic heroism which they purport to criticize, with femininity once more made synonymous with passivity, even as erotic receptivity is yet again assigned to self-destruction.

In 'Coming Out of the Real: Knots and Queries', **Elizabeth Wright** argues that the discussion of sexuality must take account of 'the historical limits of the possibilities of change, not a particular subject's object-choice'. Making use of Joan Copjec's tracing of the logical link between Kant's antinomies and Lacan's sexuation formulas arising from the failure of definitions to apply to what is strictly infinite, she argues that sexualities emerge from the real, enjoining a binary sexual difference upon all speaking beings. Nevertheless, such sexualities will always exceed the divisions laid down by any symbolic system, and this invites the subversions that a radical democracy can profit by.

Adding to a debate as urgent as it is energetic, this book is an attempt to understand how relations of contiguity and emergence may develop old debts and differences into new contentions and cooperations. In many of the essays the question of the feminine has been crucial, central as it is to both sexuality and gender, to queer, gay and straight. It remains vexed and will continue to vex (or hex?) all ways of understanding the political moment in which we write. It haunts the image with which we began, and it seems apt to end this introduction on the same question: between what comes out and what was there before, how can co-existence remain argumentative but fruitful?

Mandy Merck
Naomi Segal
Elizabeth Wright

Notes

1   Eve Kosofsky Sedgwick, *Between Men: English Literature and Male Homosexual Desire*, New York: Columbia University Press, 1985, p. 21.

2   Joseph Boone, 'Of Me(n) and Feminism', in David Porter (ed.),

Between Men and Feminism, London and New York: Routledge, 1992, p. 29.

3   Suzanne Danuta Walters, 'From Here to Queer: Radical Feminism, Postmodernism, and the Lesbian Menace (Or, Why Can't a Woman Be More Like a Fag?)', *Signs*, vol. 21 no. 41 (1996), p. 842.

4   See, for example, the introduction to Henry Abelove, Michèle Aina Barale and David M. Halperin (eds), *The Lesbian and Gay Studies Reader*, New York and London: Routledge, 1993, p. xv: 'Lesbian/gay studies does for sex and sexuality approximately what women's studies does for gender.'

5   Craig Owens, 'Outlaws: Gay Men in Feminism', in Alice Jardine and Paul Smith (eds), *Men in Feminism*, New York and London: Methuen, 1987, p. 221.

6   Ken Plummer, 'Speaking its Name: Inventing a Lesbian and Gay Studies', in Ken Plummer (ed.), *Modern Homosexualities*, London and New York: Routledge, 1992, p. 19.

7   Gayle Rubin, 'The Traffic in Women: Notes on the "Political Economy" of Sex', in Rayna R. Reiter (ed.), *Toward an Anthropology of Women*, New York: Monthly Review, 1975; Adrienne Rich, 'Compulsory Heterosexuality and Lesbian Existence', *Signs* vol. 5 no. 4 (1980), pp. 631–60.

8   Stevi Jackson and Sue Scott, 'Sexual Skirmishes and Feminist Factions: Twenty-Five Years of Debate on Women and Sexuality' in Scott and Jackson (eds), *Feminism and Sexuality*, Edinburgh: Edinburgh University Press, 1966, pp. 12–13.

9   'From the Editors', *GLQ: A Journal of Lesbian and Gay Studies*, vol. 1 no. 1, 1993, p. iii.

10 Biddy Martin, 'Sexualities without Genders and Other Queer Utopias', *Femininity Played Straight: The Significance of Being Lesbian*, New York and London: Routledge, 1996.

11 Joseph Bristow, 'Men after Feminism', in *Between Men and Feminism*, p. 57.

12 Joseph Boone, 'Of Me(n) and Feminism, in *Between Men and Feminism*, p. 29.

13 Eve Kosofsky Sedgwick, *Epistemology of the Closet*, Berkeley: University of California Press, 1990, pp. 27–8.

14 Gayle Rubin, 'Thinking Sex: Notes for a Radical Theory of the Politics of Sexuality', in Carole S. Vance (ed.), *Pleasure and Danger: Exploring Female Sexuality*, Boston, London, Melbourne: Routledge & Kegan Paul, 1984, p. 308.

15 Judith Butler, 'Against Proper Objects', *differences*, vol. 6 nos. 2–3, Summer–Fall 1994, p. 15.

16 'Sexual Traffic', *differences*, vol. 6, nos. 2–3, Summer-Fall 1994, pp. 62–99.
17 Alexander Doty, 'Introduction: What Makes Queerness Most?', *Making Things Perfectly Queer*, Minneapolis and London: University of Minnesota Press, 1993, p. xv.
18 Michael Warner, 'Introduction' to Michael Warner (ed.), *Fear of a Queer Planet*, Minneapolis and London: University of Minnesota Press, 1993, p. xxvi.

Chapter 1

Sexualities without Genders and Other Queer Utopias

Biddy Martin

For a long time I have been concerned about a tendency among some lesbian, bisexual, and gay theorists and activists to construct "queerness" as a vanguard position that announces its newness and advance over against an apparently superseded and now anachronistic feminism with its emphasis on gender. The popular gay press has been full of comparisions between the dull, literal-minded, uptight seventies and the sexually ambiguous, fun, performative nineties.[1] I welcome challenges to lesbian-feminist constructions of identity that appear to sacrifice complex analyses of sexual and social realities to desires for homogeneity and stability (see Martin). I also remain convinced of the potential of "Queer Studies" to provoke more complex accounts of gender and sexuality. But I am worried about the occasions when antifoundationalist celebrations of queerness rely on their own projections of fixity, constraint, or subjection onto a fixed ground, often onto feminism or the female body, in relation to which queer sexualities become figural, performative, playful, and fun. In the process, the female body appears to become its own trap, and the operations of misogyny disappear from view.

Before I turn my focus to specific "queer" codings of gender, I want to dwell for a moment on the helpful criticisms made by "queer theorists" of feminist theory, and in particular, on the separation in much feminist work between anatomical sex and social gender.[2] First, the separation of anatomical sex and social gender implied by the sex/gender split has had the consequence of leaving the assumption of biological sexual difference intact and of introducing a damaging body/mind split. The body, in a great deal of work that focuses exclusively on social gender, is rendered either irrelevant or conceived as an inert object of social control. The complex relations between the body and psyche often disappear from such accounts, which often conflate or equate social and political identity with identity at the psychic or psychological levels. In these moves, one becomes one's social or political identity or identities. Second, insofar as feminists have reduced the possibilities of gender to just two, that is, men and women, gender has come to do the work of stabilizing and universalizing binary opposition at other levels, including male and female sexuality, the work that the assumption of biological sex differences once did. As a number of different feminists have argued, the assumption of a core gender identity, now conceived as an effect of social construction, may also serve to ground and predict what biology, for constructionists, no longer can, namely, the putative unity or self-sameness of any given person's actual sex or gender. And, finally, to the extent that gender is assumed to constitute the ultimate ground of (women's) experience, it has, in much feminist work, come to colonize every aspect of experience, psychological and social, as the ultimate root and explanation of that experience, consigning us, once again, to the very terms that we have sought to exceed, expand, or redefine. When an uncritical assumption of the category "women" becomes the "subject of feminism," then gender politics begins to take the form of what Eve Sedgwick has characterized as the injunction to "identif[y] with/as" women (*Epistemology of the Closet* 62).[3]

For those of us who have felt constrained, even obscured, by feminists' injunctions to identify with and as women, over against men and masculinity, the celebration of an antinormative queerness has been a welcome relief.[4] The analytic and political separation of gender and sexuality has been the rallying cry of a great deal of queer theory that seeks to complicate hegemonic assumptions about the continuities between anatomical sex, social gender, gender identity, sexual identity, sexual object choice, and sexual practice. The work of complicating our theories has too often proceeded, however, by way of polemical and ultimately reductionist accounts of the varieties of feminist approaches to just one feminism, guilty of the humanist trap of making a self-same, universal category of "women" – defined as other than men – the subject of feminism. At its worst, feminism has been seen as more punitively policing than mainstream culture.

The evacuation of interior essences and normative, disciplinary assumptions of gender cores and consistencies has been critical to the shift in postmodern queer theories from biological and psychological determinisms to analyses of social norms and their complex roles in the formation of gendered identities. At the theoretical level, our efforts to clear away foundationalisms and evacuate interior essences have left us with an expanded vocabulary for talking about discursive and social complexities. I will argue here, however, that lesbian and gay work fails at times to realize its potential for reconceptualizing the complexities of identity and social relations, at moments when, almost in spite of itself, it at least implicitly conceives gender in negative terms, in the terms of fixity, miring, or subjection to the indicatively female body, with the consequence that escape from gender, usually in the form of disembodiment and always in the form of gender crossings, becomes the goal and the putative achievement. I want to suggest that race often gets cast in the terms of fixity and miring in the same moves that gender and identity itself do. I am particularly interested, here, in a resistance to something called "the feminine," played straight, and in a tendency to assume that when it is not camped up or disavowed, it constitutes a capitulation, a swamp, something maternal, ensnared and ensnaring. Too often, antideterminist accounts that challenge feminist norms depend on the visible difference represented by cross-gender identifications to represent the mobility and differentiation that "the feminine" or "the femme" supposedly cannot.

From the perspectives of those of us who have experienced the pain of being cast as queer in the most negative possible terms, or whose sense of self involves rebelliousness against the normalizing constraints of conventional femininity, the punishments that accrue to femininity itself have, perhaps, become less visible than the punitive consequences of failing to conform, and our defenses against the vulnerabilities and degradations associated with femininity have become stronger. Queer theory and politics necessarily celebrate transgression in the form of visible difference from norms that are then exposed to be norms, not natures or inevitabilities. Gender and sexual identities are arranged, in much of this work, around demonstrably defiant deviations and configurations. Surfaces, then, take priority over interiors and depths and even rule conventional approaches to them out of bounds as inevitably disciplinary and constraining. What requires more emphasis, in this context, is that the subordination of women does not follow simply from the failure to conform to convention, but also from the performance or embodiment of it. Reconfiguring gender requires reconfiguring the institutional and discursive conditions that structure and are structured by regulatory norms, but also reconfiguring interiorities, and, in particular, distributions of power, autonomy, attachment, and vulnerability.

I have become more convinced that too thorough an evacuation of interiority, too total a collapse of the boundaries between public and private, and too exclusive an understanding of psychic life as the effect of normalization can impoverish the language we have available for thinking about selves and relationships, even as they apparently enrich our vocabularies for thinking about social construction. There are connections between and among the emphasis on visible differences from norms, the evacuation of interiorities, the reduction of subjectivity to effects of power, and the invisibility or fixity attributed to the femme or to femininity. Women fade again in the face of visible signifiers of difference from norms.

It is in this context that I want to discuss the work of critics and theorists who have been most suggestive and important to my own thinking about the relations between feminist and queer projects. I will begin with Eve Sedgwick's important efforts to reconceptualize the relations between gender and sexuality, and the status of the body in that distinction. In *Epistemology of the Closet*, Sedgwick generates a set of axioms for antihomophobic analysis. The first, and my personal favorite, makes the only apparently self-evident claim that "people are different from each other" (*EC* 22). Sedgwick goes on to make the bold point that "every single theoretically or politically interesting project of postwar thought has finally had the effect of delegitimating our space for asking or thinking in detail about the multiple, unstable ways in which people may be like or different from each other" (*EC* 23). Feminism is included among those projects. In her more recent work, *Tendencies*, Sedgwick succeeds again in providing wonderfully expansive language for those potentially discontinuous aspects of self that "'sexual identity' is supposed to organize into a seamless and univocal whole" (*Tendencies* 8). "Queer," she suggests, "can refer to: the open mesh of possibilities, gaps, overlaps, dissonances and resonances, lapses and excesses of meaning when the constituent elements of anyone's gender, of anyone's sexuality aren't made (or *can't be* made) to signify monolithically." However, against any tendency to eradicate the association of queerness with homosexuality, Sedgwick warns that "for anyone to disavow those meanings, or to displace them from the term's definitional center, would be to dematerialize any possibility of queerness itself" (*Tendencies* 8).

The second axiom of Sedgwick's antihomophobic analysis in *Epistemology of the Closet* reads: "The study of sexuality is not coextensive with the study of gender; correspondingly, antihomophobic inquiry is not coextensive with feminist inquiry. But we can't know in advance how they will be different" (*EC* 27). This is a crucial observation and a remarkably spare formulation of it. Sedgwick follows the axiom with a discussion of the relations among sex, gender, and sexuality that I want to consider in more detail because of the ways in which feminism and antihomophobic analysis are cast in relation to one another. She begins with the distinctions between sex and gender. The feminist project, as she characterizes it here, has been to "chart a space between something called 'sex' and something called 'gender.'" Sex, within this scheme, might be seen as "the relatively minimal raw material" and gender as "the far more elaborated, more fully and rigidly dichotomized social production and reproduction of male and female identities and behaviors" (*EC* 27). I want to emphasize the seemingly paradoxical notion that social gender is the more fully elaborated and the more rigid, which makes the raw material of sex exceed the dictates of gender. Following Gayle Rubin's formulation, Sedgwick goes on to define sex/gender systems as "the system by which chromosomal sex is turned into, and processed as, cultural gender" (*EC* 28). According to Sedgwick, the feminist use of the notion of sex/gender systems has led us to emphasize the impact of socially constructed gender divisions and to downplay the role of biology. This, too, is a crucial observation about increasingly problematic uses of the concept of gender.

Sedgwick registers her hesitations about the possibilities of ever distinguishing clearly between sex and gender or biology and culture, a hesitation that she explains by suggesting that "a primary (or *the* primary) issue in gender differentiation and gender struggle is the question of who is to have control of women's (biologically) distinctive reproductive capability" (*EC* 27–8). Gender, and the theory of gender offered by feminism, then, are associated with reproduction and with women. Gender is primarily about control over women's bodies in Sedgwick's scheme. She follows her characterizations of gender differentiation with yet another warning against the presumption of any clear distinction between gender and sex, and then announces that she will use gender "to denominate that problematized space of the sex/gender system, the whole package of physical and cultural distinctions between women and men, more simply" (*EC* 29). I am afraid of the slide here, in which sex is now gender is now sex is now woman's reproductive potential and the political battles over its control.

Sexuality, on the other hand, is figured as that which exceeds "the bare choreographies of procreation." Invoking Freud and Foucault, Sedgwick suggests that sexuality, more than gender, occupies "the polar position of the relational, the social/symbolic, the constructed, the variable, the representational" (*EC* 29). Because her language is so compelling, my attention was caught over and over by the terms in which Sedgwick continues to cast gender throughout the introduction, as constraint, enmeshment, miring, and fixity, as she contrasts the excesses of sexuality, indicatively male, to the "coarser stigmata of gender difference" (*EC* 32).

In her introduction to the axioms, Sedgwick explains her reasons for separating feminist from gay male criticism and theory in *Epistemology of the Closet*. When faced with "the choice between risking a premature and therefore foreclosing reintegration between feminist and gay (male) terms of analysis, on the one hand, and on the other hand keeping their relation open a little longer by deferring yet again the moment of their account-ability to one another – I have followed the latter path." And she con-tinues: "Ultimately, I do feel, a great deal depends – for all women, for lesbians, for gay men, and possibly for all men – on the fostering of our ability to arrive at understandings of sexuality that will respect a certain irreducibility in it to the terms and relations of gender" (*EC* 16). It is not the argument for an analytic distinction between gender and sexuality to which I object. In fact, I applaud Sedgwick's efforts to hold open the question of how gender and sexuality or feminism and gay (male) analysis might intersect. What I find problematic is what happens to sex/gender when male homo/hetero division is made so distinct from it. The lack of conceptual clarity in our efforts to distinguish between sex and gender lead her to collapse those two terms. Yet she reacts to the irreducibility of sexuality to gender by making them more distinct, even opposed to one another. This will have the consequence of making sexuality, particularly homo/hetero sexual definition for men, seem strangely exempt from the enmeshments and constraints of gender (read: women), and, thus, even from the body. The result is that lesbians, or women in general, become interesting by making a cross-gender identification or an identification with sexuality, now implicitly (though, I think, not intentionally) associ-ated with men, over against gender and, by extension, feminism and women. Crossing becomes preferable to passing for women, at least in the context of antihomophobic analysis and its challenge to normative femi-nist identifications.

The specific issue of lesbian identity emerges in the third axiom, in which Sedgwick suggests that "there can't be an a priori decision about how far it will make sense to conceptualize lesbian and gay male identities together. Or separately." Again, I agree, but I am wary of the distinctions that ground this axiom, and I am concerned about the invisibility of the femme. Sedgwick begins her discussion of the third axiom by applauding lesbian-feminists' "stunningly efficacious re-visioning" of traditional definitions of lesbians as nonwomen, a re-visioning that characterized same-sex love as "the very definitional center of each gender" (*EC* 36). She then reminds us that the feminist "sex wars" intervened in constructions of sexuality as coextensive with gender identification and solidarity in ways that have freed up the question of lesbians' identifications and de-sires again.[5] Sedgwick goes on to suggest that "the irrepressible, relatively class-nonspecific popular culture in which James Dean has been as numinous an icon for lesbians as Garbo or Dietrich has for gay men seems resistant to a purely feminist theorization" (EC 38). Here, then, cross-gender identifications or identifications with gay men make lesbians resistant to feminist theorization. There are two potential problems with this move. First, it limits the scope of feminist inquiry. And second, it associates the cross-gender-identified lesbian with sexuality, the lesbian-feminist with gender identification, and makes the femme lesbian completely invisible.

As lesbian-femme writers and theorists Joan Nestle and Amber Hollibaugh have demonstrated, the woman-identified-woman in much lesbian-feminist work and in lesbian communities was/is as repressive of femmeness as it is of cross-gender identifications.[6] Woman-identification, then, warded off an imitative femininity as much as what was perceived to be an imitative masculinity, in favor of what many working-class femmes have demonstrated to be a class-specific move away from marked bodies and bodily or expressive specificities. If the butch threatened to move lesbianism in the direction of a "male-identification," then femmeness threatened to move lesbianism in the direction of heterosexual betrayal, and both may have threatened to keep lesbianism aligned with class specificities. Indeed, according to the contributors to Joan Nestle's *The Persistent Desire: A Femme-Butch Reader*, lesbian feminism threw out the baby of erotic and gendered specificities along with the bath water of limiting and polarized sex roles.[7] Definitions of female same-sex desire, then, are more complex than Sedgwick's helpful delineation of the two most common ways of configuring the relationship between gender and homosexual object choice, namely, that same-sex desire is indicative of cross-gender identification, on the one hand, and that it may occupy "the very definitional center of each gender" (EC 36), on the other. Adding butchness and femmeness to the equations that Sedgwick has formulated and explained multiplies the terms of these possible equations. Sedgwick gives sexuality the capacity to collapse conventional gender definitions and distinctions; I would multiply the permutations of gender with sexual aims, objects, and practices instead, so that identifications and desires that cross traditional boundaries do not efface the complexities of gender identities and expressions.

Gender is not the only social axis or element of identity that gets rendered fixed or overly proximate in Sedgwick's efforts to highlight the epistemological specificities of the male homo/hetero divide and gay coming out. Gender, in fact, often appears along with race as an identification that defies ambiguous performances. Sedgwick explicitly contrasts homosexual coming out to the affirmation of identities based on race. "Racism."

she argues, "is based on a stigma that is visible in all but exceptional cases," which "are neither rare nor irrelevant, but that delineate the outlines rather than coloring the center of racial experience" (*EC* 75). She notes that "erotic identity, of all things, is never to be circumscribed simply as itself, can never not be relational, is never to be perceived or known by anyone outside of a structure of transference and countertransference" (*EC* 81). In order to bracket the ambiguities of race, the degree to which racial identities are also performative, Sedgwick makes race readily knowable, readable. I do not mean to suggest that there is no epistemological specificity to gay coming out or to erotic identities or that racisms do not rely in part on the stigmatization of visible differences (from an illusory white homogeneity). I am worried about the ways in which these kinds of formulations project fixity onto race and gender, which then become too immediate as identifications to allow any play unless one makes cross-gender identifications with, say, a James Dean, or a person of color can pass as white, a passing that is, of course, a crossing. Racial passing, which is a crossing, and gender crossing, which may well operate as a passing (as a man), are required in this scheme in order to make visible any distance from what is otherwise the ground for differentiated figures. Such crossings have the potential to destabilize and collapse problematic boundaries. But we have to be wary of the tendency to make sexuality the means of crossing, and to make gender and race into grounds so indicatively fixed that masculine positions become the emblem again of mobility. Men do not seem gendered and whites are not racialized in accounts that make these issues too distinct.

Judith Butler's performative theory of gender is by now, perhaps, the most well-known example of the use of queer theory to challenge feminists' investment in gender binaries (see *Gender Trouble*). Sedgwick and Butler converge in their criticisms of feminist (and constructivist) work that minimizes or altogether effaces the question of the body. Whereas Sedgwick collapses gender with sex in her second axiom because of the difficulty in separating them, makes them the ground to sexuality's figural crossings, and then refuses to let them limit identifications or desire, Butler displaces the distinction in quite another way, by questioning the facticity of sex that is said to underlie the social constructedness of gender and emphasizing reconfigurations of the norms that govern sex and sexuality. If for Sedgwick, gender becomes sex, and ineluctably follows the principles of binary division, for Butler, sex becomes gender, that is, is socially constructed, and the principle of binary division is itself contested, even at the level of the body. Of course, Sedgwick, too, made the body contest binary division by leaving the work of rigid dichotomization to social and discursive determinants. By collapsing gender and sex be-

cause of the difficulty of separating them, then, Sedgwick may be closer to
Butler than it first seems. For Butler, however, the very materiality of the
body is formed in its entanglements (via the psyche) with the social world.
Her work more explicitly connects the reconfiguration of bodily gender
with the possibility of discursive resignifications. If Sedgwick casts gender
too insistently in terms of miring, Butler has been charged with failing at
times to make the body enough of a drag on signification. She achieves
a certain flexibility for the body by emphasizing the significance of
gendering to the making of psyches and bodies so that the deconstruction
or reconfiguration of gender at the discursive level promises to reshape the
body and its desires and/or to reveal their already complicated configurations. I will return to the status of gender in relation to body and person
in my conclusions.

In *Gender Trouble*, we remember, Butler used butch-femme desire to
demonstrate how homosexual practices might resignify and denaturalize
heterosexual genderbinaries. And she made the case by citing a femme
who characterized her attraction to butches by saying that she "likes her
boys to be girls" (*GT* 123). Butler goes on to suggest that "the object (and
clearly there is not just one) of lesbian-femme desire is neither some
decontextualized female body nor a discrete yet superimposed masculine
identity, but the destabilization of both terms as they come into erotic
interplay" (*GT* 123). In what I consider to be an even more suggestive
point, Butler gives her argument a different twist by introducing the
complexities of figure/ground distinctions and inversions into heterosexual desires. "Similarly," she writes,

> some heterosexual or bisexual women may well prefer that the
> relation of "figure" to "ground" work in the opposite direction
> – that is, they may prefer that their girls be boys. In that case
> the perception of "feminine" identity would be juxtaposed on
> the "male body" as ground, but both terms would, through the
> juxtaposition, lose their internal stability and distinctness from
> each other. (*GT* 123)

My students recently suggested that when the butch likes her girls to be
girls, the (female) body remains ground and femmeness becomes figural,
by way of a stress on the first "girls." But what's suggestive about the
figure-ground inversions and their many permutations is what they
ultimately say about the difficulty of knowing what may be figure and
what ground for any given person or in any given situation. And in fact,
Butler is right to point out that it is probably the specific destabilizations
of the figure-ground relation that generate what is sexually attractive.

Butler's reflections neither render the gender of the body irrelevant nor make sexuality pure excess. They focus instead on the dynamic interplay of what is considered to be embodied gender/sex, identification, and desire.

Butler has been criticized (and often misunderstood) for her efforts to make butch-femme desire do the work of parodying and destabilizing heterosexual conventions. In her recent publications, she has clarified the misunderstandings generated by her discussion of parody in *Gender Trouble* (see, in particular, "Critically Queer"). Butler joins Sedgwick in the effort to distinguish performance in the more literal, theatrical sense from performativity (see Sedgwick, "Queer Performativity"). Both cite J. L. Austin and the implications of performativity in speech-act theory to emphasize again that the performativity of gender or sexuality, or any other dimension of social life or self, does not and cannot imply that roles or identities can be assumed and/or changed voluntaristically, as if they constituted nothing more entrenched than clothing, costuming, or masks (see Austin). What performativity does suggest is the contingent, historically constituted internalization and embodiment of binary gender and sexual norms.

In "The Lesbian Phallus and the Morphological Imaginary," Butler offers a symptomatic reading of Freud and Lacan that exposes the critical moves through which the phallus becomes the putatively transcendental signifier of (sexual) difference. She demonstrates the specific ways in which both Freud and Lacan work to separate the phallus, as transcendental signifier, from the anatomical penis and the penis as imaginary body part. Butler demonstrates that both Freud and Lacan enact the idealizations that they set out to explain, that is, the idealization of the phallus by way of a psychic investment in the penis. The phallus constitutes an idealization of a psychically invested body part that is first demonstrated to be one among many parts and is then assumed to be the prototype. Through a process of substitutions in Freud and negations in Lacan, the phallus acquires, paradoxically, the status of the signifier beyond all signifieds and referents, but only by veiling its attachment to the part. The lesbian phallus is Butler's provocative figure for the plasticity, substitutability, and detachability of the phallus. That which is supposed to organize the terms of sexual difference becomes plastic, mobile, subject to substitution, and attached to the figure of the lesbian. The body has not become irrelevant but is rendered capable of representations that exceed binary divisions and that redistribute symbolic authority and routes of desire.

Butler worries, though, about the association of phallicity with lesbianism, about what it could be seen to do to femininity and its popular

degradation. "It may well be through a degradation of a feminine morphology, an imaginary and cathected degrading of the feminine, that the
lesbian phallus comes into play," she writes, "or it may be through a
castrating occupation of that central masculine trope, fueled by the kind of
defiance which seeks to overturn that very degradation of the feminine"
("Lesbian Phallus" 87). I would suggest that the lesbian phallus can come
into play without a degradation of the feminine only if that degradation is
not left unremarked in the effort to defy femininity's conventional constraints, and only insofar as feminine identifications are not excluded,
undervalued, or obscured by cross-gender investments. Perhaps still more
is required, namely, that the body constitute more of a drag on signification, that we pay more respect to what's given, to limits, even as we open
the future to what is now unthinkable or delegitimated, that we do this in
order to generate a notion of difference that is not fixed or stable in its
distribution across bodies, but is also not dispensable. I have been arguing
that in the effort to highlight obvious sexual differences and defiances of
norms, the all-too-obvious and thus invisible difference that it makes to be
a woman drops out of view. I'm reminded of one of my students' observations about Butler's reading of *Paris Is Burning*. Butler imagines that
Venus Xtravaganza was murdered by a john who discovered that she had
a penis and that she had only pretended to be a woman. "She 'passes' as a
light-skinned woman," Butler writes, "but is – by virtue of a certain failure
to pass completely – clearly vulnerable to homophobic violence; ultimately, her life is taken presumably by a client who, upon discovery of
what she calls her 'little secret,' mutilates her for having seduced him"
("Gender Is Burning" 129–30). The film does not reveal the conditions
under which Venus was murdered, and there is, of course, another possible narrative, that Venus Xtravaganza passed too successfully as a woman
and was murdered for apparently "being" one, or, at least, as one. At least
one of the "mothers" in the film makes it quite explicit that he/she resists
"passing" too successfully as a woman, that is, completely crossing, because s/he recognizes what that passing or crossing would mean in terms
of social and economic constraints. One of the goals of our analyses must
be to imagine both possibilities, one that relies on what might have been
visibly, tangibly surprising or different and one that apprehends what may
not stand out.

Cross-identifications necessarily preoccupy theorists and critics interested in more literal forms of parodic subversion and representation. And
parody depends on keeping one term stable, even to do its work of
destabilization. Carole-Anne Tyler argues that lesbians' efforts to make
butch-femme roles into parodic resignifications of heterosexual norms
paradoxically reinforce the assumption "that the 'authentic' or 'natural'

self is heterosexual, even as it inverts the hierarchy by proclaiming the 'fake' or artificial gay self to be the 'better,' smarter – more smartly dressed – self, which deconstructs itself by knowing its difference from itself and the gender role it only assumes like a costume" (56). Tyler emphasizes the difficulty for theorists who wish to make the femme appear parodic or specifically lesbian, and, indeed, this does seem to be a problem that Sue-Ellen Case and Teresa de Lauretis solve by making the butch-femme couple appear together, lest the femme remain indistinct from straight women (see Case; de Lauretis 177). I prefer Lisa Duggan's lament, her wish that she were a lesbian drag queen, so that her femmeness might be representable as something other than passing, by way of some sort of routing through a gay male form and back again, a routing that makes the crossings in all forms of identification more evident (see Duggan). Tyler accuses Butler and de Lauretis of a lesbian essentialism for importing a lesbian context to support their arguments for butch-femme parody. Such theorists, she argues, engage in tautological reasoning when it comes to femmes. Femmes are parodic because they are lesbians and are lesbians because they are parodic. The efforts to define the femme as specifically lesbian or parodic are doomed to this kind of tautological reasoning. "What ultimately makes the fem different from the r.g. for both theorists," writes Tyler, "is that she plays her role for another woman, which is supposed to make it excessive by 'recontextualizing' or 'reinterpreting' it. . . . This is the fem's (or the gay butch's) essential incongruity. But such a notion is based on" a gay essentialism (56).

Though I part ways with Tyler when she comes to her prescriptions for a way out of these problems, which she formulates as the acceptance of subjection, of just two genders, I think she highlights a genuine problem in theorists' efforts to make butch-femme roles do the work of recasting lesbianism as camp. For these reasons, the lesbian femme seems a crucial figure. The very fact that the femme may pass implies the possibility of denaturalizing heterosexuality by emphasizing the permeabilities of gay/straight boundaries. In a sense, the lesbian femme who can supposedly pass could be said most successfully to displace the opposition between imitation (of straight roles) and lesbian specificity, since she is neither the same nor different, but both. If it is true, to paraphrase Judith Butler, that the structuring presence of heterosexual roles in homosexual relations does not determine them (*GT* 31), it is also true that the structuring presence of heterosexual roles in heterosexual relations does not determine *them*. It is not possible to reimagine gender configurations outside binary frames by sustaining an absolute division between lesbianism and heterosexuality, or by stripping butch-femme roles of all social grounding and making them a metaphor for feminist subjectivity. We should also examine the positions from which the lesbian femme appears to pass, rather than cross, into heterosexuality.

Of course, the central issue for many lesbian critics continues to be visibility, the (in)visibility of the lesbian femme's incongruity and the consequent problems for lesbian representation and lesbian identity. These problems become particularly interesting when, as Tyler suggests, butch-femme roles comment parodically on heterosexuality or on conventional gender roles, but generate that parody at the expense of some other difference. "Phallic divestiture by one means," according to Tyler, "can even be congruent with phallic investiture by another" (61). Or, as Butler puts it in her recent work, "the symbolic – that register of regulatory ideality – is also and always a racial industry, indeed, the reiterated practice of *racializing* interpellations" (*Bodies* 18). Whereas Tyler warns against phallic investiture, Butler argues for an investiture that exposes the degree to which symbolic authority barely veils a male Imaginary, that is itself the effect of a changeable Symbolic. That exposure has the potential to redefine both symbolic authority and the desire to be invested with or desired by it. Butler's readings analyze the specific ways in which racial and sexual identities are articulated in and through one another. Whereas Butler focuses on the more positive possibilities of reconfiguration, Tyler suggests that there can be no benign investment in symbolic authority, at least under its current organization. Like Butler, I am convinced of the importance of rendering lesbian desire legible, despite the fact that intelligibility is not innocent. Like Tyler, I am interested in the ways in which racial markers can be used problematically in the effort to mark sexual differences between women and make lesbian desire visible. I discussed two such examples in a recent essay on changing lesbian identities (see Martin). Two additional examples are discussed in the published proceedings of the "How Do I Look?" conference on queer film and video. At the conference and in the volume, audience members draw the speakers' attention to the racialization of sexual difference in filmic and video representations of butch-femme couples.

In the discussion that followed Cindy Patton's presentation on "Safe Sex and the Pornographic Vernacular," Isaac Julien makes an effort to "open the debate to questions of racial difference in relationship to the lesbian porn tape." The lesbian porn tape that Patton had shown and to which Julien refers is called "Current Flow," and shows a sexual encounter between a black woman, who takes the position of the top, and a white woman, Annie Sprinkle, well known for her femme performances. Julien continues:

In trying to visualize safe sex or sexual desire, the creation of
porn tapes is a minefield in terms of trying to grapple with the
different dichotomies constructed around racial difference. I
felt, regarding your tape, that the butch-femme role-playing
was really based on racial difference.

Since there is already a stereotypical discourse in
representations of the black subject, how can we, as image
makers, make these identities more complex, or more
dialectical? (*How Do I Look?* 62)

In response, video-maker Jean Carlomusto suggests that "there's an unfair
burden placed on a work when it is one of the only ones out there" (*How
Do I Look?* 62–3), and goes on to explain that the casting of a black
woman in the butch role was determined by the absence of any other
willing actors. It is not necessary to doubt Carlomusto's claim or to direct
criticism at her in order to want to speculate on the implications of such
representations for the organization of race and sex.

In the last essay in the volume, which was also the last talk at the
conference, Teresa de Lauretis analyzes Sheila McLaughlin's film "She
Must Be Seeing Things," a film about a lesbian couple: Agatha, a woman
of color from Brazil and a lawyer, and Jo, a blonde, white filmmaker,
who assume, parodically, according to de Lauretis, butch-femme roles.[8]
Agatha, predictably enough, is the butch. In the course of the film, we see
Jo working to get funding for her film project, and we see her actually
making the film, "Catalina," from Thomas de Quincey's *The Spanish
Military Nun*, about a seventeenth-century cross-dressing woman. Jo also
appears to identify Catalina with her lover, Agatha, because of their
Catholic pasts and their cross-gender behaviors. Agatha spends a great
deal of time worrying about Jo's past relationships with men, to the extent
of "seeing things," when she thinks she sees Jo kissing a man on the street.

De Lauretis's subtle reading of the film focuses on the ways in which
the film treats the conventions of seeing things and what the mobility of
desire and fantasy have to do with seeing differently. She applauds the film
for "taking the question of lesbian desire seriously and trying to work
through the difficulty of representing it against this barrage of representations, discourses, and theories that negate it, from Freud to Hollywood to
contemporary feminism and film theory." And she argues that this film,
unlike a *Desert Hearts*, for example, "both addresses and questions
spectatorial desire by disallowing a univocal spectatorial identification
with any one character or role or object-choice and by foregrounding
instead the relations of desire to fantasy, and desire's mobility within the
fantasy scenario" (*How Do I Look?* 262–3).

Though de Lauretis does not focus on race, the audience points out again that the parodic assumption of butch-femme roles by these two women and the desire that that parodic play makes visible depend on a sexual difference between the two women that is made apparent by race. B. Ruby Rich suggests as much in her response to the film when she argues "that racial difference operates for lesbians in the same way as, let's say, butch-femme or s & m roles do, that is, as a form of differentiation between two people of the same gender" (*How Do I Look?* 274–5). But race does not operate just like butch-femme here; it also operates to secure butch-femme roles.

In de Lauretis's analysis, the parodic assumption of butch-femme roles, but perhaps also, implicitly, the racialization of those roles, works to distinguish lesbian desire from its heterosexist association with pre-Oedipal mother-daughter fusion, narcissistic identification, narcissistic object choice, bisexuality, or heterosexuality. Distinguishing lesbian desire from heterosexual desire from bisexual desire from narcissistic choices from identification with the other woman or with mom requires not only two lesbians but the butch-femme couple, one that parodies masculine and feminine roles and heterosexuality by playing them to excess. It requires a femme who visibly addresses her desire to another woman, because as a femme alone, her lesbianism would be invisible.

De Lauretis's analysis does not necessarily require any of the forms of racialization in the film, but we could still wonder why femme-butch couples are so frequently made visibly different by way of skin color and what it means that the femme's indifference or lack of difference from heterosexual women is often represented in the terms of whiteness. The other woman to whom her desire is visibly addressed is marked at least parodically as phallic in order to avoid any hint of identification, too much femininity, or perhaps too much lesbian-feminism. Making lesbian desire visible as desire, rather than identification, requires an added measure of difference, figured racially. Disidentification from assigned gender is accomplished through darkness, as if whiteness and femmeness could not be differentiated and as if blackness were pure difference. Blackness or color in women is associated with phallic traces and femininity with whiteness once again.

Of course, desire between any two people is much more complex, a tight braid of different forms of identification and desire, many of which are inaccessible to analysis. Again, the concern with lesbian specificity, with making lesbian desire visible, but also with parodic performance as that which makes lesbianism specific and subversive, for all its political implications, can obscure the social mobility of racial as well as sexual and gendered meanings and positions. It can obviously also seem at times to celebrate crossing and defend against passing at the level of gender by fetishistically deploying racial markers of difference. If, in these schemes, the femme needs the butch in order to cross from her apparent normalcy to queer difference, or to pass as a lesbian, and if whiteness secures her indifference, then the butch needs the femme, as well, but also a little color, to keep from passing. But to avoid passing as what? For apparently, she is in need of avoiding both femininity, lest she pass as a woman, and too literal a masculinity, lest she pass as a man. Either way, she loses her potential to render lesbian desire visible for some and unstable for others.

The potential of butch-femme discussions to challenge unproductive, static conceptions of gender and its relation to sexuality has been advanced by a range of activists, writers, theorists, and by women who wear all of those hats at once. I want to focus briefly on the particular emphasis suggested by one of the contributors to Joan Nestle's *The Persistent Desire: A Femme-Butch Reader*. In her contribution, Lyndall MacCowan revises now-popular constructions of the lesbian-feminist seventies as an asexual or antisexual decade. MacCowan suggests that we locate the problem not in a punitive puritanism among feminists but in the total rejection of roles or specificity. For her, feminists mistakenly made gender roles, indeed gender itself, the root cause of women's constraints and oppression. "Not all our experiences of 'gender' are the same, and gender roles are not the root cause of either sexism or heterosexuality," she writes. "The problem is the correlations among biological sex, gender identity, gender or sex roles, sexual object choice, sexual identity. . . . It is this system, *and the denial of any other construction of gender*, on which sexism is founded. The problem is the correlations, not the specific components." MacCowan concludes: "What's oppressive about gender, defined sex roles, in our society is that they are limited to two, rigidly correlated with biological sex, and obsolete" (MacCowan 318). What was lost when roles or erotic specificities were thrown out was language with which to conceive of one's sexual specificities or to conceive them positively. MacCowan remarks elsewhere on the hierarchical relation between masculinity and femininity and the degradation to which femininity as a role or set of roles has conventionally been consigned. She is right to suggest that the fact of specificity is not the root of oppression, and I agree that the effort to diminish the differences among women, or even internal to any given woman, has had a range of negative consequences.

MacCowan cites popular texts such as *Rubyfruit Jungle* and *Sappho Was a Right-On Woman*, the latter of which, she claims, characterizes roles in lesbian relationships as "a product of false socialization, proof of identity confusion, sexually limiting, artificial, most likely to be found among 'lower-class [*sic*]' lesbians in bars" (MacCowan 311; see Brown; Abbot and Love 92–8). I am most interested, for now, in the last charge, "most likely to be found among lower-class lesbians." MacCowan finds a number of examples of lesbian-feminists' displacement or projection of the penchant for erotic roles or gender identities onto so-called "lower-class" communities. And she makes the link between this projection of role-playing onto presumably lower-class communities and what she calls the "whore stigma," attached to women who were considered to be "too overtly sexual." This overt sexuality, combined with feminists' emphasis on women's victimization, may have made the absence of sex roles seem the obvious defense against vulnerability. But at a political level, the conception of roles as vestiges of a past that had been overcome by a lesbian vanguard goes hand in hand with the construction of working- or lower-class women as too overtly sexual, and the then-implicit construction of that hidden referent, avant-garde lesbian feminism, as the site of a role-free, disembodied higher consciousness. Here, enmeshment is associated with lower classes, with women who, according to *Rubyfruit Jungle*, have not been properly socialized, who are not conscious of what they do, and who remain too embodied.

I want to emphasize MacCowan's suggestion that refusing erotic categories and roles had clear race and class specificities in the lesbian feminist literature of the seventies. It seems important to note that at the very historical moment when lesbianism was being produced as woman-identification, when erotic roles and gender identities were rejected as limiting and oppressive, white middle-class women were also disavowing the racialization and the class-specificities of identities and relationships. Of course, a range of lesbians have made this point over and over. Joan Nestle has long insisted on the specifically middle-class norms of respectability that fueled the lesbian-feminist rejection of roles, and of butch-femme culture, in particular.

Cherríe Moraga, too, sheds light on the multiple dimensions of the rejection of erotic roles in her own personal history. In *Loving in the War Years*, Moraga writes of the dilemmas of her adolescence in terms of an impossible and culturally specific choice, or so it seemed to her, between the chingon, the macho, or male, and the chingada, who is pure passivity, defenselessness. What Moraga shows very clearly is that the rejection of erotic roles constituted the disavowal of her sexuality altogether, but also, and in the same moment, a disavowal of race, of the particular ways in which erotic and gender positions were already racialized. She saw her assumption of the position of the chingon or butch only in the terms of her lesbianism until one day

I saw in a lover, a woman, the chingón that I had so feared to
recognize in myself: "the active aggressive and closed person,"
as Paz writes, "who inflicts the wound." I had met my match. I
was forced to confront how, in all my sexual relationships I
had resisted, at all costs, feeling la chingada which, in effect,
meant that I had resisted fully feeling sex at all. (124–5)

I am particularly interested here in the associations Moraga makes between femininity, defenselessness, and feeling sexual at all, and the connection she makes between butchness and impermeability. This equation
of femmeness with sexual receptivity, with sex *per se*, occurs over and over
and seems worth pursuing. Here, racial passing is caught up in the tangled
web of gendered and racialized defenses against vulnerability. The recognition of that tangled web initiated her conscious efforts to "wrestle with
what being a *Chicana* lesbian meant." She continues:

What I never quite understood until this writing is that to be
without a sex – to be bodiless – as I sought to be to escape the
burgeoning sexuality of my adolescence, my confused early
days of active heterosexuality, and later my panicked
lesbianism, means also to be without a race. I never attributed
my removal from physicality to have anything to do with race,
only sex, only desire for women. (125)

Moraga's analysis of her own history implies a larger argument, that the
definition of feminine gender in the terms of subjection to a bodily vulnerability coexists both ideologically and often psychically with the construction of race as subjection to a body that can be escaped only in the form
of disembodied consciousness, role neutrality, and the absence of marks
or specificities.

For the femmes who have written about their experiences, of their
bodies, their psyches, their desire, and their relationships, the making
evident of a sensuality or sexuality is formulated as strength and agency
as well as risk. The proximity of femme identification to the "whore
stigma" says volumes about the prohibitions on all women's acknowledgment of themselves as sexual people, but perhaps it says most about what
might be best formulated as specifically femme or feminine active sexual
openness. The three-dimensionality lent to gender by the complicated
figure-ground relations among femmeness, femininity, and female
anatomy exposes the fallacy of conceiving feminine identifications in
passive terms, in terms of conformity, or comfort with the female body.

Femmeness is as active a structuring of organism-psyche-social relations as apparently more defiant identities, or perhaps it would be more accurate to say that femmeness is an effect of as active a structuring as butchness is, that it involves a range of crossings and surprising routings and always assumes specific forms.

But even in the literature that approaches femmeness and butchness as gender identities from a more empirically based perspective, it appears that butch identities often get constituted in negativity and always in relation to the female body as ground, comfort, and capture. In her essay on butches in *The Persistent Desire*, Gayle Rubin locates butches on a gender dysphoric scale that ranges from some butches' relative comfort with their female bodies to female-to-male transsexuals' desire for a different anatomy. While the political purpose of such a continuum seems clear and compelling, namely, to challenge the stigma attached to transsexualism, and while it is true that butch lesbians have been associated historically with gender dysphoria or dysfunction, I would suggest that making gender dysphoria or gender dysfunction too central to butchness constructs butchness in negativity, curiously makes anatomy the ground of identity, and suggests that femmes, by contrast to butches, are at least implicitly gender-conformist. It also seems problematic to put gender identities, sexual object choice, gender dysphoria, transgenderism, and transsexualism on a continuum. In keeping with the effort to separate gender and sexuality in order to expose their complex imbrications and configurations with one another, it seems productive as well to consider that the categories of experience listed above are also discrete, and that our compulsion to create coherence or political solidarities suppresses the disjunctions. In fact, in the autobiographical accounts in *The Persistent Desire*, femmes are often cast as capable of healing the butch's wounded relation to her body, a role division that makes comfort or defiance seem the two apparent options in relation to gender, and they are distributed in binary oppositions, with femmeness as ease or accession and defiance or nonconformity as phallic.

Joan Nestle consistently responds to characterizations of butchness as gender dysfunction or dysphoria by refusing that language in favor of a definition of both butchness and femmeness as different ways of enacting feelings of power, competence, and strength, as well as vulnerability and pain (see Davis, Hollibaugh, and Nestle, "Femme Tapes"). In response to Amber Hollibaugh's reflections on how the butch's "gender dysfunction" affects femme-butch interactions ("Femme Tapes" 255), Joan Nestle refuses the term and characterizes butches and femmes in a very different sense:

It's not my words, my way to say words like gender
dysfunction. I feel that what they are trying to do is have
power, and women do not have models for having power, and
so they derived their own model. I am trying to say that as
femmes we found a way to create a sexual space for ourselves
that made us different from the traditional woman and yet let
us honor our women selves. We exiled ourselves from one land
but created another. I have a feeling that butches started out
with a certain clarity also, and that clarity . . . was about how to
be powerful in their bodies and their visions of themselves, the
same way we wanted to be in our femme, giving selves. The
language binds us. I am not sure it is masculinity, even if they
say it is and it looks like it. They too chose exile from gender
to be another kind of creation. ("Femme Tapes" 267)

Here Nestle struggles with the language of gender, referring to femmes
and butches at one point as women, at another point as exiles from gender.
Nestle appears to introduce a split between the concept "women" and the
notion of gender, women who are exiles from gender, but whose
"womanness" remains undefined, capable of different representations,
even at the level of how we inhabit our bodies. At still another point, she
refuses to characterize butchness in terms of masculinity, insisting on
butches as women in search of ways to honor their bodily sense of
themselves. In response to the cultural injunction to be a woman,
butchness can be conceptualized as a defiance, as a defense, as secondary
to what we ought to be. If butchness is defense and defiance, however,
femmeness appears to become conformity and/or the healing ground for
the butch's wound. Femmeness as defiance requires a different kind of
attention, different forms of representation. While it is true that a woman
who can pass will be less subject than an obviously dykey woman to
homophobic attack, she may also be more subject to the ways in which
women are devalued, diminished, trivialized by men, but also by other
women. Here, indeed, is where the split between feminism and queer
sexual practices or identities seems evident and damaging.

Of course, Nestle reproduces conventional distinctions between
butchness and femmeness when she associates femmeness with "sexual
spaces" and with "giving selves," and butchness with "feeling powerful in
their bodies." But she concludes with their similarities, which seem
to make gender identities deep-seated stylizations, even expressions of
more fundamental aspects of self and relationship, or, if not more fundamental, then at least irreducible to the grasp or reach of gender differences. It seems that Nestle is trying to introduce or sustain a gap

between the phenomenological level of bodily or psychological experience and social injunctions. This limitation on the reach of sex/gender over selves and relationships helps correct for constructivist emphases on the discursive construction of therefore always already and thoroughly gendered bodies/psyches, emphases that lend sex/gender such imperial reach over the self that nothing seems to exceed its grasp except the inevitable failure of any individual to perform gender in a way adequate to its idealized form.

These examples bring me to my concluding point, that the opposition set up between conventional understandings of gender as stable core and postmodern conceptions of identity as the effect of discursive practice needs to be displaced, not decided in one direction or the other. It is for that reason, perhaps, that I have tried here to keep Sedgwick's and Butler's approaches to gender in a kind of tension. To make sexuality irreducible to sex/gender by rendering sex/gender of bodies the more fixed, but also potentially irrelevant, ground separates feminist and queer projects too radically. To make sex/gender and sexuality the effects of discursive practices, even at the level of the body, appears more productive, but only as long as the body, the material is conceived as a drag or a limit as well as a potential. The kind of drag it is cannot and should not be predetermined, given a shape or a content. But too little emphasis on the difference it makes risks the elimination of difference in a kind of postmodern humanism of (im)possibility. Butler has it right when she refuses to make femininity the ahistorical outside of the symbolic, of what can be made intelligible, when she challenges the tendency to associate "the feminine" over and over with Difference, but she is just as right to argue against the dream of all-inclusiveness and total intelligibility. Butler's climactic challenges to identity politics, to ahistorical assumptions of the shape of the symbolic have done the crucial ground-clearing work of opening the analysis of interiority to its construction in and through relations of power. What now seems possible are renewed and innovative approaches to the entanglements of organism/psyche/sociality. I want to pause longer over the differences that materiality and interiority make, once we introduce the crucial element of temporality into the equations. For discourse theory, as we know, does the work of introducing forms of spatialization into otherwise linear, developmental, teleological narratives of formation. When it comes to questions of gender, sexuality, and identity, however, temporality reminds us that inside/outside encounters have the effect again and again of making bodies and psyches with histories that then exert their own pressures back on the boundaries between out and in, back on what we take to be the social world around a self or a person. Though that body and psyche can be said to be effects of power, they are irreducible to it. Though never constituted outside of given social/discursive relations, power also moves from bodies/psyches/minds outward, not by virtue of will, but by virtue of the pressure exerted by what's given in the form of body and subjectivity. I worry about the degree to which normalization serves as an explanation of how power operates and about the tendency to reduce interiority to its effects, however complex those effects can be shown to be. I have focused here on the potential obfuscation of misogyny by antinormative stances, even as I have highlighted the work that has exposed feminist heterosexisms. Femininity, played straight, appears to be a problem for both. Feminist identifications have, at times, tended to enjoin women to be alike by being visibly different from conventional norms of femininity, in the direction of gender neutrality or nonspecificity, which is also, of course, gendered. Queer emphases on antinormative display enjoin us to be different from conventional norms of femininity by defiantly cross-identifying. Conceptually, then, as well as politically, something called femininity becomes the tacit ground in relation to which other positions become figural and mobile. I would conclude that some feminist and some queer conceptions of gender exaggerate its reach. Heterosexist injunctions to be a woman or a man make sex, which is always also gender, the normalizing core of the person. In our efforts to challenge forms of gender policing, we run the risk of replicating a kind of gender totalitarianism, even in the form of its deconstruction. In addition to focusing on parodic destabilizations of gender norms, which we then credit with having fundamentally undone or reworked interiorities, we might also work on diminishing our sense of gender's grasp on us, focus on exposing it as an effect, an imposition, a stylization, even an expression of more fundamental psychological and social dynamics. I do not mean to suggest that we could ever gain access to what I am calling more fundamental processes or dynamics without picking through their gendered forms. I do mean to suggest that gendered expressions or manifestations are often secondary to convergences of organism, psyche, and social realities that exceed the grasp or reach of gender divisions or differences, even if they are accessible only by way of those differences. Butler has shown the dangers of imagining gender behaviors or styles to be expressions of an underlying gender core. Displacing the assumption of binary gender division and core gender identities has been credited with having displaced identity, even interiority. But that credit can replicate the gender totalitarianism that has been the object of critique. Gender is both more and less than we make it. It is more than a fixed ground that can be easily overridden by what we call "sexuality," which, as I have tried to argue here, sometimes serves as the name for desires and identifications that defy but rely on (feminine) positions. And gender is less than that which structures everything, the deconstruction of which would take apart personhood itself. On the basis of crucial metatheoretical evacuations of supposedly natural or psychologically entrenched gendered cores, I suggest we make gender identities and expressions the site of close readings that work to expose the infinitely complex and shifting dynamics, both psychic and social, that such identities and expressions both obscure and illuminate so that gender – and "femininity," in particular – becomes a piece of what feminist and queer theories together complicate and put into motion.

Notes

1 I am thinking primarily about contributions to the lesbian/gay journal *Out/Look*, which constituted an early renewal of efforts to forge alliances between lesbians and gay men. The essays in *Out/Look*, for all their considerable significance, often cast their newness over against feminism, and lesbian-feminism, in particular.

2 For the purposes of this discussion, I am drawing primarily on the work of Eve Sedgwick and Judith Butler and their specific criticisms of feminist theory and its limitations for theories of sexuality. Both Sedgwick and Butler have relied, however, on Gayle Rubin's challenge to her own formulation of "sex/gender systems" as the object of feminist inquiry. In "Thinking Sex," Rubin led the way in suggesting that feminist theory was inadequate to the task of analyzing sexuality, which constituted a distinct social axis.

3 Sedgwick makes the point that "male-centered gay politics has tended not to be structured as strongly as feminism has by that particular ethical pressure [to identify with/as]" (EC 62).

4 For an important discussion of battles between feminists and lesbian daughter figures, see Julia Creet, "Daughter of the Movement: The Psychodynamics of Lesbian S/M Fantasy." Creet analyzes the problem in psychoanalytic terms as the mother's failure to lay down the law effectively enough, provoking the daughter's rage at disappointment as well as at constraint.

5 Sedgwick cites the important documents of those sex wars and important players in them including the Barnard conference, Heresies, Powers of Desire, and Pleasure and Danger.

6 For Nestle's criticisms of lesbian respectability, see *A Restricted Country* and her edited collection *The Persistent Desire: A Femme-Butch Reader*.

7   See, in particular, Lyndall MacCowan's contribution, where this argu-
    ment is made quite explicit.
8   I am indebted to discussions with Mandy Merck for this analysis.

References

Abbot, Sidney, and Barbara Love. *Sappho Was a Right-On Woman*. New
    York: Stein and Day, 1972.
Austin, J. L. *How to Do Things with Words*. Ed. J. O. Urmson and Marina
    Sbisa. 2nd edn. Cambridge, MA: Harvard University Press, 1975.
Brown, Rita Mae. *Rubyfruit Jungle*. Plainfield, VT: Daughters, 1973.
Butler, Judith. *Bodies That Matter*. New York: Routledge, 1993.
——. "Critically Queer." *Bodies That Matter* 223–42.
——. "Gender Is Burning." *Bodies That Matter* 121–40.
——. *Gender Trouble*. New York: Routledge, 1990. [*GT*]
——. "The Lesbian Phallus and the Morphological Imaginary." *Bodies
    That Matter* 57–92.
Case, Sue-Ellen. "Toward a Butch-Femme Aesthetic." *Discourse* 11.1
    (1988–89): 55–73.
Creet, Julia. "Daughter of the Movement: The Psychodynamics of
    Lesbian S/M Fantasy." *differences* 3.2 (1991): 135–59. Special issue on
    Queer Theory.
Davis, Madeline, Amber Hollibaugh, and Joan Nestle. "The Femme
    Tapes." Nestle, *The Persistent Desire* 254–67.
de Lauretis, Teresa. "Sexual Indifference and Lesbian Representation."
    Theatre Journal 40.2 (1988): 155–77.
Duggan, Lisa. "The Anguished Cry of an 80's Fem: 'I Want to be a Drag
    Queen.'" *Out/Look* 1.1 (1988): 62–65.
How Do I Look? Queer Film and Video. Ed. Bad Object-Choices. Seattle:
    Bay, 1991.
MacCowan, Lyndall. "Re-collecting History, Renaming Lives: Femme
    Stigma and the Feminist Seventies and Eighties." Nestle, *The Persistent
    Desire* 299–328.
Martin, Biddy. "Sexual Practice and Changing Lesbian Identities."
    Destabilizing Theories. Ed. Michele Barrett and Ann Phillips. Cam-
    bridge: Polity, 1992. 93–119.
Moraga, Cherríe. *Loving in the War Years*. Boston: South End, 1983.
Nestle, Joan, ed. *The Persistent Desire: A Femme-Butch Reader*. Boston:
    Alyson, 1991.
——. *A Restricted Country*. Ithaca, NY: Firebrand, 1990.
Paris Is Burning. Dir. Jennie Livingston. Off-White Productions, 1991.

Rubin, Gayle. "Of Catamites and Kings: Reflections on Butch, Gender, and Boundaries." Nestle, *The Persistent Desire* 466–82.

——. "Thinking Sex." *Pleasure and Danger*. Ed. Carol Vance. New York: Routledge, 1988. 267–319.

Sedgwick, Eve Kosofsky. *Epistemology of the Closet*. Berkeley: University of California Press. 1990.

——. "Queer Performativity: Henry James's *The Art of the Novel*." *GLQ: A Journal of Lesbian and Gay Studies* 1.1 (1993): 1–16.

——. *Tendencies*. Durham: Duke University Press, 1993.

Tyler, Carole-Anne. "Boys will Be Girls: The Politics of Gay Drag." *Inside/Out: Lesbian Theories, Gay Theories*. Ed. Diana Fuss. New York: Routledge, 1991. 32–70.

Chapter 2

Sexual Traffic

Gayle Rubin interviewed by Judith Butler

Gayle Rubin is an anthropologist who has written a number of highly influential articles, including "The Traffic in Women: Notes on the 'Political Economy' of Sex," "Thinking Sex," "The Leather Menace," and "Misguided, Dangerous and Wrong: An Analysis of Anti-Pornography Politics." A collection of her essays will soon be published by the University of California Press. She is currently working on a book based on ethnographic and historical research on the gay male leather community in San Francisco.

She has been a feminist activist and writer since the late 1960s, and has been active in gay and lesbian politics for over two decades. She has been an ardent critic of the anti-pornography movement and of the mistreatment of sexual minorities.

Her work has offered a series of methodological suggestions for feminism and queer studies which have significantly shaped the emergence of both fields of study.

JB: The reason I wanted to do this interview is that some people would say that you set the methodology for feminist theory, then the methodology for lesbian and gay studies. And I think it would be interesting as a way to understand the relation between these two fields for people to understand how you moved from your position in "The Traffic in Women" to your position in "Thinking Sex." But then also it would be interesting to hear a bit about the kind of work you are doing now. So, I thought I might begin at one of the beginnings, namely "The Traffic in Women," and ask you to elaborate a little bit about the context in which you wrote it, and also to ask you when you began to take distance from the position you elaborated there.

GR: Well, I guess I have a different sense of the relationship of those papers to feminist thought and lesbian and gay studies. Each was part of an ongoing process, a field of inquiry developing at the time. "Traffic in Women" had its origins in early second-wave feminism when many of us who were involved in the late 1960s were trying to figure out how to think about and articulate the oppression of women. The dominant political context at that time was the New Left, particularly the anti-war movement and the opposition to militarized US imperialism. The dominant paradigm among progressive intellectuals was Marxism, in various forms. Many of the early second-wave feminists came out of the New Left and were Marxists of one sort or another. I don't think one can fully comprehend early second-wave feminism without understanding its intimate yet conflicted relationship to New Left politics and Marxist intellectual frameworks. There is an immense Marxist legacy within feminism, and feminist thought is greatly indebted to Marxism. In a sense, Marxism enabled people to pose a whole set of questions that Marxism could not satisfactorily answer.

Marxism, no matter how modified, seemed unable to fully grasp the issues of gender difference and the oppression of women. Many of us were struggling with – or within – that dominant framework to make it work or figure out why it didn't. I was one of many who finally concluded that one could only go so far within a Marxist paradigm and that while it was useful, it had limitations with regard to gender and sex.

I should add that there were different kinds of Marxist approaches. There were some pretty reductive formulations about the "woman question," and some especially simplistic strategies for women's liberation. I remember one group in Ann Arbor, which I think was called the Red Star Sisters. Their idea of women's liberation was to mobilize women's groups to fight imperialism. There was no room in their approach to specifically address gender oppression; it was only a precipitate of class oppression and imperialism, and presumably would wither away after the workers' revolution.

There were a lot of people working over Engels' *The Origin of the Family, Private Property, and the State.* Engels was part of the Marxian canon, and he *did* talk about women, so his work was granted special status. There were dozens of little schemas about the ostensible overthrow of the supposed early Matriarchy and the invention of private property as the source of women's oppression. In retrospect some of this literature seems quaint, but at the time it was taken very seriously. I doubt people who weren't there could begin to imagine the intensity with which people fought over whether or not there was an original Matriarchy, and whether its demise accounted for class differences and the oppression of women.

Even the best of Marxist work at that time tended to focus on issues that were closer to the central concerns of Marxism, such as class, work, relations of production, and even some very creative thinking about the social relations of reproduction. There was a wonderful, very interesting literature that came up around housework, for example. There was good work on the sexual division of labor, on the place of women in the labor market, on the role of women in the reproduction of labor. Some of this literature was very interesting and very useful, but it could not get at some core issues which concerned feminists: gender difference, gender oppression, and sexuality. So there was a general effort to differentiate feminism from that political context and its dominant preoccupations. There were a lot of people looking for leverage on the problem of women's oppression, and searching for tools with which one could get different angles of vision on it. "Traffic in Women" was a part of that effort and is an artifact of that set of problems. There were many other articles dealing with similar issues; one of my favorites was "The Unhappy Marriage of Marxism and Feminism," by Heidi Hartman.

The immediate precipitating factor of "Traffic" was a course on tribal economics given by Marshall Sahlins at the University of Michigan, about 1970. That course changed my life. I had already been involved with feminism, but this was my first experience of anthropology, and I was smitten. I was utterly seduced by Sahlins' theoretical approach, as well as the descriptive richness of the ethnographic literature.

I was co-writing with two friends a term paper for the course, and our topic was the status of women in tribal societies. Sahlins suggested that I read Lévi-Strauss's *The Elementary Structures of Kinship*. To use the vernacular of the time, "it completely blew my mind." So did some of the other literature of French structuralism. I read the Althusser article on Freud and Lacan from *New Left Review* right around the time I was reading *The Elementary Structures of Kinship* and there was just some moment of revelation that these approaches had a relationship. Then I went and read most of the classic psychoanalytic essays on "femininity." The confluence of those things was where "The Traffic In Women" came from. I was very excited about all these connections and wanted to incorporate them into the term paper for Sahlins' class. One of my co-authors was reluctant to include this wild stuff in the body of the paper, so I wrote the first version of "Traffic" as an appendix for the paper. Then I kept reading and thinking about it.

At that time, the University of Michigan allowed students to declare an independent major through the honors program. I had taken advantage of the program to construct a major in Women's Studies, in 1969. There was no Women's Studies program at Michigan then, so I was the first Women's Studies major there. The independent major required a senior honors thesis, so I did half on lesbian literature and history, and half on this analysis of psychoanalysis and kinship. I finished the senior thesis in 1972 and kept reworking the "Traffic" part until Rayna Rapp (then Reiter) extracted the final version for *Toward An Anthropology of Women*. A penultimate version was published in an obscure Ann Arbor journal called *Dissemination* in 1974.

Something that people now probably forget is how little of the French structuralist and poststructuralist literature was available then in English. While Lévi-Strauss, Althusser, and Foucault were very well translated by 1970, Lacan was not readily available. Besides the Althusser essay on him, Lacan was mostly represented in English by one or two articles, Anthony Wilden's *The Language of the Self*, and a book by Maud Mannoni. I remember seeing maybe one or two articles by Derrida. Most of Derrida, as well as Lyotard, Kristeva, Irigaray, and Bourdieu were still pretty much restricted to those fluent in French. This kind of thinking was virtually unknown in the United States. When I wrote the version of "Traffic" that was finally published, one of my friends edited it. She thought only ten people would read it. I thought maybe 200 people would read it, and I think we agreed on 50.

JB: You were saying that in some ways you wanted to make an intervention in Marxist feminism, and make feminism something other than a kind of subsidiary movement in Marxism. Would you elaborate on that?

GR: I felt that if people privileged Marxism as the theory with which to approach the oppression of women, then they were going to miss a lot, and they did. I think of "Traffic" as a neo-Marxist, proto-promo exercise. It was written on the cusp of a transition between dominant paradigms, both in progressive intellectual thought in general, and feminist thought in particular. But the basic problem was that Marxism had a weak grasp of sex and gender, and had intrinsic limitations as a theoretical framework for feminism. There were other issues, such as the whole problem of trying to find some theoretical basis for lesbianism.

JB: It seemed to me that you based much of what you say about sexuality and gender in "The Traffic In Women" on an understanding of kinship that you were taking from Lévi-Strauss. To the extent that you could show that kinship relations were in the service of compulsory heterosexuality you could also show that gender identities were in some sense derived from kinship relations. You then speculated that it might be possible to get beyond gender – maybe "gender identity" is the better word – if one also could so something like overthrow kinship . . .

GR: Right . . . and the cultural residue and the symbolic manifestations and all of the other aspects of that system, and the inscription and installation of those structures and categories within people.

JB: It was a utopian vision of sorts.

GR: Well, we were all pretty utopian in those days. I mean this was about 1969 to 1974. I was young and optimistic about social change. In those days there was a common expectation that utopia was around the corner. I feel very differently now. I worry instead that fascism in our time is around the corner. I am almost as pessimistic now as I was optimistic then.

JB: Yes. So could you narrate something about the distance you took from that particular vision and what prompted the writing of "Thinking Sex"?

GR: There was a different set of concerns that generated "Thinking Sex." I suppose the most basic differences were that, theoretically, I felt that feminism dealt inadequately with sexual practice, particularly diverse sexual conduct; and practically, the political situation was changing. "Thinking sex" came from the late 1970s, when the New Right was beginning to be ascendant in US politics, and when stigmatized sexual practices were drawing a lot of repressive attention. 1977 was the year of Anita Bryant and the campaign to repeal the Dade County gay rights ordinance. Such campaigns are now, unfortunately, the common stuff of gay politics, but at that time the bigotry and homophobia that emerged in that fight were shocking. This period was when Richard Viguerie's direct mail fundraising operation was underwriting a new era of radical right-wing political organizing. By 1980 Reagan was in office. This shifted the status, safety, and legal positions of homosexuality, sex work, sexually explicit media, and many other forms of sexual practice.

"Thinking Sex" wasn't conceived in a direct line or as a direct departure from the concerns of "Traffic." I was trying to get at something different, which had some implications for my previous formulations. But I think those last few pages have been overinterpreted as some huge rejection or turnabout on my part. I saw them more as a corrective, and as a way to get a handle on another group of issues. I wasn't looking to get away from "Traffic in Women." I was trying to deal with issues of sexual difference and sexual variety. And when I use "sexual difference" I realize from reading your paper "Against Proper Objects" that you are using it in a very different way than I am. I am using the term to refer to different sexual practices. You seem to be using it to refer to gender.

JB: You mean, I am using "sexual difference" in the way that you were using "gender" in "Traffic in Women"?

GR: Well I'm not sure. Tell me how you are using "sexual difference," because I'm not clear on it.

JB: Yes, well, I think that for the most part that people who work in a "sexual difference" framework actually believe in some kind of symbolic position of the masculine and the feminine, or believe there is something persistent about sexual difference understood in terms of masculine and feminine. At the same time they tend to engage psychoanalysis or some theory of the symbolic. And what I always found interesting in "The Traffic in Women" was that you used the term gender to track that same kind of problem that came out of Lacan and Lévi-Strauss, but that you actually took a very different direction than most of the – what I would call – sexual difference feminists who now work almost exclusively within psychoanalytic domains. And what interested me in "The Traffic in Women" was that you, by using a term that comes from American socio-logical discourse – "gender" – by using that term, you actually made gender less fixed, and you imagined a kind of mobility to it which I think would be quite impossible in the Lacanian framework. So I think that what you produced was an amalgamation of positions which I very much appreciated, and it became one of the reasons I went with gender myself in *Gender Trouble*.

GR: Well, I didn't want to get stuck in the Lacanian trap. It seemed to me, and with all due respect to those who are very skilled at evading or manipulating the snares, that Lacan's work came with a dangerous ten-dency to create a kind of deep crevasse from which it would be hard to escape. I kept wanting to find ways not to get caught in the demands of certain systems, and Lacanian psychoanalysis both provided leverage and posed new challenges. Lacanian psychoanalysis is very useful in dealing with structures of gender and desire, but it comes with a price. I was concerned with the totalizing tendencies in Lacan, and the non-social qualities of his concept of the symbolic.

JB: Yes. This is actually an interesting problem. My sense is that in British feminism, for instance, in the seventies, there was a belief that if you could reconfigure and change your kinship arrangements that you could also reconfigure your sexuality and your psyche, and that psychic transformation really followed directly from the social transformation of kinship arrangements. And then when everybody had done that and found out that their psyches were still in the same old pits that they had always been in, I think that the Lacanian position became very popular. I guess the problem became how to describe those constraints on sexuality which seem more persistent than what we can change through the trans-formation of social and kinship relations. Maybe there is something intractable, maybe there is something more persistent . . .

GR: Leaving aside such issues as how much these social and kinship relations have actually been transformed at this point, the magnitude of such changes and the time-spans required to make them, and the fact that most of our psyches were long since formed and are resistant to such swift re-education, what is the something that is *intractable*? One of the nifty things about psychoanalytic approaches is that they explain both change and intractability. But there is something about the particular intractabil-ity of what is called the symbolic that I don't understand. Is there sup-posed to be something in the very nature of the structure of the brain and the way it creates language?

JB: I would say the structure of language, the emergence of the speaking subject through sexual differentiation, and how language subsequently creates intelligibility.

GR: . . . that makes it somehow necessary to have a masculine and a feminine?

JB: As you know from some of the reading of Lacan that you have done, there is a tendency to understand sexual difference coextensive with language itself. And that there is no possibility of speaking, of taking a position in language outside of differentiating moves, not only through a differentiation from the maternal which is said to install a speaker in language for the first time, but then further differentiations among speakers positioned within kinship, which includes the prohibition on incest. To the extent to which that is done within the constellation of, say, Mother/Father as symbolic positions . . .

GR: There is something intrinsically problematic about any notion that somehow language itself or the capacity for acquiring it requires a sexual differentiation as a primary differentiation. If humans were hermaphroditic or reproduced asexually, I can imagine we would still be capable of speech. A specific symbolic relation that precedes any social life whatsoever – I have a problem with that. One of the problems I have with Lacan was that his system didn't seem to allow quite enough latitude for the social structuring of the symbolic.

JB: Right. I agree with you on this. But I think that it is one of the reasons why the social doesn't have such a great name and is really not of interest for many who work in the Lacanian domain. I guess what I always found really great about "The Traffic in Women," is that it actually did give us a way to understand psychic structures in relationship to social structures.

GR: Well that is what I wanted to do, and I didn't want to get entangled in a symbolic that couldn't be socially accessed in some way. People often assume that if something is social it is also somehow fragile, and can be changed quickly. For example, some right-wing anti-gay literature now argues that since homosexuality is socially constructed, people can (and should) easily change their sexual orientation. And as you were saying earlier, frustration with the enduring quality of certain things sometimes leads people to think that they can't be socially generated. But the kind of social change we are talking about takes a long time, and the time-frame in which we have been undertaking such change is incredibly tiny.

Besides, the imprint of kinship arrangements on individual psyches is very durable. The acquisition of our sexual and gender programming is much like the learning of our native cultural system or language. It is much harder to learn new languages, or to be as facile in them as in our first language. As Carole Vance has argued, this same model can be useful for thinking about gender and sexual preferences (Vance 1989). As with languages, some people have more gender and erotic flexibility than others. Some can acquire secondary sexual or gender languages, and even fewer will be completely fluent in more than one position. But most people have a home language, and home sexual or gender comfort zones that will not change much. This doesn't mean these things are not social, any more than the difficulties of acquiring other languages means that languages are not social. Social phenomena can be incredibly obdurate. Nonetheless, I wanted in "Traffic" to put gender and sexuality into a social framework, and I did not want to go completely in the direction of the Lacanian symbolic and be stuck with a primary category of gender differences which might as well be inscribed in granite.

JB: So, if you would, talk about the theoretical and political circumstances that made you turn toward "Thinking Sex."

GR: "Thinking Sex" was part of a movement away from an early structuralist focus on the binary aspects of language, such as the binary oppositions you see very much in Lévi-Strauss and Lacan, toward the more discursive models of later poststructuralism or postmodernism. If you are really going to take seriously that social life is structured like language, then you need complex models for how language is structured. I think these binary models seemed to work better for gender, because our usual understandings posit gender as in some ways binary; even the continuums of gender differences often seem structured by a primary binary opposition. But as soon as you get away from the presumptions of heterosexuality, or a simple hetero–homo opposition, differences in sexual conduct are not very intelligible in terms of binary models. Even the notion of a continuum is not a good model for sexual variations; one needs one of those mathematical models they do now with strange topologies and convoluted shapes. There needs to be some kind of model that is not binary, because sexual variation is a system of many differences, not just a couple of salient ones.

We were talking earlier about the ostensible relationship of "Thinking Sex" to MacKinnon's work. Retrospectively, many people have interpreted "Thinking Sex" as a reaction to MacKinnon's work against pornography.

JB: I'm doubtless guilty of that . . .

GR: While the early feminist anti-pornography movement was an issue, most of the work for "Thinking Sex" was done before MacKinnon became a visible figure in that movement. To many, MacKinnon has come to represent the feminist anti-porn movement, but actually she was a relative latecomer to it. She became visible as an important actor in the porn wars about 1984, after the passage of the so-called "civil rights" anti-porn ordinances, first in Minneapolis late in 1983, and subsequently in Indianapolis. Her fame tends to eclipse the early history of the feminist anti-porn movement, which is represented better by the anthology *Take Back the Night*. I mostly knew about MacKinnon from those two articles in *Signs*. The first was published in 1982, and I had seen an earlier version. I had already been working on versions of "Thinking Sex" for some time. But I could see where MacKinnon was heading, at least at the theoretical level, and I was going in a different direction. She wanted to make feminism the privileged site for analyzing sexuality and to subordinate sexual politics not only to feminism, but to a particular type of feminism. On the grand chessboard of life, I wanted to block this particular move. But it was not the impetus for the paper. At some level, I think there were some underlying social and political shifts that produced "Thinking Sex," the feminist anti-porn movement, MacKinnon's approach, and the right-wing focus on homosexuality and other forms of variant sexual conduct, among other things.

JB: You are referring to MacKinnon's "Marxism, Feminism, Method and the State."

GR: Yes. "Thinking Sex" had its roots back in 1977–78, and I started doing lecture versions of it in 1979. I think you were at one of these, at the Second Sex Conference at the New York Institute for the Humanities.

JB: Right. The first time I saw a copy of Michel Foucault's *The History of Sexuality* . . .

GR: Was I waving it around?

JB: Yes. You introduced it to me.

GR: I was really, just totally hot for that book.

JB: Yes, you made me hot for it too . . .
[laughter]

GR: The paper actually began before I ran into Foucault, but his work clarified issues and inspired me. In any event, the sources of this paper were earlier, and a little different. First of all, I started to get more and more dissatisfied with what were then the stock feminist explanations for certain kinds of sexual behaviors. A number of different debates, incidents, and issues forced me to start questioning the wisdom, if not the relevance, of feminism as the privileged political movement or political theory for certain issues of sexuality and sexual difference. One was the debate on transsexuality. Even before that debate hit print toward the late 1970s, the discussion really flipped me out because it was so biologically deterministic. When it finally erupted over the hiring of Sandy Stone, a male to female transsexual, by Olivia Records, there were a number of articles in the lesbian press about how women were born and not made which I found rather

GR & JB: [in unison] distressing.

GR: To say the least (House and Cowan). And then there were other issues that came up. Around 1977–78, there was a repression, to use an old fashioned term, going on in Michigan, directed against gay male public sex. All of a sudden men were being arrested in a much more aggressive way for sex in parks and tearooms. There were a couple of old cruising areas on the Michigan campus, one in the Union and the other in Mason Hall. The cops came in and arrested some people. There was a truckstop on I–94 between Ann Arbor and Detroit where a number of men were arrested, and in one park sweep I think one of the officials of the Detroit public school system was nabbed and subsequently fired. And as these stories started to percolate through the feminist and lesbian communities, the most common opinion I heard was that these were just men doing horrible masculine, patriarchal things and they probably should be arrested. This was not a position I could accept. No one was going around arresting all the people having heterosexual sex in parks and automobiles. To support or rationalize the arrests of anyone for engaging in consensual homosexual sex was abhorrent to me.

There was another set of incidents that happened, again in Ann Arbor in the late 1970s, around sex work and prostitution. There was a really interesting woman named Carol Ernst. We had disagreed on many things over the years; she was very involved with ideas for which I had little patience, like matriarchy theory and the patriarchal revolt as an explanation for women's oppression, and the idea that women had political power in societies that worshiped female deities. But you know how in small communities people tend to talk to each other even if they disagree or have really different perspectives. That was the case there, and we were friends. Carol did a number of things which were very important in that community. At one point she went to work for a local massage parlor. She ended up trying to unionize the sex workers, and sometime in the early 1970s she spearheaded a labor action against the parlor management. There were hookers with picket signs on the street in front of this dirty bookstore in downtown Ann Arbor, and the striking sex workers even filed an unfair labor practice complaint with the Michigan Labor Relations Board. It was amazing.

Then Carol left the massage parlor and went to work for the bus company, where she was also deeply involved in labor issues and unionization. Many Ann Arbor lesbians ended up working either at the massage parlor or the bus company, which we fondly referred to as "dial-a-dyke." During the mid-1970s, the three major employers of the lesbian community in Ann Arbor were the university, the bus company, and the massage parlor. It's pretty comic but that's how it was.

Then the massage parlor where many of the dykes worked was busted. One of the arrested women was a really wonderful, good-looking, athletic butch who happened to be the star left-fielder of the lesbian softball team. The local lesbian-feminist community suddenly had to deal with the fact that many of their friends and heroes had been arrested for prostitution.

JB: Fabulous.

GR: Most of the rest of us initially had a stock response, which was that they shouldn't be doing this work and that they were upholding the patriarchy. The arrested women and their supporters formed an organization, called PEP, the Prostitution Education Project. They put the rest of us through quite an educational process. They asked how what they did was so different from what anyone else did for a living. Some said they liked the work more than other kinds of work available to them. They asked why it was more feminist to work as secretaries and for longer hours and less money. Some said they liked the working conditions; the busted parlor even had a weight room where the jocks worked out while waiting for clients. They demanded that we deal with prostitution as a work issue rather than a moralistic one. They brought in Margo St. James and had a big hookers' ball to raise funds for the legal defense.

Carol Ernst was later tragically killed in an automobile accident. But she was a visionary, and her peculiar combination of feminist and labor politics really left an imprint. She challenged me on my rhetorical use of prostitution to make debating points about the horror of women's oppression. I used to convince people to feel moral outrage by comparing the situation of women in marriage and similar sexual/economic arrangements to prostitution. Carol argued that I was using the stigma of prostitution as a technique of persuasion, and that in so doing I was maintaining and intensifying such stigma at the expense of the women who did sex work. She was right. I finally realized that the rhetorical effectiveness came from the stigma, and decided that my rhetorical gain could not justify reinforcing attitudes which rationalized the persecution of sex workers. All of these incidents began to eat away at some of my preconceptions about how to think about power and sex, and the politics of sex.

I was also getting more and more alarmed at the way the logic of the woman-identified-woman picture of lesbianism had been working itself out. By defining lesbianism entirely as something about supportive relations between women, rather than as something with sexual content, the woman-identified-woman approach essentially evacuated it – to use a popular term – of any sexual content. It made it difficult to tell the difference between a lesbian and a non-lesbian. These were tendencies of thought common in local lesbian communities. Adrienne Rich in a way codified a certain approach that was widespread at the time, in which people didn't want to distinguish very much between lesbians and other women in close supportive relationships. And I found this both intellectually and politically problematic. A lot of things that were not by any stretch of the imagination lesbian were being incorporated into the category of lesbian. And this approach also diminished some of what was interesting and special about lesbians. I had initially been incredibly excited about the woman-identified-woman ideas, but I was starting to get a sense of their limitations.

JB: Is it that you objected to calling "lesbian" the whole domain of female friendship?

GR: In part. I objected to a particular obfuscation of the categories, and of taking the limited world of nineteenth-century romantic friendship, bound as it was by rigid sex role segregation and enmeshed in marriage relations, as some kind of ideal standard for lesbian existence. I objected to the master narrative that was then developing in lesbian historiography, in which the shifts which undermined that world were seen as entirely negative, a fall from grace, an expulsion from Eden engineered by nasty sexologists with their knowledge of carnal desires. I did not like the way in which lesbians motivated by lust, or lesbians who were invested in butch/femme roles, were treated as inferior residents of the lesbian continuum, while some women who never had sexual desire for women were granted more elevated status. This narrative and its prejudices were expressed in the title of the Nancy Sahli article, which was called "Smashing: Women's relationships Before the Fall." It is highly developed in Lillian Faderman's *Surpassing the Love of Men*. Carroll Smith-Rosenberg's original 1975 essay deliberately blurred some of the distinctions between categories of lesbianism as a sexual status and other types of female intimacy, but she refrained from using romantic friendship as the standard by which lesbianism should be measured. I suppose the most vulgar reduction of this "paradise lost" narrative of lesbian history can be found in Sheila Jeffreys' work.

JB: But then Rich's notion of the continuum, I take it you . . .

GR: Rich's piece shares many of the same elements and assumptions that turn up in the historical work. I was not opposed to historical research on these relationships, but thought it was a mistake to privilege them in defining the category of "lesbian," either historically or in a contemporary context, and to judge other forms of lesbianism as wanting, degraded, or inferior. For example, from reading *Surpassing the Love of Men*, you might conclude that "mannish lesbians" were concocted by the sexologists as a plot to discredit romantic friendship. In addition, both Sahli's and Faderman's analyses imply that the conditions which enable the emergence of sexually aware lesbians, conscious lesbian identities, and lesbian subcultures in the late nineteenth century are regrettable, because they undermined the old innocent passions and pure friendships. Then nothing much good happened for lesbians until the emergence of lesbian-feminism in the early 1970s. Unfortunately, this ostensible dark age happens to coincide with much of the early development of lesbian cultures, literatures, identities, self-awareness, and politics.

This narrative structure oversimplified the complexities of these friendships, obscured their class components, and obliterated many important distinctions. This is a much longer discussion than we can have here, but the point I want to make is just that this categorical system submerged many historical and social complexities in a romantic, politicized, and limited notion of lesbianism. It, moreover, displaced sexual preference with a form of gender solidarity. The displacement was both moral and analytical. While female intimacy and solidarity are important and overlap in certain ways with lesbian erotic passions, they are not isomorphic and they require a finer set of distinctions.

Another problem in the late 1970s was presented by gay male politics. Feminism was also used quite a bit as the political theory of gay male politics, and it didn't work very well. Very little gay male behavior actually was granted the feminist seal of approval. Most of the actual practice of gay male culture was objectionable to many feminists, who mercilessly condemned drag and cross-dressing, gay public sex, gay male promiscuity, gay male masculinity, gay leather, gay fist-fucking, gay cruising, and just about everything else gay men did. I could not accept the usual lines about why all this stuff was terrible and anti-feminist, and thought they were frequently an expression of reconstituted homophobia. By the late 1970s, there was an emerging body of gay male political writing on issues of gay male sexual practice. I found this literature fascinating, and thought it was not only helpful in thinking about gay male sexuality, but also that it had implications for the politics of lesbian sexual practice as well.

And then there was just the whole issue of sexual difference. I am using the terminology of "sexual difference" here to refer to what has otherwise been called perversion, sexual deviance, sexual variance, or sexual diversity. By the late 1970s, almost every sexual variation was described somewhere in feminist literature in negative terms with a feminist rationalization. Transsexuality, male homosexuality, promiscuity, public sex, transvestism, fetishism, and sadomasochism were all vilified within a feminist rhetoric, and some causal primacy in the creation and maintenance of female subordination was attributed to each of them. Somehow, these poor sexual deviations were suddenly the ultimate expressions of patriarchal domination. I found this move baffling: on the one hand, it took relatively minor, relatively powerless sexual practices and populations and targeted them as the primary enemy of women's freedom and well-being. At the same time, it exonerated the more powerful institutions of male supremacy and the traditional loci for feminist agitation: the family, religion, job discrimination and economic dependency, forced reproduction, biased education, lack of legal rights and civil status, etc.

JB: OK. Well let's go back for a minute. You spoke earlier about how you were forced to rethink the notion of prostitution, and I gather that it became for you something very different. You spoke about rethinking prostitution both as a labor question and a question of women's work. You then talked about the desexualization of the lesbian, and you also talked about how gay male politics had feminism as its theory, and yet that theory didn't really fit with the kinds of practices that gay men were engaged in.

GR: Toward the late seventies and early eighties, just before AIDS hit and changed everyone's preoccupations, there was an emergent literature of gay male political theory of sexuality. Much of this appeared in North America's two best gay/lesbian newspapers at the time, *The Body Politic*, and *GCN* (*Gay Community News*). There were articles on public sex, fistfucking, man–boy love, promiscuity, cruising, public sex, and sex ads. Gay men were articulating an indigenous political theory of their own sexual culture(s). This body of work evaluated gay male sexual behavior in its own terms, rather than appealing to feminism for either justification or condemnation.

Looking back, it seems clear to me now that many things were happening almost at once. Somehow, the political conditions of sexual practice were undergoing a shift in the late 1970s, and the emergence of creative gay male sexual political theory was part of that. The major development was the phenomenal growth of the New Right. By the late 1970s it was mobilizing explicitly and successfully around sexual issues. The New Right had a strong sexual agenda: to raise the punitive costs of sexual activity for the young, to prevent homosexuals (male and female) from obtaining social and civic equality, to coerce women to reproduce, and so forth. Then the anti-porn movement erupted into feminism in the late 1970s. WAVPM (Women Against Violence in Pornography and Media) was founded around 1976–77, and WAP (Women Against Pornography) followed in 1979. Samois, the first lesbian SM organization, was founded in 1978. There was something profound going on; some larger underlying shift in how sexuality was experienced, conceptualized, and mobilized. "Thinking Sex" was just one response to this change in the social and political weather. I think my work shifted because something different was happening and my set of operating assumptions and tools was not adequate for helping me navigate the shifts.

JB: I gather that you also objected to the available language in which so-called sexual deviants were described . . .

GR: I looked at sex "deviants," and frankly they didn't strike me as the apotheosis of patriarchy. On the contrary, they seemed like people with a whole set of problems of their own, generated by a dominant system of sexual politics that treated them very badly. They did not strike me as the avatars of political and social power in this society. So I asked myself, what's wrong with this picture? It seemed to me that many feminists had simply assimilated the usual stigmas and common hatreds of certain forms of non-normative sexual practice which they then rearticulated in their own framework.

I was also becoming dissatisfied with the dominance of certain kinds of psychoanalytic interpretations of variant sexualities, and the common presumption that psychoanalysis was the privileged site for interpreting differences of sexual conduct. Despite its limitations and its problems, psychoanalysis has a certain power and utility for thinking about issues of gender identity and gender difference. By contrast, much of the psycho-analytic approach to sexual variation, also known as perversion, struck me as incredibly reductionist and oversimplified. Moreover, many of these

traditional approaches to "perversion" had come into feminism almost
uncriticized. For me, the explanatory potency of psychoanalysis seemed
much more limited with regard to sexual variation.

For example, to look at something like fetishism and say it has to do
with castration and the lack, or maybe it's the knowledge of castration,
or maybe it's the denial of the knowledge of castration, or maybe it is
the foreclosure of the knowledge of, or the displacement of the
knowledge . . . Well, it says very little to me about fetishism.

When I think about fetishism I want to know about many other things.
I do not see how one can talk about fetishism, or sadomasochism, without
thinking about the production of rubber, the techniques and gear used for
controlling and riding horses, the high-polished gleam of military foot-
wear, the history of silk stockings, the cold authoritative qualities of
medical equipment, or the allure of motorcycles and the elusive liberties of
leaving the city for the open road. For that matter, how can we think
of fetishism without the impact of cities, of certain streets and parks, of
redlight districts and "cheap amusements," or the seductions of department store counters, piled high with desirable and glamorous goods?
(Walkowitz, Peiss, Matlock) To me, fetishism raises all sorts of issues
concerning shifts in the manufacture of objects, the historical and social
specificities of control and skin and social etiquette, or ambiguously experienced body invasions and minutely graduated hierarchies. If all of this
complex social information is reduced to castration or the Oedipus complex or knowing or not knowing what one is not supposed to know, I
think something important has been lost.

I want to know about the topographies and political economies of erotic
signification. I think that we acquire much of our grammar of eroticism
very early in life, and that psychoanalysis has very strong models for the
active acquisition and personalized transformations of meanings by the
very young. But I do not find the conventional preoccupations of psychoanalysis to be all that illuminating with regard to the shifting historical
and social content of those meanings. So much of the input gets – to
borrow some phrasing – foreclosed, denied or displaced. There is a lot of
very interesting and creative and smart psychoanalytic work. But when I
wanted to think about sexual diversity, psychoanalytic approaches seemed
less interesting to me. They seemed prone to impoverish the rich complexity of erotic meaning and conduct.

Moreover, it seemed that many psychoanalytically based approaches
made a lot of assumptions about what certain variant erotic practices or
preference meant. These interpretations, mostly derived *a priori* from
the literature, were then applied to living populations of individual

practitioners, without any concern to check to see if such interpretations had any relevance or validity.

There has also been a kind of degradation of psychoanalytic approaches, when the language and concepts are applied with great enthusiasm and little discrimination. Instead of vulgar Marxism, we now have a kind of vulgar Lacanianism. Even the best ideas from truly creative minds can be overused and beaten into the ground. I remember sitting in the audience of one conference and thinking that there was now a "phallus ex machina," a kind of dramatic technique for the resolution of academic papers. I was remembering an image form a famous Japanese print, where the men have these very large cocks, and one man has a member so huge that he rolls it around in a wheelbarrow. I had this image of the phallus being brought up to the podium on a cart. I have heard a few too many papers where the phallus or the lack were brought in as if they provided profound analysis or sudden illumination. On many of these occasions, they did neither.

At some point, I went back and read some of the early sexology and realized that Freud's comments on the sexual aberrations were a brilliant, but limited, intervention into a pre-existing literature that was very dense, rich, and interesting. His brilliance and fame, and the role of psychoanalytic explanation within psychiatry, have given his comments on sexual variation a kind of canonical status. Even though many of his successors ignored or reversed his insights, Freud's prestige has been used to legitimate the later psychoanalytic literature as the privileged discourse on the "perversions." This has eclipsed a vast sexological enterprise that was roughly contemporary with Freud and which was actually more directly concerned with the sexual "aberrations" than he was.

Early sexology has many problems of its own. Besides being sexist and anti-homosexual, the earliest sexology treated pretty much all sexual practice other than procreative heterosexuality as a pathology. Even oral sex was classified as a perversion. The dominant models were drawn from evolutionism, particularly a kind of Lamarckian social evolutionism that was deeply embedded in ideologies of the ostensible superiority of the societies of white Europeans. But sexology, particularly after Krafft-Ebing, actually looked at sexual variety, taking sexual "aberrations" or "perversions" as its primary subject. Sexologists began to collect cases, and to record studies of living, breathing, speaking inverts and perverts. Their data collecting was very uneven – some were better at it than others. And many historians are pointing out the limitations of their empirical practices. For example, from her work on the Alice Mitchell trial, Lisa Duggan has discussed how sexologists unsceptically treated newspaper

reports, or reports from other sexologists, as primary data. Robert
Nye and Jann Matlock have analyzed assumptions and prejudices, especially about men and women, which shaped the early configurations of
the categories of sexual fetishism and perversion. Nonetheless, early
sexological compendia are incredible sources to mine. Even Krafft-Ebing
is useful. For example, actual "inverts" and "perverts" read his early work
and wrote him. They sent him their life histories, their anguished self-
examinations, and their angry social critiques. Some of these were duly
published in the later editions of *Psychopathia Sexualis*. So there are these
amazing voices, like the early activist invert who eloquently denounces
the social and legal sanctions against homosexuality. Or there is an account of what was called the "woman-haters" ball, but was actually a drag
ball in turn-of-the-century Berlin. The detailed description notes that
the dancing was accompanied by "a very fine orchestra" and that many
beautifully bedecked "women" suddenly lit up cigars or spoke in a deep
baritone.

JB: Who were the other sexologists you were thinking of?

GR: Well Havelock Ellis is one of the best of them. Magnus Hirschfeld
was also very important. Ellis and Hirschfeld probably did the most,
before Freud, to normalize and destigmatize homosexuality and other
sexual variations. An indication of Ellis' power as a polemicist can be seen
in the famous letter Freud wrote to an American mother who was worried
about her homosexual son. Freud assured her that many great individuals
were homosexual, and that homosexuals should not be persecuted. He
advised her, if she didn't believe him, to go "read the books of Havelock
Ellis" (Abelove, 381).

Ellis and Freud both acknowledge a considerable debt to Hirschfeld.
Virtually everyone who writes about homosexuality at the turn of
the century cites Hirschfeld's journal, the *Jahrbuch für sexuelle
Zwischenstufen* [*The Journal for Intermediate Sexual Stages*]. Other
important sexologists included Albert Moll, Albert Eulenberg, and
Iwan Bloch. In the first footnote to his famous essay on the sexual aberrations, Freud lists several of the most influential sexologists. These are the
writers with whom he is in dialogue. They each have their own approach,
and some are more interesting that others. Despite a limited theoretical
apparatus, there is a rich social, historical, and cultural complexity
reflected in this literature that gets lost in much later psychoanalytic
writings.

My sense is that Freud was not all that interested in "perverts" or
"inverts;" he seemed much more excited by neurosis and the psychic costs

of sexual "normality." Yet his interventions into turn-of-the-century sex-ology have overshadowed the context in which he was writing and the memory of that substantial and fascinating literature. In any event, instead of just taking off from Freud or later psychoanalysis, I thought it would be a good idea to go back to that literature before the psychanalytic branch became so dominant, and see what could be learned from the issues and materials that were salient to those who first looked at sexual diversity as their main object of study.

JB: And Foucault, I presume he offered you an alternative to psychoanalysis. You were reading the first volume of Foucault's *History of Sexuality* somewhere around this time as well.

GR: Yes. That was published in English in 1978. I immediately gravi-tated to it. As you can see from my copy here it is very marked up and dog-eared. That was a very important book. I do think, that because of his undoubted stature, other work in the field of sexuality is retrospectively credited to him. There was a debate recently on one of the gay studies lists on the Internet, in which Foucault was credited as the originator of "social construction" theory. The key roles of people like Mary McIntosh, Jeffrey Weeks, Kenneth Plummer, and a host of other historians, anthropologists, and sociologists were completely erased in the context of this discussion. It astonishes me how quickly people forget even recent history, and how much they are willing to project current attitudes back as a fictive chrono-logical sequence. I was influenced by Jeffrey Weeks as much as Foucault. In my opinion, Weeks is one of the great underappreciated figures in gay studies and the social theory of sexuality. He published the basic state-ment of social construction of homosexuality in 1977, the year before Foucault's *History of Sexuality* was translated.

Many others who were working in the field of gay or lesbian history were rapidly coming to the same kinds of conclusions. I had been re-searching the history of lesbianism in the early 1970s, and quickly became aware that there was some discontinuity in the type of available data and the kinds of characteristic persons called "lesbian" before and after the late nineteenth century. There were earlier records of women who had rela-tionships with women, and records of cross-dressing or passing women. But it seemed there was little evidence of self-conscious, self-identified lesbians, or lesbian communities, or a kind of lesbian political critique, until the late 1800s.

In 1973, I took another course that changed my life. It was "The Urbanization of Europe, 1500–1900," and was given by Charles Tilly (also at the University of Michigan). Tilly described how industrialization resulted in massive transfers of population from countryside to cities, how urban life was subsequently transformed, and how the forms of voluntary association available to city-dwellers differed from those in peasant villages. Another major theme of the course was how the language and repertoire of political action changed in different historical periods. We spent a lot of time on different structures of revolutionary action and political protest in France, and how these changed over time and were specific to particular historical circumstances. Another theme of the course was the way in which forms of individual consciousness changed in the course of all these developments. We discussed E. P. Thompson's work on shifts in how people experienced time, and I was already familiar with Althusser's discussions of different forms of historical individuality (Althusser 251–3). It was a short jump from the impact of urbanization and industrialization on repertoires of political protest, the conventions of time, and forms of historical individuality, to thinking about how different forms of sexual identity and subjectivity might have resulted from the same large-scale social changes. These ideas seemed to make sense of what I was finding in my explorations of lesbian history. I didn't label any of this as "social construction," but I was reaching for ways to think about such issues. But many different scholars were taking the common approaches of social history, anthropology, and sociology, and applying these in a consistent way to homosexuality. There was a widespread convergence of this kind of thinking about male and female homosexuality, and a sudden paradigm shift, in the mid-1970s.

I was unaware of the extent of Foucault's involvement in this emerging paradigm, but I had some idea that he was doing research on sexuality and homosexuality. I had met Foucault earlier, when I was studying in France in the summers of 1972 and 1973. One of my friends was a wonderful man named Larry Shields. We were both completely obsessed with "structuralism," which was what we then called most of the contemporary French thought. We had read Lévi-Strauss and what there was of Lacan, and books of Foucault's such as *The Order of Things*. But there was so little of this material around, and we wanted to go to the source. We got grants to go off to Paris to do research on structuralism. Well, Larry dutifully sat in the main reading room at the Bibliothèque Nationale reading Godelier, Lyotard, Kristeva, and Baudrillard.

But I found that my French was inadequate to this task. As a game to find my way through the labyrinthine catalogue of the Bibliothèque Nationale, I started looking for some obscure lesbian novels that I had not been able to get my hands on for the part of my senior thesis on lesbian literature. When I found that they had Liane de Pougy's *Idylle Sapphique* (her *roman à clef* about her affair with Natalie Barney), I went up to the Reserve room to read it. I found a whole deposit of books by the Natalie Barney and Renée Vivien crowd, with penciled marginalia containing incredible biographical information on the cast of characters. So I ended up spending the summer in the Reserve, clutching my dictionary and verb book, reading dirty lesbian novels.

GR/JB: [in unison] My/Your French was good enough for that!

GR: Well, one day Larry spotted Foucault in the main reading room, and we got up our nerve and asked him out for coffee. We were totally dumbfounded when he accepted. So we went out for coffee, and he asked us what we were doing. Larry enthusiastically reported on his explorations of cutting-edge theorists. When Foucault asked me what I was doing, I very sheepishly admitted that I was reading lesbian novels upstairs in the Reserve. To my surprise, he seemed completely nonplussed, and just said, "Oh, I've been studying sodomy convictions." He explained that while sodomy laws were on the books for most of European history, they were only sporadically enforced. He was curious about what determined such patterns of enforcement. This was totally unexpected; I was astonished.

He was incredibly friendly and approachable, and gave us his address and phone number. I thought no more about it until I saw the *History of Sexuality* in 1978. I was just starting my research on the gay male leather community in San Francisco. I was going to France for a feminist conference. I mailed Foucault the very rough draft of my dissertation proposal, and told him how much I loved his new book. I thought my work might interest him at a theoretical level, but I expected him to be put off by specific things, like the focus on gay male SM. Once again he surprised me, by inviting me to dinner. It was not until I got to the dinner that I finally realized that he was homosexual, that he seemed perfectly comfortable about SM, and that I could stop worrying about offending him.

JB: So what was it in Foucault that you found useful to your thinking about sexual practices and sexuality in general?

GR: I thought his discussion of the emergence of a new relationship between systems of alliance and sexuality, at least in certain western industrial countries, was very insightful. You know, I said earlier that many people seem to have overinterpreted the last few pages of "Thinking Sex." I was not arguing there that kinship, gender, feminism, or psychoanalysis no longer mattered in any way. Rather, I was arguing that there were systems other than kinship which had assumed some kind of relative autonomy and could not be reduced to kinship, at least in the Lévi-Straussian sense. When I wrote about that, I very much had in mind the section from the *History of Sexuality* where Foucault says: "Particularly from the eighteenth century onwards, Western societies created and deployed a new apparatus which was superimposed on the previous one" (p. 106). He never says it replaces, he says "superimposed."

JB: Right, right.

GR: "And which, without completely supplanting the latter helped reduce its importance." That is the actual phrase. It does not supplant, it simply reduces its importance. "I am speaking of the deployment of sexuality: like the deployment of alliances it connects up with the circuit of sexual partners, but in a different way. The systems can be contrasted term by term." And then he says, "For the first" – that is, alliance – "what is pertinent is the link between partners and definite statutes. The second is concerned with the sensations of the body, the quality of the pleasures, and the nature of impressions, however tenuous or imperceptible these may be." Then on the next page he goes on to explain that "it is not exact to say that the deployment of sexuality supplanted the deployment of alliance" (p. 107). He writes, "One can imagine that one day it will have replaced it, but as things stand at present, while it does tend to cover up the deployment of alliance, *it has neither obliterated the latter, nor rendered it useless. Moreover, historically it was around, and on the basis of the deployment of alliance that the deployment of sexuality was constructed*" [GR's emphasis]. And then he goes on to write, "Since then it has not ceased to operate in conjunction with a system of alliance on which it had depended for support" (p. 108). He even says the family is the "inter-change" of sexuality and alliance. "It conveys the law in the juridical dimension in the deployment of sexuality, and it conveys the economy of pleasure, and the intensity of sensations in the regime of alliance." He even calls the family "the most active site of sexuality" (p. 109). Echoing this discussion, it never occurred to me that anyone would think I was arguing that kinship or the family, and their respective dynamics, have ceased to have any relevance. What he was saying helped me to think about the outlines of another system that had different dynamics, a different topography, and different lines of force. In this whole section by Foucault, you can hear the echoes of his conversations with Lévi-Strauss and Lacan. I felt that his assessment of those relationships was novel, insightful, and accurate.

There were so many things I loved about this book – the brilliance and descriptive richness of his writing, his rearrangement of the dominant concepts of sexuality, his interpretations of Freud, Lacan, Reich, and Lévi-Strauss, the dazzling insights, his models for social power, his ideas about resistance and revolution, the depth of his commitment to social and historical causality.

He generated many wonderful phrases – such as the proliferation of perversions. It gave me new ideas, provided some really clear and vivid language, and confirmed that my own preoccupations at the time were not completely absurd. I had given a couple talks on the emergence of modern lesbianism and homosexuality, and many people who heard them probably thought, politely, that I was out of my mind. Finding out that Weeks in *Coming Out* and Foucault in *The History of Sexuality* had already come to similar conclusions and had a similar understanding of a set of historical and theoretical issues was immensely reassuring and helped shape my subsequent approach.

JB: I realize that you don't want to discount the force of kinship altogether, but isn't there another issue here, namely, developing a vocabulary to articulate contemporary configurations of kinship. I guess another question for me is whether various supportive networks within the lesbian and gay community can't also be understood as contemporary forms of kinship.

GR: You can understand them that way, but then you are using kinship in a really different way. When people talk about gay kinship, for example, they are using a different model of kinship. Instead of Lévi-Strauss, it is based more on the work of David Schneider, who wrote about kinship in America. You have to be specific about how the term is used. In a Lévi-Straussian sense, kinship is a way of generating a social and political structure from manipulations of marriage and descent. In a more vernacular sense, particularly in complex societies like this one, kinship can mean simply the social relations of support, intimacy, and enduring connection. This use of kinship is very different from the Lévi-Straussian notion of kinship.

JB: Well of course it is. But doesn't that mark the conservatism of the Lévi-Straussian notion?

GR: Yes, but I'm saying that the terms are not quite commensurate. In feminist theory, a lot rides on that Lévi-Straussian notion of kinship, which can't just be switched into a more fluid notion of modern or gay-type kinship systems. So one has to be careful about what one is then saying about kinship in this different sense. A system of voluntary association is very different from a system in which obligatory marriages create dynastic systems or other forms of political organization.

Lévi-Strauss is talking about societies in which those relations of marriage and descent *are* the social structure. They either organize almost all of the social life, or they are the most important and visible institutional apparatus. In modern systems, kinship is already a structure that is much reduced in institutional importance. It is not radical to say, in anthropology, that kinship doesn't do in modern urban societies what it used to do in pre-modern cultures. Furthermore, gay kinship closely resembles what anthropologists would call "fictive" or "informal kinship." Such systems of informal or fictive kinship are even less institutionalized and structurally stable than those relationships which are reinforced by state authority.

JB: Right. Well, I would certainly say that kinship can't possibly be the predominant way in which we try to take account of the complexity of contemporary social or sexual life. I mean, that seems clear. On the other hand, it seems to me that the Foucauldian historiography that you have just noted takes for granted the Lévi-Straussian account of kinship and presumes that this form of kinship is itself something in the past.

GR: No. I don't mean to suggest that. Again, one issue is how we are defining kinship.

JB: OK. Because if we understand kinship as obligatory relations, or we think about societies that are governed by obligatory kinship relations, then certainly we would be able to say that is not commensurate with social life as we live it. On the other hand, it seems to me that kinship itself may have lost some of that obligatory status, or is in the process of losing it. And I am wondering if there is some value in holding on to the term "kinship" precisely in order to document that shift in the way in which the social life of sexuality is reconfigured and sustained.

I guess this becomes important when people want to say that feminism, especially in its psychoanalytic or structuralist mode, could talk about kinship. But that particular discourse can't possibly describe the complexity of more modern arrangements or regulatory powers that are governing sexuality. And I think that the problem has been that some people have taken this distinction to be the basis of the distinction between what feminism ought to do, namely look at kinship and gender and psychoanalysis, and what sexuality studies ought to do. And then some people, I think, have taken that a step further and have said that sexuality is the proper "object," as it were, of gay and lesbian studies, and have based the whole methodological distinction between feminism and gay and lesbian on the apparent autonomy of those two domains. So maybe it would be better if I just asked you to address that question now.

GR: You have several different issues here. To take one pertinent at the time I wrote "Traffic," there was a still a kind of naïve tendency to make general statements about the human condition that most people, including me, would now try to avoid. When you read Lévi-Strauss or Lacan, they make pretty grandiose generalizations. Plus they never hesitate to call something *the* theory of this and *the* theory of that. I often wonder if that usage reflects a grandiosity that is no longer possible or, if it is only an artifact of the translation. In French everything has an article in front of it. So "*la* théorie" in French can mean something quite different from *the* theory in English. In "Traffic," I simply absorbed the idioms and innocent universalism of the time. By the time I wrote "Thinking Sex," I wanted to make more modest claims. That was part of why, in "Thinking Sex," I noted that the Lévi-Straussian/Lacanian formulations might or might not be accurate for other societies, even as I was certain that they had limited applicability to our own. I had acquired some scepticism about the universality of those models.

As for this great methodological divide you are talking about, between feminism and gay/lesbian studies, I do not think I would accept that distribution of interests, activities, objects, and methods. I see no reason why feminism has to be limited to kinship and psychoanalysis, and I never said it should not work on sexuality. I only said it should not be seen as the privileged site for work on sexuality. I cannot imagine a gay and lesbian studies that is not interested in gender as well as sexuality and, as you note in your paper, there are many other sexualities to explore besides male homosexuality and lesbianism. But I am not persuaded that there is widespread acceptance of this division of intellectual labor between feminism, on the one hand, and gay and lesbian studies on the other. And it was certainly never my intention to establish a mutually exclusive disciplinary barrier between feminism and gay and lesbian studies. That was not an issue I was dealing with. I was trying to make some space for work on sexuality (and even gender) that did not presume feminism as the obligatory and sufficient approach. But I was not trying to found a field. For one thing, at that time the institutionalization of gay and lesbian studies was a fond dream that seemed far removed from the realm of immediate possibility. And yet, on the other hand, gay and lesbian studies as an enterprise was well under way. "Thinking Sex" was part of that ongoing process.

Some of the context for "Thinking Sex" was the developing project of gay and lesbian studies, especially gay and lesbian history and anthropology. There now seems to be a certain amnesia about the early work of lesbian and gay studies, as if the field only just started in the early or mid-1980s. This just isn't true. There are whole strata of work in lesbian and gay scholarship which date from the early 1970s and which came out of the gay liberation movement. These in turn built on even earlier research based in the homophile movement. Gay scholarly work was not institutionalized in academia, and many of the people who did that work in the 1970s have paid a high price in terms of their academic careers. Lesbian and gay studies certainly didn't start with me, or at such a late date.

For example, the San Francisco Lesbian and Gay History Project started 1978. A lot of work was begun in the excitement of that time: Allan Berubé's work on gays in the military, Liz Kennedy and Madeline Davis's work on the Buffalo lesbian community, and my research on gay male leather were all undertaken then. By that time, there were many other scholars involved, and most of us were in communication and dialogue with one another and with one another's work.

Jonathan Ned Katz' *Gay American History*, John D'Emilio's *Sexual Politics, Sexual Communities*, Jim Steakley's *The Homosexual Emancipation Movement in Germany*, and Jeffrey Weeks's *Coming Out: Homosexual Politics in Britain* were from an even earlier period. There was another book on the German gay rights movement by John Lauritsen and David Thorstad published in 1974. By the very early 1970s, lesbian scholars were starting to build on the earlier, pathbreaking bibliographic studies by Jeannette Foster and Barbara Grier. I bring this work up to note that gay and lesbian studies preceded "Thinking Sex" and that it was a thriving scholarly enterprise long before it began to be institutionalized.

JB: Well, tell us what you had in mind then when you wanted to designate the provisionally autonomous status of sexuality as a field.

GR: I wanted to have better scholarship on sexuality, and a richer set of ideas about it than were readily available. I wanted to be able to articulate a sexual politics that did not assume that feminism was the last word and holy writ on the subject. Just as I had a decade earlier wanted a way to think about gender oppression as distinct from class oppression (though not necessarily unrelated or in opposition), I later wanted to be able to think about oppression based on sexual conduct or illicit desire that was distinct from gender oppression (although, again, not necessarily unrelated or in opposition to it). I felt that we had to be able to articulate the structures of sexual stratification and make them visible in order to contest them. I thought that if we did not, progressive constituencies would unwittingly play into a very reactionary sexual agenda, which has, alas, too often been the case. I was afraid that if there were no independent analysis of sexual stratification and erotic persecution, well-intentioned feminists and other progressives would support abusive, oppressive, and undeserved witch-hunts.

I think by then a certain kind of feminist orthodoxy had become an edifice with some of the same problems that had earlier plagued Marxism. Instead of class, gender was often supposed to be the primary contradiction from which all social problems flowed. There was an attitude that feminism now had the answers to all the problems for which Marxism was found wanting. I remember that one Marxist scholar made a wonderful comment about a certain approach to Marxism, which I thought was beginning to be applicable to a certain kind of feminism as well. I cannot recall who made the comment, although I think it was Martin Nicolaus. But the comment criticized those Marxists who treated *Capital* as if it were a lemon, as if by squeezing it hard enough all the categories of social life would come dripping out. By the early 1980s, there were many people who approached feminism in the same way. For some, feminism had become the successor to Marxism and was supposed to be the next grand theory of all human misery. I am sceptical of any attempt to privilege one set of analytical tools over all others, and all such claims of theoretical and political omnipotence.

I approach systems of thought as tools people make to get leverage and control over certain problems. I an sceptical of all universal tools. A tool may do one job brilliantly, and be less helpful for another. I did not see feminism as the best tool for the job of getting leverage over issues of sexual variation.

I certainly never intended "Thinking Sex" as an attack on feminism, any more than I intended "Traffic" as an attack on Marxism. "Traffic" was largely addressed to an audience drenched in Marxism, and can be easily be misunderstood in an era whose preoccupations are so different. I find the current neglect of Marx a tragedy, and I hope to see a revival of interest in his work. Marx was a brilliant social thinker, and the failure to engage important and vital issues of Marxist thought has weakened social and political analysis.

"Thinking Sex" similarly assumed a largely feminist readership. It was delivered at a feminist conference, aimed at a feminist audience, and written within the context of feminist discussion. I do not consider it an attack on a body of work to say that it cannot do everything equally well.

Finally, I wanted to add sexual practice to the grand list of social stratifications, and to establish sexuality as a vector of persecution and oppression. In the 1960s, the important stratifications were pretty much understood to be caste, class, and race. One of the great contributions of feminism was to add gender to that list. By the early 1980s, it had become clear to me that adding gender did not take care of the issues of sexual persecution, and that sexuality needed to be included as well.

JB: Your own work has become descriptively very rich, especially the ethnographic work, and earlier, with respect to the sexologists, you applaud their efforts for being full of valuable descriptive data. You mention as well that they "looked at" cases and practices. Is "looking at" in this sense a theoretical activity? In other words, don't we look with or through certain kinds of theoretical suppositions? And are certain kinds of practices "seeable" or "unseeable" depending on which theoretical presuppositions are used? Perhaps you would like to take this opportunity to speak a bit more about the relationship between descriptive and theoretical work?

GR: Yes, of course. Whenever we look at anything we are already making decisions at some level about what constitutes the "seeable," and those decisions affect how we interpret what it is that we "see." The paradigms that informed early sexology produced a certain set of interpretations and explanations which I would reject, particularly the presumption that sexual diversity equals sexual pathology. The assumptions of sexology structured many of the categories and presuppositions that we are still dealing with today, for example, the idea that women are less capable of, less prone to, and less adept at sexual perversions than men. At the same time, their approach enabled sexologists to bring sexual diversity, however misperceived, into their field of view. It is, as it were, at the center of their lens, at the focal point of their enterprise. While Freud had, in general, a lens with better optics and higher resolution, sexual diversity was more at the edge of his field of view. In a way, it remains there in much subsequent work, including large parts of feminism.

But your question raises another issue for me, and that is the way in which empirical research and descriptive work are often treated as some kind of low-status, even stigmatized, activity that is inferior to "theory." There needs to be a discussion of what exactly is meant, these days, by "theory," and what counts as "theory." I would like to see a less dismissive attitude toward empirical work. There is a disturbing trend to treat with condescension or contempt any work that bothers to wrestle with data. This comes, in part, from the quite justified critiques of positivism and crude empiricism. But such critiques should sharpen the techniques for gathering and evaluating information rather than becoming a rationalization for failing to gather information at all.

One friend of mine likes to say, "all data are dirty." I take this to mean that data are not just things out there waiting to be harvested, with intrinsic meanings that are readily or inevitably apparent. Data, too, are socially constructed, and there are always perspectives that determine what constitutes data or affect evaluations of what can be learned from data. Nonetheless, it is a big mistake to decide that since data are imperfect, it is better to avoid the challenges of dealing with data altogether. I am appalled at a developing attitude that seems to think that having no data is better than having any data, or that dealing with data is an inferior and discrediting activity. A lack of solid, well-researched, careful, descriptive work will eventually impoverish feminism, and gay and lesbian studies, as much as a lack of rigorous conceptual scrutiny will. I find this galloping idealism as disturbing as mindless positivism.

I also find preposterous the idea that empirical work is always easy, simple, or unanalytical. Unfortunately, virtuoso empirical work often goes unrecognized. Good empirical research involves as much thought and is as intellectually challenging as good conceptual analysis. In many ways, it is more challenging. I know this is a completely heretical opinion, but it is often more difficult to assemble, assimilate, understand, organize, and present original data than it is to work over a group of canonical texts which have been, by now, cultivated for so long by so many that they are already largely digested. There is plenty of "theory" in the best empirical studies, even if such studies often fail to cite the latest list of 25 essential authorizing or legitimizing "theorists."

Moreover, many people who deal with data are trained to be sophisticated about how to evaluate empirical material. Some who proclaim the supremacy of theory and who are contemptuous of empirical research can be quite naïve about the material used in their own "theoretical" work. Often, data come in, as it were, by the back door. In the absence of empirical research or training, some ostensibly theoretical texts end up relying on assumptions, stereotypes, anecdotes, fragments of data that are out of context, inaccurate details, other people's research, or material that is recycled from other so-called "theoretical texts." So some extremely dirty data get enshrined as "theory." The opposition between "theoretical" and "empirical" work is a false, or at least, distorted one; the imbalance between conceptual analysis and data analysis needs some redress. In short, I would like to see more "interrogation" of the contemporary category of "theory," and of the relationships between such "theory" and empirical or descriptive research.

There is another specific problem I see with regard to sexuality. There is a common assumption that certain kinds of conceptual analysis or literary and film criticism provide descriptions or explanations about living individuals or populations, without establishing the relevance or applicability of such analyses to those individuals or groups. I have no objection to people performing dazzling analytic moves upon a body of assumptions or texts in order to say interesting things about those assumptions or texts. I have nothing against philosophy, literary analysis, or film criticism *per se*. But I have a problem with the indiscriminate use of such analyses to generate descriptions of living populations or explanations of their behaviors.

For example, there is a trend to analyze sexual variance by mixing a few privileged "theoretical" texts with literary or film criticism to produce statements about either the thing (e.g. "masochism") or the population (e.g. "masochists"). The currently fashionable "theory" of sadomasochism is Deleuze's long 1971 essay on "masochism." Despite the fact that Deleuze based much of his analysis on fiction, primarily Sacher-Masoch's novel, *Venus in Furs*, and some texts of de Sade, he is taken to be an authority on sadism and masochism in general. Since he is known as a theorist, his comments on sadism and masochism are surrounded with the penumbra of "Theory."

Deleuze treats differences in the literary techniques of Sade and Sacher-Masoch as evidence for ostensible differences between "sadism" and "masochism." But what are the "sadism" and "masochism" of which he speaks? Are they literary genres? Desires of living sadists and masochists? Floating formations of desire? He makes sweeping generalizations about "sadism" and "masochism," such as "sadism negates the mother and inflates the father; masochism disavows the mother and abolishes the father. . . . There is an aestheticism in masochism, while sadism is hostile to the aesthetic attitude. . . ." (p. 115). I find statements like these fairly meaningless, intelligible only because of a psychoanalytic tradition that has equated particular constellations of sexual desire with alleged universals of childhood development. What troubles me is that such generalizations are and will be taken as descriptive statements about those persons and populations who might be considered "masochistic" or "sadistic."

Deleuze is very smart, and it also seems clear from his text that he had some acquaintance with practicing perverts. But his empirical knowledge enters primarily as anecdote. He seems familiar with female dominance, particularly by professional Mistresses. He seems to generalize from some literature and some kind of personal knowledge to make statements about "masochism" and "sadism" in a broader context. This essay is fascinating, yet hardly definitive. It is nonetheless becoming an authoritative text for writing about masochism and sadism.

Now there are discussions which draw on Deleuze to analyze the "masochistic aesthetic," "the masochistic text," "masochism's psycho-dynamics," or "masochistic narrativity." Such usage implies that maso-chism is an "it," a unitary phenomenon whose singular psychodynamic, text, aesthetic, or narrativity are not only knowable but known. Leaving aside the issue of what terms like this mean, I see a danger that statements about what "masochism" in this sense "is" or "does" or "means" will be taken as descriptions or interpretations of what actual masochists are, do, or mean. Yet, the authority of these statements is not derived from any systematic knowledge of masochism as it is practiced by masochists. It is derived from an analytic apparatus balanced precariously upon Deleuze's commentary, Sade's fiction and philosophical writings, Sacher-Masoch's novels, psychoanalytic writings on the etiology of masochism, various other texts and films, and personal anecdote.

I have this quaint, social science attitude that statements about living populations should be based on some knowledge of such populations, not on speculative analysis, literary texts, cinematic repre-sentations, or preconceived assumptions. And I can hear the objection to what I'm saying already: "but Deleuze," someone is bound to say, "is Theory."

JB: So tell us more about the kind of work you are currently doing, and how it negotiates this tension between conceptual and descriptive domains. You just completed your study on the gay male leather community in San Francisco. What is it that you sought to find there?

GR: Well, when I started this project I was interested in the whole question of sexual ethnogenesis. I wanted to understand better how sexual communities form. This question came out of work I had done in lesbian history, and initially I was trying to figure out where lesbian communities came from, or how they come to exist. I became curious about gay male as well as lesbian communities. Then I realized that many sexualities were organized as urban populations, some quite territorial. I started to wonder about what stork brought all of these sexual populations, and how it happened. This was all part of reorienting my thinking about such catego-ries as lesbianism, homosexuality, sadism, masochism, or fetishism. In-stead of seeing these as clinical entities or categories of individual psychology, I wanted to approach them as social groups with histories, territories, institutional structures, modes of communication, etc.

As an anthropologist, I wanted to study something contemporary. There were a number of reasons why I picked this community, but one was that it had crystallized since World War II. There were still individuals around who were involved then, from the late 1940s on. I had access to them, and could study this fascinating process whereby some sexual practice or desire that was once completely stigmatized, hidden, and despised could actually be institutionalized in a subculture in which it was considered normal and desirable. The building of subcultural systems designed to facilitate non-normative sexualities is an interesting process.

And in many ways, the gay male leather community is a textbook case of sexual social formation, although the sexualities within it are more complex than I initially thought. For one thing, "leather" does not always mean "SM." Leather is a broader category that includes gay men who do SM, gay men who are into fisting, gay men who are fetishists, and gay men who are masculine and prefer masculine partners. Leather is a multivalent symbol that has different meanings to different individuals and groups within such communities. Among gay men, leather and its idioms of masculinity have been the main framework for gay male SM since the late 1940s. Other groups organize similar desires in different social and symbolic constellations. For example, heterosexual SM for most of the same period was not organized around the symbol of leather, idioms of masculinity, or urban territories. "Leather" is a historically and culturally specific construct in which certain forms of desire among gay men have been organized and structured socially.

I also did not know when I began this research that at least one sexual activity, fist-fucking, seems to have been a truly original invention. As others have pointed out, fisting is perhaps the only sexual practice invented in this century. It may have been practiced in the early 1960s. But it really became popular in the late 1960s and early 1970s, and then spawned its own unique subcultural elaboration and institutionalization.

Within the gay male leather community, you get this particular unity of the kinky and the masculine in a way that you don't see among heterosexuals or lesbians where those things are mapped out differently. It is a very unique and interesting way of putting certain sexual practices together.

JB: What is the significance about the combination of masculinity and kinkiness?

GR: That is a huge subject, and requires a much longer discussion than we can have here. Among gay men, the adoption of masculinity is complicated, and has a lot to do with rejecting the traditional equations of male homosexual desire with effeminacy. Since the mid-nineteenth century, there has been a slowly evolving distinction between homosexual object choice and cross-gender or transgender behavior. A masculine homosexual (like a feminine lesbian) was once considered an oxymoron; such persons existed but were "unthinkable" in terms of the hegemonic models of sexuality and gender. The development of the leather community is part of a long historical process in which masculinity has been claimed, asserted, or reappropriated by male homosexuals. Gay male leather, including gay male SM, codes both desiring/desired subjects and desired/desiring objects as masculine. In this system, a man can be overpowered, restrained, tormented, and penetrated, yet retain his masculinity, desirability, and subjectivity. There are also symbolics of effeminate homosexual SM, but these have been a relatively minor theme in the 50 years of gay male leather.

Other communities don't combine these things in the same way. During most of the same time period, heterosexual SM was organized more through sex ads, professional dominance, and some private social clubs. For heterosexual SM, leather was a fetish, but not the core symbol which anchored institutionalization. Straight SM was not territorial, and if anything, the dominant stylistic idioms were feminine.

The imagery of heterosexual SM and fetishism draws on a lot of feminine symbolism. SM erotica aimed at male heterosexuals often has mostly female characters, and the few male characters are often effeminized. There are many reasons for this, including the idiosyncracies of the history of legal regulation of SM erotica. But evidently many heterosexual men have fantasies of being lovely young ladies. Most of the better equipped houses of dominance have a special room for cross-dressing male clients who pay handsomely for the privilege. These "fantasy" rooms are distinguished from "dungeons" or "medical" rooms. They are often decorated in pink frills and ruffles. So one typical heterosexual SM coupling may involve a woman dressed in feminine attire, dominating a man who may be overtly or covertly "effeminized." I do not mean to imply that there are no "masculine" heterosexual male masochists or sadists. Moreover, this feminine imagery is not as hegemonic for heterosexual SM as is masculine imagery for gay male SM. But a visible and common style of heterosexual SM involves a feminine woman and an effeminized man, a sort of fantasy "lesbian" couple. Meanwhile, among actual lesbian sadomasochists, there seems to be a pretty even distribution of masculine and feminine styles, genders, and symbolism.

JB: I'd like to bring us back to gender . . .

GR: You would! I will only say that I never claimed that sexuality and gender were always unconnected, only that they are not identical. Moreover, their relationships are situational, not universal, and must be determined in particular situations. I think I will leave any further comments on gender to you, in your capacity as the reigning "Queen" of Gender!

San Francisco, August 1994

References

Abelove, Henry. "Freud, Male Homosexuality, and the Americans," in Henry Abelove, Michele Barale, and David Halperin, eds, *The Lesbian and Gay Studies Reader*, New York: Routledge, 1993.

Althusser, Louis. "Freud and Lacan," *New Left Review*, no. 55, May–June (1969), pp. 48–66.

——. *Reading Capital*, London: New Left Books, 1970.

Berubé, Allan. *Coming Out Under Fire: the History of Gay Men and Women in World War II*, New York: Free Press, 1990.

D'Emilio, John. *Sexual Politics Sexual Communities: The Making of a Homosexual Minority in the United States, 1940–1970*, Chicago: University of Chicago Press, 1983.

Deleuze, Gilles. *Masochism: An Interpretation of Coldness and Cruelty*, New York: George Braziller, 1971.

Duggan, Lisa. "The Trials of Alice Mitchell: Sensationalism, Sexology and the Lesbian Subject in Turn-of-the-Century America," *Signs*, Summer (1993), pp. 791–814.

Engels, Friedrich. *The Origin of the Family, Private Property and the State*, Intro. Eleanor Burke Leacock (1st edn), New York: International Publishers, 1942, 1972.

Faderman, Lillian. *Surpassing the Love of Men: Romantic Friendship and Love Between Women from the Renaissance to the Present*, New York: Morrow, 1981.

Foster, Jeannette D. *Sex Variant Women In Literature*, New York: Vantage, 1956.

Foucault, Michel. *The Archaeology of Knowledge*, Trans. A. M. Sheridan Smith, New York: Pantheon, 1972.

——. *The History of Sexuality, Vol. I*, Trans. Robert Jurley, New York: Pantheon, 1978.

——. *Madness and Civilization: A History of Insanity in the Age of Reason*, Trans. Richard Howard, New York: Pantheon Books, 1965.

——. *The Order of Things: An Archaeology of the Human Sciences*, New York: Pantheon, 1970.

Sigmund Freud, "The Sexual Aberrations," *The Basic Writings of Sigmund Freud*, 1966, New York: Modern Library, pp. 553–79.

Grier, Barbara. *The Lesbian in Literature*, Tallahassee, FL: Naiad, 1981. (Note: the first edition of *The Lesbian in Literature* was published in 1967, when Barbara Grier still published under the name of Gene Damon.)

Hartman, Heidi. "The Unhappy Marriage of Marxism and Feminism," in *Women and Revolution*, Ed. Lydia Sargent, Boston: South End Press, 1981.

House, Penny and Liza Cowan. "Can Men Be Women? Some Lesbians Think So! Transsexuals in the Women's Movement," *Dyke, A Quarterly*, vol. 5, Fall (1977), pp. 29–35.

Jeffreys, Sheila. *The Spinster and her Enemies: Feminism and Sexuality*, London, Boston: Pandora Press, 1985.

Katz, Jonathan. *Gay American History: Lesbians and Gay Men in the USA*, New York: Crowell, 1976.

Kennedy, Elizabeth Lapovsky and Madeline Davis. *Boots of Leather Slippers of Gold: the History of a Lesbian Community*, New York: Routledge, 1993.

Krafft-Ebing, R. von. *Psychopathia Sexualis, with Special Reference to the Contrary Sexual Instinct: A Medico-Legal Study*, Philadelphia: F. A. Davis Company, 1899.

Lacan, Jacques. *The Language of the Self: the Function of Language in Psychoanalysis*, Trans. Anthony Wilden, Baltimore: Johns Hopkins Press, 1968.

Lauritsen, John and David Thorstad. *The Early Homosexual Rights Movement*, New York: Times Change Press, 1974.

Lederer, Laura. *Take Back the Night: Women on Pornography*, New York: William Morrow, 1980.

Lévi-Strauss, Claude. *The Elementary Structures of Kinship*, Trans. Bell, Strurmer, and Needham, Boston: Beacon Press, 1969.

MacKinnon, Catherine. "Marxism, Feminism, Method and the State," Parts I and II, *Signs*, vol. 7, no. 3 (1982) and vol. 8, no. 4 (1983).

Mannoni, Maud *The Child, his "Illness" and the Others*, New York: Pantheon Books, 1970.

Matlock, Jann. "Masquerading Women, Pathologized Men: Cross-Dressing, Fetishism, and the Theory of Perversion, 1882–1935,"

Fetishism as Cultural Discourse, Ed. Emily Apter and William Pietz, Ithaca, NY: Cornell University Press, 1993, pp. 31–61.

Nye, Robert A. "The Medical Origins of Sexual Fetishism," in *Fetishism as Cultural Discourse*, Ed. Emily Apter and William Pietz, Ithaca, NY: Cornell University Press, 1993, pp. 13–30.

Peiss, Kathy. *Cheap Amusements: Working Women and Leisure in Turn-of the Century New York*, Philadelphia: Temple, 1986.

Pougy, Liane de. *Idylle Sapphique*, Paris: La Plume, 1901.

Reiter, Rayna R. *Toward An Anthropology of Women*, New York: Monthly Review Press, 1975.

Adrienne Rich. "Compulsory Heterosexuality and Lesbian Existence, *Signs*, vol. 5, no. 4, pp. 631–60 (1980).

Rubin, Gayle. "The Traffic in Women: Notes on the 'Political Economy' of Sex," *Toward an Anthropology of Women*, Ed. Rayna R. Reiter, New York: Monthly Review Press, 1975: 157–210.

——. "Thinking Sex: Notes for a Radical Theory of the Politics of Sexuality," in *Pleasure and Danger: Exploring Female Sexuality*, Ed. Carole S. Vance, Boston: Routledge & Kegan Paul, 1984, pp. 267–319.

——. "Misguided, Dangerous, and Wrong: An Analysis of Anti-Pornography Politics," in Allison Assiter and Avedon Carol, eds, *Bad Girls and Dirty Pictures: the Challenge To Reclaim Feminism*, London: Pluto, 1993, pp. 18–40.

——. "The Leather Menace," in Samois, *Coming To Power*, Boston: Alyson, 1982, pp. 192–227.

——. "A Contribution to the Critique of the Political Economy of Sex and Gender," Part I, *Dissemination* vol. 1, no. 1, pp. 6–13; Part II, *Dissemination* vol. 1, no. 2, pp. 23–32 (1974).

Sacher-Masoch, Leopold von. *Venus in Furs*. In Gilles, Deleuze, *Masochism* New York: Zone Books, 1991.

Sahli, Nancy. "Smashing: Women's Relationships Before the Fall," *Chrysalis*, vol. 8, pp. 17–27.

Schneider, David M. *American Kinship: A Cultural Account*, Englewood Cliffs, NJ: Prentice-Hall, 1968.

——. *A Critique of the Study of Kinship*, Ann Arbor: University of Michigan Press, 1984.

Smith-Rosenberg, Caroll. "The Female World of Love and Ritual: Relations Between Women in Nineteenth-Century America," *Signs*, vol. 1, no. 1 (1975) pp. 1–29.

Steakley, James D. *The Homosexual Emancipation Movement in Germany*, Salem: H. H. Ayer, 1975.

Thompson, E. P. "Time, Work-Discipline, and Industrial Capitalism," in *Customs in Common: Studies in Traditional Popular Culture*, New York: New Press, 1993.

Vance, Carole S. *Pleasure and Danger*, Boston: Routledge & Kegan Paul, 1984.

———. "Social Construction Theory: Problems in the History of Sexuality," in Dennis Altman et al., *Homosexuality, Which Homosexuality?* London: Gay Men's Press, 1989.

Walkowitz, Judith. *City of Dreadful Delight: Narratives of Sexual Danger in Late-Victorian London*, Chicago: University of Chicago, 1992.

Weeks, Jeffrey. *Coming Out: Homosexual Politics in Britain from the Nineteenth Century to the Present*, London, New York: Quartet Books, 1977.

Chapter 3

Sissies and Sisters: Gender, Sexuality and the Possibilities of Coalition

William J. Spurlin

The varieties of feminist criticism of the past two to three decades have helped to dismantle hegemonic constructions of gender and culture and have provided new lenses for reading texts and reading the world. More recently, and not without the insistent pressures of lesbians, women of color, and non-western women, feminism has begun to question gender as a single category of analysis and as a singular subject position from which to speak. For me, feminism also has personal value because it was a pathway to lesbian and gay studies. Many gay men like myself came to feminism in their graduate training before coming to lesbian and gay studies, having been taught by second-wave feminist thinkers who formed a significant part of our academic history and intellectual formation. It would not be reductive to say that feminism, because it allowed us to retheorize our positions as gay men in a patriarchal culture and to question radically the (straight) male gaze, enabled gay inquiry or, at the very least, helped us to develop an intellectual position from which to speak and work in the academy.

As a gay critic, I remain excited by the explosion of lesbian and gay scholarship over the past decade, the proliferation of lesbian and gay studies courses, the development of centers and institutes for lesbian and gay studies at major research universities, and, indeed, the arrival of the "queer moment" in the humanities. Yet I worry over the cost of such institutional recognition and success. Despite early feminist support, I find it surprising that to date, gay (male) studies has neither significantly nor sufficiently theorized and developed its relation to feminism politically or intellectually;[1] it is still often assumed that one's own self-identical authority as a gay man is sufficient to articulate queer identity. Teresa de Lauretis has observed that gay critics seldom make more than a perfunctory gesture in the direction of feminist or lesbian studies (De Lauretis 1991, viii). I also share Ed Cohen's concern that, while collectively and individually "we may want to claim or create positions from which to make visible and intelligible diverse bodies of practices (or practices of bodies) that have historically been excluded from intellectual inquiry, to do so in the name of any one such position will ultimately repeat the problematic oppositions of sameness and difference that have plagued earlier attempts to institutionalize identity politics" (Cohen 1990, 172). Contemporary feminist work has already noticed this uncritical reinscription of oppositions in identity politics, and women of color, especially, have urged new alliances focusing on interarticulations of power. As bell hooks writes:

> Feminism, as liberation struggle, must exist *apart from* and *as a*
> *part of* the larger struggle to eradicate domination in all of its
> forms. We must understand that patriarchal domination shares
> an ideological foundation with racism and other forms of group
> oppression, that there is no hope that it can be eradicated while
> these systems remain intact. (hooks 1989, 22; emphasis added)

Including homophobia as a significant axis of domination implies further thinking about where various forms of power intersect in culture and how this may lead to the restructuring of political alliances. With these preliminary thoughts in mind, I am interested in how we may retheorize the relation between gender and sexuality (the supposed "proper" objects of feminism and queer studies respectively).[2] One can also ask how the projects of feminist and gay male inquiry may operate in coalition to disrupt further the structures of patriarchal domination responsible for oppressive social relations. To what extent do the political positions of women (both straight and lesbian) and gay men converge by virtue of being situated in (ef)feminized positions in relation to patriarchal power (which is the not the same as assuming that there is an automatic or transhistorical relation between feminist, lesbian, and gay male inquiry)? Crucial to this analysis is attention to how identities are produced through what Teresa de Lauretis has elsewhere referred to as "technologies of gender," that is, how subjects are engendered through the process of taking on or assuming "the positionalities and meaning effects specified by a particular society's gender system" (de Lauretis, 1994, 302).[3] Such attention to gender must also ensure that the axes of gender and sexuality operate as dialogically as possible. In the particular context of my focus on theorizing sites of cultural and political alliance between feminist and gay male inquiry, it is especially important to ensure that the axis of sexuality not obscure that of gender so that the specificity of lesbian difference, which arises out of apparent parallels, is not rendered invisible.

Acknowledging that the projects of feminism and gay studies are not coextensive, one can ask whether it might be helpful theoretically and politically to argue for their interimplication, not globally or causally, but by asking how the struggle against homophobia by gay men may also in part be feminist struggle insofar as it is a struggle against gender oppression. As Eve Sedgwick has pointed out in *Between Men*, homophobia directed by men against men is misogynistic, and not only oppressive of the so-called feminine in men, but oppressive of women (Sedgwick 1985, 20). Because in western culture a man perceived as feminine is similar to being perceived as gay, and a man identified as gay is thought to be feminine (that is, not a "real" man), the struggles against gender oppression and homosexuality become linked, though one is not reducible to the other. Although homophobia may be the more prominent axis of oppression used against gay men, and misogyny the more prominent one against lesbians (often in a more pronounced way than the ways in which it is used against heterosexual women), the apparent differences of these oppressions may be matters of degree, of back and forth movement. This should not blind us to the ways in which an emphasis on one may also include or implicate the other and how either can apply to both lesbians and gay men, though not necessarily in equal measure. But in *Epistemology of the Closet*, where Sedgwick brilliantly shows the pervasiveness of the hetero/homo split in western cultural representations in the twentieth century, arguing that readings of western culture are flawed unless cultural works across the disciplines are (re)read through the lenses of antihomophobic analyses, she, through citing Gayle Rubin's essay "Thinking Sex," speaks of the analytic usefulness of disjoining gender and sexuality while acknowledging their relatedness (Sedgwick 1990, 30–1).[4] Certainly Sedgwick's argument is useful to expose the limits of the hetero/homo opposition, which she sees as operating foundationally and substitutively for the category of sexuality. According to Sedgwick, the hetero/homo opposition fails to acknowledge the possibility of theorizing dimensions of sexuality that may not have a *distinctive* or *explicit* connection with the gender of object choice, and it breaks down when we consider instances in which the issue of gender may not be the distinguishing feature of sexual choice, as in certain autoerotic and alloerotic practices and erotic acts between generations, species, etc., that cannot be easily or fully subsumed under the auspices of either heterosexuality or homosexuality (Sedgwick 1990, 31, 35).

These are useful distinctions with which I fully agree. But in the specific context of lesbian and gay studies, I think it is a mistake to theorize gender and sexuality as distinct, as, for instance, a means to resist effeminophobia, a form homophobia may take, in the fairly recent addition of "Gender Identity Disorder in Childhood" (GID), which first appeared in the *DSM-III*.[5] Because psychoanalytic and psychiatric clinical literature have historically conflated gender and sexuality, Sedgwick once again suggests in her essay "How to Bring Your Kids Up Gay," though with more caution this time, the usefulness of theorizing gender and sexuality as distinct though intimately entangled axes of analysis (Sedgwick 1993, 157). Sedgwick's argument here stems from revisionary psychoanalytic developments (which I shall discuss shortly) that depathologize *atypical sexual object-choice* while in the same move, through the inclusion of gender identity disorder in the *DSM*, pathologizing *atypical gender identification* (Sedgwick 1993, 158). But are gender and sexuality necessarily separated in this shift of focus? It seems that the diagnosing of GID in feminine boys, its usual target, is intimately tied to the prevention of gay outcome, that interpreting feminine identification in boys as a gender "disorder" is not distinct, as I shall argue, from homophobia. As the imperatives of compulsory heterosexuality, which serve patriarchy, conflate gender and sexuality by prescribing that identification as one sex must necessarily result in the desire for the other, it does not follow that the combined efforts of an oppositional antimisogynistic and antihomophobic analysis will necessarily reproduce the same simplistic, causal logic between gender and sexuality already in place. To destabilize and resist the apparatus of compulsory heterosexuality, it seems necessary to develop an analysis that *re*theorizes the relation between gender and sexuality. Speaking to this point in *Bodies that Matter*, Judith Butler writes:

> Precisely because homophobia often operates through the attribution of a damaged, failed, or otherwise abject gender to homosexuals, that is, calling gay men "feminine" or calling lesbians "masculine," and because the homophobic terror over performing homosexual acts, where it exists, is often also a terror over losing proper gender . . . , it seems crucial to retain a theoretical apparatus that will account for how sexuality is regulated through the policing and the shaming of gender. (Butler 1993, 238)

According to Butler, gender and sexuality are linked as they are produced as effects of juridical systems of power, specifically the heterosexual matrix, which Butler defines as that grid of *cultural* intelligibility through which bodies, genders, and desires are "naturalized." In other words, the heterosexual matrix sets up imaginary relations between gender identification and desire in assuming "that for bodies to cohere and make sense there must be a stable sex expressed through a stable gender (masculine expresses male, feminine expresses female) that is oppositionally and hierarchically defined through the compulsory practice of heterosexuality" (Butler 1990, 151n). "True" sexuality comes to be defined as heterosexuality supported by "true" genders.[6]

Following Butler's argument, because gender and sexuality figure in the matrix of power relations delimited by phallogocentrism and compulsory heterosexuality, it would not be feasible to treat them as separate categories of analysis. If sexuality is culturally constructed within existing regimes of power, it is not possible to theorize gender apart from regulatory sexual regimes. There are instances when gender does not follow from sex and when desire does not follow from either sex or gender, "follow" here denoting not a natural continuity but "a *political* relation of entailment instituted by the cultural laws that establish and regulate the shape and meaning of sexuality" (Butler 1990, 17; emphasis added). The proliferation and persistence of gender identities that do not adhere to the norm of cultural intelligibility (and are thereby marked as abject within that domain) enable critical opportunities, Butler argues, to expose the limits of cultural intelligibility and to open up subversive matrices of gender disorder within the very terms of that matrix of intelligibility (Butler 1990, 17). I would add, however, that sexuality and gender may be linked, though not in the way demanded by compulsory heterosexuality. For Butler, gender is a performance that is not a singular act, but a reiteration of a set of norms linked to heterosexual hegemony creating the illusion of an inner sex or essence. To inhabit a viable subjectivity, we are not required simply to obey gender norms as commands, but to respond to their material demands, to take them up, to cite them. But as Butler elaborates in *Bodies that Matter*, gender is an assignment that is never quite carried out to expectation; the addressee who takes up the imperative of gendering through the embodying of norms never quite fully meets the ideal or expectation (Butler 1994, 231–2). Thus, although compulsory heterosexuality operates through the stabilization of gender norms, gender designates a diverse site of significations that *contain* and *exceed* the heterosexual matrix (Butler 1994, 238), a site densely occupied with possibilities for resistance. In this light, contentious practices of queerness are examples of performativity and citational politics that not only rework the abjection of homosexuality into political agency, defiance, and legitimacy (Butler 1994, 21), but *resignify* new relations between gender and sexuality rather than seeing their interimplication as part of the problem. In other words, if I understand Butler correctly, queer performativity does not transcend the regimes of power it seeks to contest, but redeploys them to seek new modalities of agency and resistance. Butler's analysis teaches that while the relation between sexuality and gender is not one that is structurally determined, the two need to be thought of in dynamic relation to one another in other ways in order to destabilize the heterosexist presumption that structures their relationship.

I have given significant space to Butler's analysis of gender because it creates a space to retheorize gender, sexuality, and both the ways in which feminism may potentially, if provisionally, intersect with lesbian and gay studies and the ways in which queer inquiry works through feminist positions and practices. The point is that gender and sexuality are always already interimplicated to the extent that sexual practices are differentially structured according to the relations of gender in which they occur. The *causal* and reductive relation between gender and sexuality posited by the regime of compulsory heterosexuality is not one that is natural, but is an imaginary construct that may lose its imposing power through the persistence of other configurations between them.

Theorizing gender and sexuality beyond the positions they occupy in the heterosexual matrix not only has important analytic implications, like those I have been discussing, but important political ones as well in terms of how we think about the relation of gender and sexuality in *gendered* terms. Biddy Martin has indicated that queer theorists often see gender differences as constraining, as if they can be overridden by the greater mobility of queer desires. But such representations of gender, she argues, get "coded implicitly, when not explicitly, as female while sexuality takes on the universality of man" (Martin 1994a, 102). By privileging sexuality as the more avant-garde, more volatile site of resistance to normalization, and in some cases as an escape from gender, rendered as fixed on the one hand or as irrelevant on the other, to what extent do queer theorists reinvent the logic of masculine privilege? Martin makes a similar argument in "Sexualities without Genders and Other Queer Utopias" (chapter 1 in this volume) where she critiques Sedgwick's representation of gender in *Epistemology of the Closet* as constraint, enmeshment, miring, and fixity in contrast to the excesses of sexuality (Martin 1994b, 107).[7] Yet despite her compelling argument and her critique of Sedgwick's theorization of gender and sexuality, Martin claims she does not object to Sedgwick's argument for an analytic distinction between them. When Sedgwick asks us to try and arrive at understandings of sexuality that "will respect a certain irreducibility in it to the terms and relations of gender" (Sedgwick 1990, 16), Martin, through her skepticism of such irreducibility, rightly argues that "this will have the consequence of making sexuality, particularly homo/hetero sexual definition for men, seem strangely exempt from the enmeshments and constraints of gender (read: women)" (Martin 1994b, 107). But why *not* object to the fallibility of an analytic distinction if it allows for the privileging of sexuality over gender in gay male analysis and the obscuring of gender in lesbian inquiry whereby "lesbians, or women in general, become interesting by making a cross-gender identification or an identification with sexuality, now implicitly . . . associated with men, over [and] against gender and, by extension, feminism and women" (Martin 1994b, 107)?

Further, such analytic and methodological distinctions between gender and sexuality often result in the allocation of the territorial space one may occupy institutionally, intellectually, and politically as is the case with the term "lesbian and gay studies," which assumes first, a kind of symmetry between lesbians and gay men, as if they both occupy the same political ground as a result of sexual orientation, and second, a splitting between feminism and lesbian studies insofar as they analyze gender and sexuality respectively. Besides, such moves tend to reinvent hegemonic masculinity, not only through insisting on sharply demarcated divisions of labor and "turf," but because, as Butler notes, "the sexuality that is [supposedly] 'liberated' from feminism will be one which suspends the reference to masculine and feminine, reenforcing [sic] the refusal to mark that difference, which is the conventional way in which the masculine has achieved the status of the 'sex' which is one" (Butler 1994, 20). If we understand gender and sexuality as linked, it makes no sense for feminists to analyze only gender (as if this were a stable category) just as it makes no sense for gay and lesbian studies to analyze only sexuality. Analyses of gender and sexuality remain incomplete if they are not interrogated by each other and by other axes of social positioning including race, class, and geopolitical location.

Not distinguishing sexuality as a more privileged site of resistance to normativity, or as a "corrective" to the errors of feminism, allows us to subject queer studies, especially gay male studies, to feminist interrogation and critique. Gay studies in particular has not sufficiently interrogated its own hegemonic impulses, or in Sedgwick's words, "how a variety of forms of oppression intertwine systemically with each other; and especially how the person who is disabled through one set of oppressions may *by the same positioning* be enabled through others" (Sedgwick 1990, 32). This is especially important to consider in the case of gay men; while self-identifying as gay or being "outed" as such may, in some contexts, mean the loss of male privilege, it is still possible for gay men, whether or not they are consciously aware of it, to retain their proximity and access to male privilege when they decide to remain in the closet, when they self-identify as gay only in nonhomophobic or "safe" contexts, or in situations and contexts where sexual orientation may not surface because of the cultural presumption of heterosexuality which often works in the political and economic favor of gay men. As Adrienne Rich notes, "the systems men have created are homogeneous systems, which exclude and degrade women. . . . [Yet] both straight and homosexual men take refuge in those systems" (Rich 1986, 210–11). While the more gender-typical gay man may retain a great deal of male privilege in a way unlike the lesbian femme in that the politics of gender prevents them from occupying the same social, political, and economic ground, gay studies needs to move away from universalizing the oppression of gay men by more seriously addressing the specific contexts in which oppression operates, and by more rigorously theorizing gay male subjectivity in relation to gender, race, and class. This will enable a better analysis of the more-or-less slippery relation between privilege and struggle among gay men.

One cultural space where I see gender oppression and homophobia as axes of power intersecting and working together toward repressive ends is in revisionary psychoanalytic and psychiatric work on "Gender Identity Disorder in Childhood." While the American Psychiatric Association (APA) decided in 1973 to remove homosexuality as a diagnostic category of psychopathology from the third edition of the DSM which appeared in 1980,[8] the *DSM-III* was the first to contain the addition of GID as a new diagnosis. Rather than signaling a change in perspective regarding the psychological health of gay people following the deletion of homosexuality from the *DSM-III*, traces of a former predisposition toward pathology that marked American psychoanalytic clinical literature at its most homophobic height (from the period following the Kinsey Report of 1948 until the beginning of serious debates that led to the 1973 decision)[9] still seem to inform the new diagnostic category of GID. According to the *DSM-IV*, published in 1994, gender identity disorder in children is manifested by such criteria as a repeated desire to be the other sex, a strong preference for cross-dressing, strong and persistent preferences for cross-sex roles in make-believe play, an intense desire to participate in the games and pastimes of the other sex, and a strong preference for playmates of the other sex (*DSM-IV* 1994, 537). In boys, the *DSM* says that cross-gender identification is manifested by a preoccupation with traditionally feminine activities which may include dressing in women's and/or girl's attire, or improvising by using towels, aprons, or scarves when authentic female clothing is not available. Other manifestations of cross-gendered identification in boys range from preferences for the stereotypical games and pastimes of girls, including playing with "female-type" dolls, drawing pictures of beautiful girls and princesses, identifying with female characters in books or on television, and taking the role of the mother in playing house, to avoiding "rough-and-tumble play" as well as "nonaggressive" but stereotypical boys' toys (*DSM-IV* 1994, 533). Girls with GID are described in the *DSM-IV* with such characteristics as rejecting feminine attire, having fantasy heroes that are powerful male figures such as Batman and Superman, preferring boys as playmates, and having a strong interest in contact sports, rough-and-tumble play, and traditional boyhood games (*DSM-IV* 1994, 533). It is important to note that the diagnosis of GID is therapeutically imposed mostly on feminine boys; though the *DSM-IV* does describe how GID may operate in girls, it stipulates that boys are more commonly referred with GID at a ratio of about five to one (*DSM-IV* 1994, 535). This difference in diagnosis in boys and girls, and the subsequent lack of sufficient clinical literature on GID in girls, is a social and cultural phenomenon which psychoanalysis and psychiatry have yet to acknowledge and address. June Statham, in speaking to this issue in her book on nonsexist childraising, suggests that boys do not have to stray far beyond the boundaries of "acceptable" male behavior to stimulate "concern" for their psychological well-being (Statham 1986, 87). The true "concern" is for the male child to assume his proper (i.e. privileged) place in a masculinist world, while tomboyism, often left to develop unimpeded by clinical intervention and management, is socially dismissed as a "cute" transitional stage to be outgrown later. This does not mean that girls are not forced to conform to gender-typical behavior, as they often are once they reach adolescence, but that parents and caretakers tend to be more flexible nowadays in raising girls in nonsexist ways and are generally more tolerant of cross-gendered identification in girls because it is less tied to the fear of homosexual outcome.[10] But this still leaves us with unanswered questions: though tomboyishness may be regarded as a way of exploring and being in the world, as well as a counter-identity girls may more freely adopt (in most cases without therapeutic intervention), what sexist assumptions are operating in the clinical, institutional, and familial prohibitions for boys to take on feminine identifications?

What I find interesting is how gender identity disorder is interpreted in psychoanalytic research based on clinical data that is gathered from the treatment of patients. The study of research on gender identity disorder and its close relation to pre-*DSM-III* psychoanalytic work on homosexuality, which more blatantly operated as a form of cultural reproduction serving the interests of dominant social groups during a period of rigid

social conformity and political repression, provides a salient site of inquiry
to examine how sexuality is regulated through what Butler has referred to
as "the policing and the shaming of gender." After all, what has not to date
been asked is why the behaviors and preferences of gender-atypical children are deemed pathological. Nor has it been considered how far the
enforcement of gender norms in children, who are the least empowered to
resist them, is homophobic, in that gender nonconformity in children,
especially in boys, stirs up anxieties about homosexuality. Moreover,
whose purposes are really served in pathologizing and "treating" nonconformity to gender norms as a "disorder"?

Richard Friedman's book, *Male Homosexuality: A Contemporary Psychoanalytic Perspective*, published in 1988, is an important example of
revisionary work on homosexuality, not only because it attempts to take
a more sympathetic stance toward homosexuality than did earlier work by
Edmund Bergler, Irving Bieber, and Charles Socarides, but also because of
the author's membership on the Advisory Committee on Psychosexual
Disorders for the *DSM-III*. While Friedman applauds the decision of the
APA to drop homosexuality from the *DSM* as based on "sound clinical
reasoning," he goes on to say that when "homosexual phenomena" are
symptoms of primary psychiatric disorder, such as gender identity disorder, they should be so specified in the manual (Friedman 1988, 186). As a
result, Friedman has much to say about the new shift to issues of gender
identity, yet very much like his predecessors, from whom he tries to
distance himself, he still retreats to the authority of the clinic and "scientific" method. Though he does recognize that concepts of "masculinity,
femininity, and androgyny may have personal meanings far removed from
commonly accepted social norms without the implication of psychopathology," and although he recognizes the imprecision of clinical concepts to describe the rich varieties of behavior, he nonetheless concludes
that he uses "such obviously value-laden terms as disorder . . . to indicate
behavior that most clinicians, relying upon *common sense*, clinical experience, and the scientific and clinical literature, would place in the clinical
domain" (Friedman 1988, 34; emphasis added). It seems that the clinician
knows best. But not only is the clinical domain not disembodied from
heteronormativity, as it has historically ratified and been informed by it,
little attention is given to how what is proffered in the name of "clinical
common sense" may have social and political consequences insofar as
"treatment" of GID, usually at the behest of "concerned" parents, is often
aimed at the prevention of gay outcome. Issues left undertheorized in
Friedman's position are not only the conflation of gender and sexuality,
but the way in which psychological health is conflated with social conformity, and, as Ronald Bayer more pointedly notes, the way in which the

category of "health" can become a moral category to ideologically justify
discriminatory social practices (Friedman 1988, 13).

Two recurring themes that seem most descriptive in the so-called revisionary clinical literature on gender-atypical boys are femininity and the
relationship with the mother. Not surprisingly, these were the same distinguishing features that appeared in earlier studies on the etiology of
homosexuality, especially the influential study by Irving Bieber and his
colleagues in 1962, which was seen by both the psychiatric/psychoanalytic
community, and eventually by the general public, as the standard pro-
nouncement on male homosexuality.[11] In the ten-year investigation,
largely in response to a growing public awareness around issues of homosexuality in the years following the Kinsey Report of 1948, Bieber found
"effeminacy" in the childhoods of the 106 gay male patients studied to be
a significant distinguishing factor from the childhoods of the 100 heterosexual men in the control group. Childhood "effeminacy," as reported by
the patient in therapy and then on a questionnaire submitted by the
patient's analyst, revealed "patterns of prehomosexual childhood," such as
excessive fear of physical injury in 75 percent of the homosexual men
studied, girls as primary playmates in a third, participation in the usual
games of boys in less than one-fifth (Bieber et al. 1988, 204), and other
behaviors not remarkably different from the description of boys with
GID in the current edition of the *DSM*. Twenty-five percent of patients in
the homosexual group exhibited such behaviors as exaggerated shrugging,
"wrist-breaking," lisping, hand-to-hip posturing, and effusiveness [?!];
but Bieber points out that these patterns of effeminate behavior in males
are less an emulation of femininity than a caricature of it, as such behavior
observed in women would seem "bizarre" rather than feminine (Bieber
et al. 1988, 188–9).

Though Bieber's work is no longer recognized as the leading authority
on homosexuality because of its predisposition to pathology and for only
studying gay men in treatment, it nonetheless has left an indelible mark on
more recent work on gender identity disorder in childhood. Friedman
speaks of gender-atypical boys as having "female-like symptoms"
(Friedman 1988, 199), and postulates that most childhood effeminacy
results in homosexuality, that cross-gendered behavior in childhood is
more common in homosexual than in heterosexual men, and that most
adult homosexuality is preceded by some type of *pre-pubertal gender
disturbance* (Friedman 1988, 212).[12] He does acknowledge that research
cannot prove that every instance of homosexuality results from childhood
gender identity disturbances, but argues that a theoretical model derived
from this research need not be based on 100 percent association (Friedman
1988, 192). Again, clinician knows best. Even though Friedman admits

that there are cases where there may not be a correlation between childhood effeminacy and homosexuality, the association is for him still clinically valid. Yet what remains blatantly unanswered is why atypical gender identification is necessarily a disorder and how the entire heterosexual matrix, upon which studies of GID are based, is thwarted by the occasions when some feminine boys turn out to be heterosexual adults, and when other boys, who identify with conventional masculinity, become gay adults.[13]

Not only does Friedman's revisionary psychoanalytic work on homosexuality still, for the most part, view homosexuality in terms of abject gender, that is, the failure to reach the masculine ideal, like the older pathological model which serves as his intertext, it still relies on certain types of family dynamic that lead to gender atypicality and homosexual possibility. Bieber's study, in an effort to shift psychoanalytic attention away from the role of constitutional factors in the development of homosexuality (which Freud thought it was also important to consider) to oedipal and pre-oedipal experiences, also promulgated and popularized the by now all-too-familiar view that a high proportion of gay men had "close-binding" mothers who sexually stimulated their sons through seductiveness and over-close intimacy, thwarted the development of their heterosexual drives, showed undue concern for health and safety, and interfered with the father–son relationship and peer-group participation. As a result, "close-binding" mothers frequently minimized opportunities for masculine identification (Bieber et al. 1988, 79–81). The study also concluded that fathers played an essential and determining role in the homosexual outcome of the gay men studied; in the majority of instances the father was explicitly detached and hostile (Bieber et al. 1988, 310). Tables 1 and 2, taken from the Bieber study, list the distinguishing traits of mother–son and father–son relationships in the group of homosexual men (the "H" group) and in the control group of heterosexual men (the "C" group). Insofar as these family constellations inform current work on the treatment of GID in boys, they raise crucial implications for coalitional feminist and antihomophobic critiques of psychoanalysis. Notice, for example, not only the sheer difference in size of the "significant" items for mothers as compared to the list for fathers, but the placement of the mother in the active role (i.e. the subject of most of the sentences in each item) that casts her behavior as encouraging homosexuality. In table 2, sons are differentially cast according to how well they earned the respect and admiration of their father. Unlike the mother, the father does not seem to actively demonstrate or exhibit behaviors that would lead to gay outcome; the greater degree of hostility, rejection, and distance that characterize the fathers of homosexual men is a reaction to their sons' lack of masculine identification as children, exacerbated by the close-binding mother.

Similarly, despite assertions of a more progressive post-*DSM-III* stance, Friedman indicates that the families of gender-atypical boys seem

Table 3.1 Significant items regarding mother–son relationships which distinguish homosexuals from comparisons (in percentages)

		Answered Yes	
		H N = 106	C 100
1	Sibling preference: Was patient mother's favorite?[a]	66	50*
2	Did mother demand to be the prime center of the patient's attentions?	61	36[†]
3	Was she dominating?	81	65*
4	Was she seductive?	57	34*
5	Amount of contact (time spent between mother and patient):		
	(a) Great deal	56	27[†]
	(b) Average	20	53
	(c) Little	15	11
	(d) Very little	7	9
	(e) Absent	2	0
6	Did mother encourage masculine activities and attitudes?	17	47[†]
7	Did mother discourage masculine activities and attitudes?	37	16**
8	Did mother encourage feminine activities and attitudes?	35	11[†]
9	Was mother considered to be puritanical?	62	48*
10	Was mother considered to be sexually frigid?	64	47**
11	Did mother try to ally with son against husband?	62	40**
12	Did mother openly prefer patient to husband?	58	38**
13	Did mother want patient to grow up to be like some particular individual?	26	27
	(a) Like mother?	6	0*
	(b) If male, was he a virile male?	9	21*
14	Were there families with other male siblings?	64	63

Table 3.1 *Continued*

	Answered Yes	
	H N = 106	C 100
15 If yes, was mother, as compared to other siblings:[b]		
(a) More intimate with patient?	56	29*
16 Does analyst believe mother interfered with patient's heterosexual activity?	58	35**
17 Was patient the mother's confidant?	52	36*
18 Was mother the patient's confidante?	39	23*
19[c] Was mother *unduly* concerned about protecting the patient from physical injury?	58	39*
20 Did mother's concern about health or injury cause her to interfere with or restrict his play, social or other activities?	49	26[†]
21 Does the patient consider his mother to have been overprotective?	61	46*
22 Does analyst consider patient's mother to have been overprotective?	67	43**
23 In childhood, was the patient *excessively* dependent on his mother for advice or direction in making decisions?	64	42**
24 Does patient feel his mother "babied" him?	61	41**
25 Did mother administer frequent enemas?	15	4*
26 Which parent does the patient feel he could cope with more easily? Mother?	64	48**
27 Did patient use the technique of rebellion to cope with mother?	9	23*

[a] Based on number of families in which patient had siblings.
[b] Based on number of families in which patient had male siblings.
[c] Questions 19–27 were derived from equal samples of 96 homosexuals and comparisons. These questions were on the Third (Second Supplementary) Questionnaire and there was no Third Questionnaire for 10 homosexual cases (106 − 10 = 96) and 4 comparison cases (100 − 4 = 96).
* 0.05 level of significance.
** 0.01 level of significance.
† 0.001 level of significance.
Source: Bieber et al. 1988, pp. 45–6.

Table 3.2 Items distinguishing fathers of homosexual and control groups (in percentages)

		H N = 106	C 100
1	Patient is father's favorite[a]	7	28[†]
2	Another sibling is father's favorite[a]	59	36**
3	Patient is least favored child[a]	44	24**
4	Patient felt accepted by father	23	47**
5	Time spent with patient: little, very little, father absent	87	60[†]
6	Father encouraged masculine attitudes	45	60*
7	Patient knowingly hated father	60	37[†]
8	Patient both hated and feared father	57	31[†]
9	Patient respected father	28	48**
10	Patient accepted father	20	50[†]
11	Father expressed affection for patient	25	51**
12	Father had less respect for patient than for other male siblings[b]	42	19*
13[c]	Patient sided with father in parental arguments: in childhood	7	23**
	in adolescence	11	25*
14	Patient coped with father more easily than with mother	21	40**
15	Technique for coping with father: rebellion	8	20*
16	Patient feared his assertiveness would: anger father	76	55**
	hurt father	7	18*
17	Patient feels father considered his needs	6	20**
18	Patient feels currently respected by father	30	50**
19	Patient regards father as admirable	16	47[†]
20	Patient was excessively dependent on father	7	19*

[a] Based on number of families with siblings.
[b] Bascd on number of families with male siblings.
[c] Items 13–20 based on 96 cases.
* 0.05 level of significance.
** 0.01 level of significance.
[†] 0.001 level of significance.
Source: Bieber et al. 1988, p. 86.

strikingly similar to the families of homosexual men described in much clinical literature, that is, negative maternal attitudes toward men, especially male aggression, active maternal involvement in discouraging separation and individuation, and the absence or detachment of the father (Friedman 1988, 193). He specifically notes that boys develop their gender identity in the context of separating from the mother and that psychological movement away from intimacy (which threatens male gender identity) stems from the necessity to create distance from the mother (Friedman 1988, 238). Other researchers have corroborated Friedman's position. Susan Coates and Kenneth Zucker, internationally known experts on GID in children and directors of childhood gender identity disorder centers in New York City and Toronto respectively, comment that mothers of "gender-disturbed" boys fear male aggression, which often leads them to confuse "normal" boyhood assertiveness and rambunctiousness ("rough-and-tumble play") with aggressive and destructive behavior. Coates and Zucker found that mothers of boys with GID typically "were often proud of their sons' nonviolent qualities and saw their sons as special and better than the neighborhood boys, whom they considered roughnecks" (Coates and Zucker 1988, 18). Richard Green, in The "Sissy Boy Syndrome," another "revisionary" work on homosexuality, found mothers of feminine boys often to be the source for increased female identification. Mothers in Green's research were studied through data collected in interviews for the ways in which they supported and/or discouraged such cross-gendered behaviors as playing with dolls, cross-dressing, and female roleplaying, as well as for the extent to which they encouraged and/or discouraged traditionally "boyish" behavior such as playing sports and games such as cops and robbers. The study found a high correlation between parental support (especially among mothers) for early cross-gender behavior and the subsequent appearance of boyhood femininity. Fathers were studied in terms of their support of cross-gendered behaviors, whereby it was found that a more accepting attitude resulted in greater femininity in already feminine boys. But it also must be pointed out that the parents in the control group of conventionally masculine boys generally saw less femininity to which to respond. While this more recent work, unlike that of Bieber, appears to be less harsh on parents generally, it is still mired in the etiology of homosexuality, based on negatively construed family configurations in which the mother plays a pivotal "domineering" role in influencing boyhood femininity and eventual homosexuality.

This research remains blatantly indifferent to the ways in which it might be read, specifically to the rhetorical strategies that might be employed in a misogynistic and homophobic world to interpret affectionate, loving mothers, absent fathers (or fathers who may, through feminist influence, support nonsexist ways of raising children), and the nontraditional family structures in which children are now being raised as prototypes and familial sources of the prehomosexual child. Further, how might this research promote, encourage, and extend institutional practices that sanction violence, both physical and psychic, in order to "make a man" out of feminine or otherwise unmasculine boys by assuming, if not the role of the father, then, indeed, the Law of the Father as a means to enforce maternal separation and rectify the "consequences" before it is "too late"? Sedgwick has spoken of the lack of social resistance to the wish endemic in culture that gay people not exist:

> [T]he scope of institutions whose programmatic undertaking is to prevent the development of gay people is unimaginably large. There is no major institutionalized discourse that offers a firm resistance to that undertaking: in the United States, at any rate, most sites of the state, the military, education, law, penal institutions, the church, medicine, and mass culture enforce it all but unquestioningly, and with little hesitation at even the recourse to invasive violence. (Sedgwick 1993, 161)

Some of these institutions, such as schools, the military, children's camps, and children's sports organizations, take it upon themselves to develop (heterosexual) male socialization often through institutionally sanctioned teasing, bullying, hazing, and physical assault by peers and superiors, which are not only aimed to "toughen up" feminine boys and young men, but are similarly directed at those who may not exhibit stereotypically masculine behavior as well (such as boys who are "too sensitive"). As Lynne Segal notes, such terms as "pansy" (as well as "sissy," "pussy," and others), often synonymous with physical or emotional inadequacy, make all males potentially vulnerable to the "unmanliness" of failure in such misogynistic contexts (Segal 1990, 143). How does this help to reproduce and sustain patriarchal hierarchies that denigrate women? Equally disturbing, such destructive indoctrinations into the cult of phallic masculinity, with its culturally and institutionally sanctioned violence, seem to have Green's support as he speaks of them as "informal" forms of therapy "delivered by the peer group and the larger society via teasing and sex-role standards" (Green 1987, 388). Not only is he indifferent to the homophobic and sexist implications of the cultural enforcement of gender norms, he is quite blatant about what purpose and whose purposes "treatment" for GID serves: "Who," writes Green, "is to *dictate* that parents may not try to raise their children in a manner that maximizes the possibility of a heterosexual outcome" (Green 1987, 260; emphasis added)?

Since psychoanalysis and psychiatry, as clinical and cultural practices, have not sufficiently interrogated how their systems of inscription and intelligibility reproduce dominant social norms while, at the same time, being affected by them, feminist and gay analysis may subvert the mutually exclusive relation posited between gender identification and desire that still persists in clinical literature despite the removal of homosexuality from the *DSM* as a diagnostic category. Feminist and gay inquiry, in mobilizing around this issue, may ask how nonconformity to gender assignment among children ruptures the heterosexual matrix (which rests on an ontological view of gender) and impairs its efficient manageability. Such inquiry may specifically ask psychoanalytic and psychiatric scholars and practitioners, first, how atypical gender identification in children points to the failure of the heterosexual matrix ever to fully legislate itself, and, second, how, in our postmodern, post-theoretical times, such a rupture, such an epistemological crisis, could be welcomed as producing new identificatory sites, as well as new theoretical apparatuses for understanding the psychological growth of gender-nonconforming children (who may or may not turn out to be gay) and gay people (who may or may not conform to prescribed gender expectations).

One possible way of looking at this may be by taking Butler's work on drag one step further which may help to provide yet another illustration of gender as performativity, as a reiteration of norms, rather than as a psychic truth or as reducible to surface appearance. While Bieber theorized a high correlation between feminine boyhood and subsequent homosexuality, thereby pathologizing feminine boys as having gender disturbance, his observation of their feminine behavior as being a *caricature* of femininity, very interestingly I think, helps support Butler's contention that gender is an assignment never quite carried out to expectation, in that one who takes up the imperative of gendering through the embodying of norms never fully attains that ideal. Gender-atypical children, then, not only help to illustrate gender as a diverse site of significations that destabilizes normative regimes of cultural intelligibility but also show how gender never quite inhabits the "ideal" to which one is compelled to approximate. Gender-atypical children, not unlike drag, represent an effort "to negotiate cross-gendered identification," thereby subverting the heterosexual matrix, with the important stipulation (in both cases, I believe) that cross-gender identification is not the exemplary paradigm for thinking about homosexuality (Butler 1994, 235). More important, gender-atypical children, following Butler's analysis of drag, expose the "normal" constitution of gender performed as disavowed attachments of identification which allegorize heterosexual melancholy whereby "heterosexualized genders form themselves through the renunciation of the *possibility* of homosexuality, a foreclosure that produces . . . at the same time . . . a domain of those whom it would be impossible to love" (Butler 1994, 235). It is precisely this renunciation that is more overtly performed and dramatized, that is (re)cited, in the clinical "treatment" of gender-atypical children, especially in light of the concomitant anxiety over the possibility of homosexuality that informs and accompanies it.

Concerning the role of mothers, Adrienne Rich offers insight into how work on GID reproduces the logic of etiology and serves the interests of compulsory heterosexuality and its concomitant misogyny and homophobia. According to Rich, as a result of psychoanalytic opinion that the "son of the mother" becomes homosexual in flight from the power of women he sees embodied in his mother, or in protest at the traditional male role which she supposedly tries to prevent him from achieving (Rich 1986, 210), women who have never read Freud nonetheless raise their sons on the belief that to show them physical affection is to be "seductive." To discourage those forms of conventional masculine behavior they abhor (such as contempt for women, regarding women as sexual objects), they believe, is to "castrate" their sons or to become the domineering woman sons will have to reject in order to become psychologically healthy (Rich 1986, 196). It is easy to see how this came about given the growing attention to homosexuality in the postwar years, especially through its diagnosis by "experts." The position of Bieber and his colleagues was disseminated not only in such prestigious professional journals as the *American Journal of Psychoanalysis*, but was popularized and often applauded in such news magazines as *Time*, *Newsweek*, and *Life* which entered middle-class homes at the time, a kind of (re)specification of "the homosexual" as a distinct species in the Foucauldian sense.

An issue of *Life* magazine in 1964, in a voyeuristic exposé, "Homosexuality in America," cites Bieber's findings in explaining how "on the one hand, the homosexual's mother kept him utterly dependent on her, unable to make his own decisions. On the other, she pampered him, catered to his every whim and smothered him with affection. Often she openly preferred him to his father" (*Life* June 26, 1964, 78). The myth of the "too-loving" mother has caused great anxiety among mothers of the last four decades in terms of how best to love and raise their sons. This is most evident to me in the numerous coming-out stories I have heard over the years from gay male friends, colleagues, and acquaintances from the baby-boom years, where, invariably, I am told, following the disclosure, mothers have asked their gay sons "Was it my fault?" "What did I do wrong?"

"Did I love you *too much*?" It is for this reason, I think, that mothers, including those who are actively feminist and/or do not condemn homosexuality, find it difficult to advocate and practice nonsexist, nontraditional ways of parenting boys; as Rich notes, the self-serving, self-legislating ideology of patriarchy makes people who care for children (including parents, teachers, counselors, etc.) believe that it is better for the boy in the end to be a "real" man (Rich 1986, 211). According to June Statham, nonsexist parenting for girls and the breaking down of pre-scribed gender roles for daughters are seen as opening opportunities for them to attain higher educational levels and achieve higher social status and economic power, whereas for sons, nonsexist parenting often means teaching boys to forego some of the power and privilege (Statham 1986, 91). In describing the conflicts she experiences between protecting her son from the regime of phallic masculinity and her fears of the possible conse-quences of this, Jane Lazarre, in *On Loving Men*, writes: "I have a fear of his losing his bearing altogether; that without masculinity in its most conventional sense, at least a part of it, he will falter, stay so close to me that he will not be able to walk away at all" (Lazarre 1981, 156). This presents a dilemma for mothers who, on the one hand, are all too familiar with the view that maternal strength and influence may alienate the male child from "his" culture, and whose feminist work or feminist inclina-tions, on the other hand, seek to undermine that very culture of male privilege and power.[14] But to what extent are concerns about holding the male child back still inscribed by the myth of the all-consuming, over-indulgent mother (which is really symptomatic of a more pervasive mi-sogyny that fears any power or influence women may possess or exert) when, in actuality, boys who identify closely with their mothers, boys who are not conventionally masculine, as well as feminine boys, are ex-posed to patriarchy in other contexts, and, often with remarkable resil-ience, develop strategies for coping with it? Raising gender-flexible children in a patriarchal culture does not isolate them from patriarchy, but may help them to see its flaws and provide them with a rich context for theorizing their own positions in relation to it.

But what still has not been asked is the following: if we accept the psychoanalytic notion that feminine boys resist familial, cultural, and clinical imperatives to separate from their mothers unlike more gender-typical boys who conform, how might feminist and gay inquiry reread the feminine boy's resistance against dominant interpretations that pathologize the closeness of the mother–son relationship? Psychoanalysis might consider the positive outcomes of this relationship and ask why we need necessarily to think of intimacy and attachment as threatening mas-culine gender identity. Offering an alternative psychoanalytic trajectory,

Leo Bersani has suggested that an exclusively heterosexual orientation in men may depend on a misogynous identification with the father and a permanent equating of femininity with castration, while male homosexual desire, if we accept that it depends on an identification with the mother, "has already detraumatized sexual difference (by internalizing it) *and* set the stage for a relation to the father in which the latter would no longer have to be marked as the Law, the agent of castration" (Bersani 1995, 58). It seems that parents of both sexes, especially those in traditional family structures, need to ask themselves critically whether their reluctance to raise gender-flexible boys is truly based "on the best interest of the child," which is the same justification used to treat GID in children, or if they, too, fear the possibility of homosexual outcome, tolerating it, if at all, only when it occurs in adult life and is unlikely to change. Raising gender-flexible boys does not amount to sending them to school in dresses, or encouraging their participation in the stereotypical activities of girls, as these approaches reduce gender to surface appearances and fail to address how such moves could be as potentially repressive as the gender norms one is trying to contest. They also result in tokenism rather than in a sustained engagement by children and parents as to how prescribed gender roles and inequalities are the effects of power rather than a reflection of a natural order. Rather, the issue for parents seems to be seriously to question their motives for actively or subtly *discouraging* atypical gender identification and behavior, as well as reflecting not only on the possibility, but on the *desirability* of parenting a queer child.

It is also important to point out that gender atypicality is not the only site for the coalitional efforts of feminist and queer inquiry and to foreground issues of gender in other contexts. While the enforcement of gender norms, as well as the homophobia enjoined on gender-atypical boys, is informed by misogynistic impulses, and while tomboyishness in girls may be less informed by homophobic anxiety (and therefore less resisted through therapeutic intervention), butch lesbians, as Biddy Martin reminds us, have historically been associated with gender dysphoria or dysfunction, making them subject to homophobic attack in addition to being subject to the ways in which women are devalued, diminished, and trivialized in patriarchal culture (Martin 1994b, 117–18). In the absence of a more pronounced clinical surveillance of gender (and [homo]sexuality) in girls, another question that must be addressed is at what point, to what degree, or in what circumstances atypical gender identification becomes "attached" to the homophobia enjoined on butch lesbians, while its attachment to feminine boys seems clear from the start.

More important to this argument, the specificity of lesbian subjectivity teaches us that an over-emphasis on cross-gender identification is limiting; as Martin notes, it makes lesbians more resistant to feminist theorization and renders the femme lesbian invisible (Martin 1994b, 108). Psychoanalytic theory, when it does speak of lesbian desire, promulgates a view of lesbians as cross-gender-identified; Freud, for instance, claimed that women inverts "exhibit masculine characteristics ... with peculiar frequency and look for femininity in their sexual objects" (Freud 1962, 11), whereas in men "the most complete mental masculinity can be combined with inversion" (Freud 1962, 8). The problem here is not only a gender bias in terms of the development of gender identity in gay women and men, but the historical difficulty of reducing lesbian desire to masculine identification, which, as Mandy Merck points out, has been, to explain the "feminine" women that the "masculine" kind are supposed to desire. "If a masculine libido is what produces female homosexuality," Merck writes, "what makes these other women do it" (Merck 1993, 24)? Still another problem with reading queer identity only in terms of cross-gender identification is the uncritical tendency to lump femme lesbians and more conventionally masculine gay men together as gender-conforming, as "passing" for straight, and therefore more protected from homophobic attack, without accounting for how the politics of gender prevents them from occupying the same social and political ground. On the other hand, foregrounding the axis of gender does not mean that we wipe the axis of sexuality out of the picture altogether; to what extent are femme lesbians truly "gender-conformists," that is, "capable of healing the butch's wounded relation to her body, a role division that makes comfort or defiance seem the two apparent options in relation to gender ... with femmeness as ease or accession and defiance or nonconformity as phallic" (Martin 1994b, 117)? Putting femme lesbians on a par with heterosexual women not only discursively limits lesbian relationships to a masculine/feminine binary opposition and subjects them to heterosexist readings, but ignores the erotic significance of these identities, as well as their radical potential to transgress the opposition between "true" (heterosexual) femininity and lesbian specificity. In this regard, lesbian femmes, as Butler notes, "may recall the heterosexual scene, ... but also displace it at the same time" (Butler 1990, 123), and in so doing, subvert normative heterosexuality as a political regime and expose its pretense to reflect merely a natural order of "true" genders defined exclusively by heterosexual desire.

In writing this essay, I do not entertain fantasies of a family romance through highlighting some of the ways in which feminism has influenced gay studies and by theorizing possibilities of alliance between these fields of study. Making connections between feminism and gay studies, through the influence of feminism on gay studies and an analysis of gender and sexuality that accounts for their interimplication, further implies that feminism need not operate as a master discourse, as a site of privilege or as the originary force of gay studies. Engaging the two disciplines dialogically is potentially productive of insights into each and enables us to ask new questions of identity politics. One may also ask how lesbian and gay studies, especially lesbian studies, has helped feminism revise many of its heterosexist assumptions. As Landry and MacLean note, existing feminist debates on sexuality have focused relentlessly on psychoanalysis as *the* language of sexuality, which not only familializes sexuality but heterosexualizes it as well, whereas the work of lesbian and gay critics, they argue, has critiqued such paradigms for understanding sexuality through challenging a strictly psychoanalytic, family-based model for understanding it (Landry and MacLean 1993, 160). Psychoanalysis has yet to theorize a more elastic view of the family and call into question the primacy it places on oedipal development in consideration of children raised in nontraditional families, such as those headed by single mothers or fathers, lesbian couples, and gay male couples. Many gay male academics have also been supportive of feminist work, and gay studies in particular has helped feminism to rethink and differentiate the category of "masculinity" as a structure of social relations not reducible to men in general. To totalize "men," masculinity, or masculine signifying economies in the absence of historical or contextual considerations only offers a mirror image of the sexual order one is opposing; as Butler notes in this regard, the colonizing gesture is not primarily or irreducibly masculinist (Butler 1990, 13).

Finally, my focus on theorizing gender and sexuality, the sites where misogyny and homophobia may intertwine in patriarchal culture, and the possibilities for alliance, with neither feminism nor gay studies serving as the foundational term, helps to address a significant problem in contemporary identity politics and critical practice. A unity or self-sameness is projected on to identities and cultures without engaging the disputes and differences within a particular social group about its identity and its relationship to the wider social world. Such an appropriation often leads to another problem whereby differences of race, gender, sexuality, and class are articulated as if they are in parallel relation to one another without accounting for their differential structures and their intersecting and converging formations within the social field. Speaking to this, Butler points out that any analysis of power which foregrounds one of its vectors of domination (racism, sexism, homophobia) over others becomes vulnerable to the criticism that it ignores or devalues the others, and any

analysis that pretends to encompass every vector of power risks epistemological imperialism (Butler 1994, 18). Yet the difficulty of this position
need not signal a theoretical impasse or obstacle. It is rather a reminder as
to the *interarticulations* of power through more than one specific vector
and to the correlative idea that an axis of social positioning, such as sexual
orientation, is never experienced in isolation, based on "common" identifications, but is always mediated by other axes of social positioning, in the
case of sexual orientation, by race, gender, and social class. The challenge
for future work in identity politics is to ask how theories of difference will
not occlude the politics of solidarity and coalition.

Notes

1   One exception perhaps is some of the essays by gay male academics
   in Boone and Cadden's *Engendering Men: The Question of Male
   Feminist Criticism*, though the book as a whole deals with the question of men in feminism generally.

2   See Judith Butler's essay "Against Proper Objects" for an excellent
   critique of reducing feminism to the study of gender and lesbian and
   gay studies to the study of sexuality. I will also address the
   problematics and limitations of such a conception of the two fields
   later in my discussion.

3   See also Teresa de Lauretis, *Technologies of Gender: Essays on
   Theory, Film, and Fiction* (Bloomington: Indiana University Press,
   1987).

4   Rubin has since clarified in a recent interview with Judith Butler that
   she never claimed that gender and sexuality were always unconnected, "only that their relationships are situational, not universal,
   and must be determined in particular situations" (see p. 70).

5   The *DSM* refers to the *Diagnostic and Statistical Manual* published
   by the American Psychiatric Association (APA) and used to diagnose
   psychiatric disorders. The third edition (*DSM-III*), published in
   1980, was the first to remove homosexuality as a category of psychopathology as a result of the APA's historic 1973 decision.

6   In Butler's theory, sex is not thought to be inherently biological,
   prediscursive, immutable, or a prior ontological reality on which
   culture acts, but produced as the effect of the apparatus of cultural
   construction, as already gendered, as part of an overall juridical regime of (hetero)sexuality based on foundational categories where
   gender follows from sex and sexuality from gender. Sex, then, does

not signify in and of itself, but is *always already* read through the lens of gender.

7 In addition to pointing out that sexuality, *even more* than gender, could occupy a more constructed, variable, representational, and relational position (Sedgwick 1990, 29), Sedgwick further proposes that the *greater* potential of sexual orientation for "rearrangement, ambiguity, and representational doubleness . . . would offer the apter deconstructive object," with the disclaimer that though she is not arguing for the epistemological privileging of sexuality over gender, the argument is nonetheless a powerful one for the distinctness of one from the other (Sedgwick 1990, 34). Despite the disclaimer, it is difficult to see how sexuality would not still occupy a more privileged position than gender.

8 The *DSM-III* retained "ego-dystonic homosexuality" which was reserved for individuals who where distressed by homosexual arousal and desired to acquire or increase heterosexual arousal. The revised edition of *DSM-III* (*DSM-III-R*), published in 1987, deleted ego-dystonic homosexuality as well.

9 Within this period, the APA produced two editions of the *DSM*. The first, published in 1952, listed homosexuality as a sociopathic personality disturbance. The *DSM-II* (1968) still considered homosexuality as indicative of psychopathology, but removed it from the category of sociopathic disturbance, listing it instead under "sexual deviations" alongside fetishism, pedophilia, transvestism, exhibitionism, and others. For psychoanalytic work on homosexuality from this period, see Sandor Rado, "An Adaptational View of Sexual Behavior" in *Psychosexual Development in Health and Disease* (Eds. P. Hoch and J. Zubin, New York: Grune and Stratton, 1949); Edmund Bergler's "The Myth of a New National Disease: Homosexuality and the Kinsey Report," *Psychiatric Quarterly*, 22, pp. 66–8 and *Homosexuality: Disease Or Way of Life?* (New York: Hill and Wang, 1956); Irving Bieber, et al., *Homosexuality: A Psychoanalytic Study of Male Homosexuals* (New York: Basic Books, 1962), reprinted as *Homosexuality: A Psychoanalytic Study* (Northvale, NJ: Aronson, 1988); and Charles Socarides, *The Overt Homosexual* (New York: Grune and Stratton, 1968).

10 The non-linking of tomboyishness with female homosexuality is also supported by the *DSM-IV*, which states that about three-quarters of boys who had a childhood history of GID report a homosexual or bisexual orientation by late adolescence or adulthood, whereas the corresponding percentages for girls are not known (*DSM-IV* 1994, 536). Interestingly, the three-fourths figure for boys with GID be-

coming homosexual is also Richard Green's finding (see my note 12), a study which I discuss later.

11 This book, originally published in 1962 under the title *Homosexuality: A Psychoanalytic Study of Male Homosexuals*, was republished in its entirety in 1988 under the names of the same team of co-authors who were also the researchers in the 1962 study. All references in my text are to the 1988 edition of the 1962 study. The 1988 edition contains a new foreword by Irving Bieber and Toby Bieber which aims to familiarize the reader with the ideas and observations of the 1962 study since the time it was originally published. Bieber et al. specifically state that "the republication of this book deals with those same aspects [of the development of homosexuality, family dynamics, adaptive techniques, and the results of psychoanalytic therapy] *exactly* as written twenty-five years ago" (Bieber et al., 1988, ix–x; emphasis added). While the foreword acknowledges some of the debates and changed thinking about homosexuality since the 1950s and early 1960s when the study was carried out, and acknowledges some of the critiques launched against the study, it is still largely a defense of the findings and points out how subsequent clinical studies by the researchers have corroborated the original data. The foreword ends by pointing out that after the 1962 study was published, follow-up work showed that one-third of the patients had shifted to heterosexual adaptation and that many have remained exclusively heterosexual (i.e. "cured") in the intervening years (Bieber et al. 1988, xxiii).

12 Similarly, Richard Green's 15-year study *The "Sissy Boy Syndrome,"* wherein he studies 66 feminine boys between the ages of four and twelve at the beginning of the study, with two-thirds of this group available for follow-up interviews in adolescence and/or young adulthood, concludes that because three-fourths of the boys in this group turned out to be homosexual or bisexual, while only one of the two-thirds of conventionally masculine boys (the control group) available for follow-up was bisexually-oriented, feminine boys are far more likely to mature into homosexual or bisexual men than are most boys (Green 1987, 99). Interestingly, the causal links between gender-atypical boys and homosexuality of which I have been speaking are most apparent in the full title of Green's book: *The "Sissy Boy Syndrome" and the Development of Homosexuality.*

13 While there is still little research in these areas, Friedman has also done work on gender-conforming gay men (who were also gender-conforming children – i.e. conventionally masculine). These include, for example, Tim, who grew up doing "solitary heavy labor" on a

rural farm and was an excellent athlete and captain of his wrestling team (Friedman 1988, 205, 207). Luke, a career army officer, was "an honors student and a track star" (Friedman 1988, 152); and Bob, an engineer, "had regular sexual activity with a few different partners but never cruised or visited gay bars or baths" (Friedman 1988, 93). These men are represented as "psychologically healthy" and as having "good coping skills and a generally high level of ego functioning" (Friedman 1988, 205). Yet they may also be considered to be "well-integrated" and psychologically healthy because they do not *overtly* challenge the status quo through their conformity to social expectations about gender as children and as adults and through pursuing their sexual lives in private.

14 Another problem is that while both feminist and lesbian activism have encouraged and supported nonsexist roles for girls, at present no comparable social movement exists for gender-atypical boys. Feminism and the gay movement may be sympathetic, but the gender-atypical boy is not central to their causes, though he would be for the gay movement if he were to self-identify as gay.

References

Bayer, Ronald. *Homosexuality and American Psychiatry: The Politics of Diagnosis*. New York: Basic Books, 1981. Princeton: Princeton University Press, 1987.

Bersani, Leo. *Homos*. Cambridge: Harvard University Press, 1995.

Bieber, Irving, et al. *Homosexuality: A Psychoanalytic Study*. Northvale, NJ: Aronson, 1988.

Boone, Joseph A. and Michael Cadden, eds. *Engendering Men: The Question of Male Feminist Criticism*. New York: Routledge, 1990.

Butler, Judith. *Gender Trouble: Feminism and the Subversion of Identity*. New York: Routledge, 1990.

——. *Bodies That Matter: On the Discursive Limits of "Sex"*. New York: Routledge, 1993.

——. "Against Proper Objects." *differences: A Journal of Feminist Cultural Studies*. 6, 2–3 (1994), pp. 1–26.

Coates, Susan and Kenneth Zucker. "Gender Identity Disorder in Children." *Clinical Assessment of Children: A Biopsychosocial Approach*. Eds. C. J. Kestenbaum and D. T. Williams. New York: New York University Press, 1988.

Cohen, Ed. "Are We (Not) What We Are Becoming? 'Gay' 'Identity,' 'Gay Studies,' and the Disciplining of Knowledge." In Boone and Cadden 1990, pp. 161–75.

De Lauretis, Teresa. "Queer Theory: Lesbian and Gay Sexualities." *differences: A Journal of Feminist Cultural Studies*. 3, 2 (1991), pp. iii–xviii.

——. "Habit Changes." *differences: A Journal of Feminist Cultural Studies*. 6, 2–3 (1994), pp. 296–313.

Diagnostic and Statistical Manual of Mental Disorders. 4th edn. Washington, DC: American Psychiatric Association, 1994.

Freud, Sigmund. *Three Essays on the Theory of Sexuality*. Trans. James Strachey. New York: Basic Books, 1962.

Friedman, Richard C. *Male Homosexuality: A Contemporary Psychoanalytic Perspective*. New Haven: Yale University Press, 1988.

Green, Richard. *The "Sissy Boy Syndrome" and the Development of Homosexuality*. New Haven: Yale University Press, 1987.

"Homosexuality in America." *Life*. June 26, 1964, pp. 66–80.

hooks, bell. *Talking Back*. Boston: South End Press, 1989.

Landry, Donna and Gerald MacLean. *Materialist Feminisms*. Cambridge, MA: Blackwell, 1993.

Lazarre, Jane. *On Loving Men*. London: Virago, 1981.

Martin, Biddy. "Extraordinary Homosexuals and the Fear of Being Ordinary." *differences: A Journal of Feminist Cultural Studies*. 6, 2–3 (1994a), pp. 100–25.

——. "Sexualities without Genders and Other Queer Utopias." *Diacritics*. 24, 2–3 (1994b), pp. 104–21.

Merck, Mandy. *Perversions: Deviant Readings*. New York: Routledge, 1993.

Rich, Adrienne. *Of Woman Born: Motherhood as Experience and Institution*. New York: W. W. Norton, 1986.

Rubin, Gayle. "Sexual Traffic," *differences: A Journal of Feminist Cultural Studies*. 6, 2–3 (1994), pp. 62–99.

Sedgwick, Eve Kosofsky. *Between Men: English Literature and Male Homosocial Desire*. New York: Columbia University Press, 1985.

——. *Epistemology of the Closet*. Berkeley: University of California Press, 1990.

——. "How to Bring Your Kids Up Gay: The War on Effeminate Boys." *Tendencies*. Durham: Duke University Press, 1993, pp. 154–64.

Segal, Lynne. *Slow Motion: Changing Masculinities, Changing Men*. New Brunswick: Rutgers University Press, 1990.

Statham, June. *Daughters and Sons: Experiences of Non-Sexist Childraising*. New York: Blackwell, 1986.

Chapter 4

Reflections on Gynophobia

Emily Apter

Cette catastrophe: être femme.
Natalie Clifford Barney, *Les Pensées d'une Amazone*

Why would a feminist critic write a piece devoted to gynophobia? Isn't there sufficient antagonism toward feminine subjects within institutionally entrenched practices of misogyny? Admittedly, there is something perverse in investigating why a still embattled sex might want to reject itself or to expose parts of itself to negative critique. But I have been struck by the fact that feminist aversion to femininity in women (as distinct from male effeminophobia, where the phobics are men, or homophobia, in which effeminate men are objects of phobia), is a relatively little-discussed area within feminism.[1] I would argue that in contrast to misogyny, gynophobia stresses feminine agency and designates the ambivalence women harbor toward the enhanced cosmetic bodies and warped social formations characteristic of conventional femininity. It is a form of femme-phobia that precludes neither women nor femmes as objects of desire. For me, the term gynophobia refers first and foremost to a kind of resistance to bearing femininity as a professional liability, performative history, and weight of existence. Femininity makes itself known to the feminine subject as an interiorized negation, often identifiable as a socially sanctioned egoic deficiency that sends the superego into spasms of self-punishing overdrive. As a "gender identity" femininity seems riveted to philosophic and psychoanalytic paradigms of prosthetic consciousness: the logic of the supplement, the phallic veil, the scaffold of the unconscious, defensive armature, maternal compensation, narcissistic self-augmentation, mimeticism, virile display, *Penisneid*, and fetish envy. Archaic in its traditions, conventions, and psychoanalytic constructions, femininity as a gender code remains intractable in social practices and daily life; ill-conducive to discursive and ontological reordering despite the goads provided by feminist theory and politics. Though at times femininity feels like a symptom one enjoys, it nonetheless retains the status of a stigma that one wears, a kind of being that "sticks" despite attempts to reconfigure it "otherwise," (the lesbian phallus, the lesbian fetish, femme aesthetics, the feminine Symbolic, surgical transformation, etc).

As with the subject of maternal desire (acknowledged but under-theorized), feminist gynophobia may be one of the last remaining taboos in an era of intense reflection on gender, sexuality, and identity. There are obvious reasons why: in addition to being virtually impossible to define systematically as a subject position or psychoanalytic condition equipped with specific traits, the term yields caricatures of "self-hating feminism," of women fleeing the *odor de femina* or sharing the putative masculine horror of the *vagina dentata*. As an umbrella term, it slides confusingly between a politics of antifemininity (one that stigmatizes femininity as a masculine tool), and an erotics of femme-ness that radically resignifies the feminine. The concept of gynophobia also (potentially) undermines principles of feminist solidarity in designating strategic defection from the fold of what Judith Butler has critically referred to as the feminist "we." "The feminist 'we,' " she writes, "is always and only a phantasmatic construction, one that has its purposes, but which denies the internal complexity and indeterminacy of the term and constitutes itself only through the exclusion of some part of the constituency that it simultaneously seeks to represent."[2]

Given these concerns, the principal reasons for attempting to identify a possible discourse of gynophobia derive from the wish to examine problems that the feminist "we" has traditionally occluded, and to explore overlooked areas where feminism and queer theory may converge, albeit in the negative mode of shared phobia. In a recent special issue of the journal *differences*, centering on the encounter between queer theory and feminism, attempts are made to redress the perceived alienation of feminism by queer theory.[3] Queer theory, in arrogating desire, transgression and sexuality to itself, is seen to have left feminism in the dust-gathering gender spot, associated, in Biddy Martin's words, with "a maternal, anachronistic, and putatively puritanical feminism . . . a homogeneous field in need of the intervention of desire and conflict."[4] Martin's observation emerges from a moment in the 1990s in which gender melancholia, transgender, bisexuality, butch/femme dynamics, queer parenting, and queer-envy appear to be the privileged locations of sexuality in feminism's cultural ethos, even though the term queer, as a nomenclature for variously sexed positions has been assailed for its anti-identitarian politics and erasure of gay and lesbian history. In this context, as linked neither with gender nor with sexuality in any fixed or obvious way, gynophobia would be a theme that disrespects the politics/desire split implicit in gender/sex, straight/lesbian or feminist/ queer antinomies. It would also be a theme that takes up the problem of gender claustrophobia characterized by Denise Riley as an unsustainable ontological condition: "Can anyone fully inhabit a gender without a de- gree of horror? How could someone 'be a woman' through and through, make a final home in that classification without suffering claustrophobia?" Riley surmises that "being a woman" is a part-time, temporally fluctuating existential investment: "there are always different densities of sexed being in operation, and the historical aspects are in play here."[5] Though I fully grant that the degree to which a subject identifies itself through a sexuality or gender will vary historically and biographically, what interests me here is the durability of that sense of phobia-inducing claustration in a sexed ontology. Riley herself admits of such a predicament when she acknowl- edges that "'women' is a simultaneous foundation of and irritant to feminism."[6] With the word "irritant" she evokes the congeries of negative affect submerged within eugenic theorizations of feminist consciousness: irritability, spleen, depression, anxiety, embarrassment, repulsion, panic, nausea – a spectrum of antipathies to the personal and public claims of *woman* on the female subject.

Femininity has historically been identified with an ethically and intellectu- ally disabled or impoverished subjectivity. As early as 1792, Mary Wollstonecraft, in *A Vindication of the Rights of Woman*, deplored the traits of character typical of upperclass women: irrationality, infantilism, artifice, weakness, dependency, inertia, a crippling modesty and forbear- ance, non-purposeful thought and speech ("flowery diction"), frivolity, and a taste for "littleness" (sartorial fetishes, mundane pursuits). The repudiation of practices identified with eighteenth-century English femi- nine life and survival – presented as hindrances to moral development and equality – becomes in her essay the basis for a feminophobic vision that has instrumental value in the service of political "vindication" (particu- larly in that word's sense of "to claim or establish possession of, for oneself or another"). Though Wollstonecraft may well have been a gynophobe in the sense of being repelled by her own sexual desire,[7] more importantly, her critique of feminine gender prefigures a view of feminin- ity as, in Freud's terms, an array of neurotic symptoms "formed to escape an otherwise unavoidable generating of anxiety," itself the product of the ego's "attempt at flight from the demand by its libido," and substitution of external danger with an internal one.[8]

Wollstonecraft's distillation of socially and psychically endorsed properties of femininity has persisted as a kind of phantasmatic inventory to be abjected by the western feminist subject, thereby precipitating an enduring uncertainty about whether to exile or to incorporate the kind of "little-woman" attitudes that came to be fictionally enshrined by Louisa May Alcott. Predictably, Wollstonecraft's dim view of the deficits of female character prompted her to look to "the imitation of manly virtues, or more properly speaking, the attainment of those talents and virtues, the exercise of which ennobles the human character."[9] Wollstonecraft's acknowledgment of a perdurable masculinism productively linked to political feminism offers the prospect of an empowering gynophobia. Though in the present climate, this kind of gynophobia might well be regarded with justified suspicion as, that which "reduces femininity to masculinity's other,"[10] I would suggest that, at the very least, gynophobia provides a conceptual frame for negotiating the place of new masculinities within feminist theory, practice and subcultures.

Though there is no precise date or historic locale on which to pin "the birth of gynophobia" (and I have already hedged enough against defining it monolithically at all), it would seem that the Parisian *demi-monde* at the turn of the century created a singular space for social experiments in erotic life convergent with a psychoanalytically informed critical consciousness of the transmutability of sex and gender stereotypes. Paris 1900 was the inaugural moment of what is generally perceived (by Shari Benstock, Herbert Lottman, Sue-Ellen Case, Andrea Weiss, Mary Louise Roberts, and many others) to be the apotheosis of first-wave feminist self-fashioning. Though British and American suffragettism may well have contributed more significantly to a feminist politics of equal rights, I would suggest that in the sphere of identity politics the privileged world of the Parisian expat salon provided a unique occasion for acting out or working through nonconformist feminine ontologies. Gynophobia emerged from this feminist avant-gardism as a leitmotif. Consider, for example, Mina Loy's violently anti-woman pronouncements in her "Feminist Manifesto" of 1914:

> Women, if you want to realize yourselves (for you are on the brink of a devastating upheaval) all your pet illusions must be unmasked. The lies of centuries have got to be discarded. Are you prepared for the WRENCH?
> [. . .] The fictitious value of woman as identified with her physical purity is too easy a standby. It renders her lethargic in the acquisition of intrinsic merits of character by which she

could obtain a concrete value. Therefore, the first self-enforced
law for the female sex, as protection against the manmade
bogey of virtue (which is the principal instrument of her
subjugation) is the *unconditional* surgical *destruction of
virginity* throughout the female population at puberty. [. . .]
 Woman must destroy in herself the desire to be loved.[11]

If Loy gave gynophobia the radical trope of surgically removed maiden-
hood, Djuna Barnes's sapphic *roman-à-clef*, *Ladies Almanack* (1928),
commemorated gynophobia through the Mina Loy-inspired character,
Patience Scalpel, who is admitted into Evangeline Musset's (Natalie
Barney's) inner circle as the token heterosexual because she shares the
group's uncompromising contempt for femme-ness:

> Patience Scalpel was of this Month, and belongs to this
> Almanack for one Reason only, that from Beginning to End,
> Top to Bottom, inside and out, she could not understand
> Women and their Ways as they were about her, above her and
> before her.
> [. . .] Thus her voice was heard throughout the Year, as
> cutting in its Derision as a surgical Instrument, nor did she use
> it to come to other than a Day and yet another Day in which
> she said, "I have tried all means, Mathematical, Poetical,
> Statistical and Reasonable, to come to the Core of this
> Distemper, known as Girls! Girls![12]

Taking their cue from George Sand and Rosa Bonheur in the nineteenth
century, the *garçonnes*, flappers, and literary *vedettes* of the Parisian *demi-
monde* produced a prototype of the gynophobe: a female dandy whose
outward signs were her trousers, cravat and top hat, cropped hair, ciga-
rette, skill in equitation, and aspirations in the fields of art, culture, and
savoir vivre.[13] Colette's lover, Matilde de Morny (a.k.a. "Missy"), Natalie
Barney's lover, Romaine Brooks, and her friend, Elisabeth de Gramont,
Duchesse de Clermont-Tonnerre, epitomized the type at the turn of the
century. Colette described the coterie to which they belonged:

> The adherents of this clique of women exacted secrecy for their
> parties, where they appeared dressed in long trousers and
> dinner jackets and behaved with unsurpassed propriety [. . .].
> Where could I find, nowadays, messmates like those [. . .]
> Baronesses of the Empire, lady cousins of Czars, illegitimate
> daughters of grand-dukes, exquisite examples of the Parisian
> bourgeoisie, and also some aged horsewomen of the Austrian
> aristocracy, hands and eyes of steel.[14]

The mannish costume sported by these belle epoque aristocrats often inspired horror in their femme sisters. The famous courtesan and lover of Natalie Barney, Liane de Pougy, deplored Missy's cross-dressing in her famous blue notebooks:

> Never will I understand such an error: the desire to resemble a
> man, abandon feminine grace, with its charm and sweetness. To
> create the illusion, Missy crushed her breasts under a large
> rubber strap. How horrible! [. . .] Cuts her hair when this
> feature can become a woman's most beautiful attribute![15]

What makes Liane's reaction interesting is the way in which it encapsulates a "phobia of phobia" within early lesbian identity politics. It is not so much, I would argue, the spectacle of a constricted poitrine or transvestic aesthetic that arouses Liane de Pougy's "horror," as the *transparency* of femme-phobia that Missy's chest-flattening operation signifies to the exterior world. The outing of gynophobia through butch aggression to the female body is tantamount to being incriminating evidence of femininity's self-recognition as a site of negative or aversive affect. Butch gynophobia, at least for Pougy, seems to qualify as a paramount betrayal of lesbian gynophilia, featured implicitly as the desire to promote a feminized ideal untainted by imitative androcentric stereotypes. Pougy's phobia of gynophobia ultimately represents a futile, but nonetheless symptomatic attempt to banish butchness from the sapphic city of women. Her tirade would seem to suggest that, as the most specular form of "outed" gynophobia, butch cross-dressing, and by extension gynophobia itself, is identifiable with parasitic masculinity.

Butchness, masculinity, and gynophobia would certainly seem to be complexly and irrevocably imbricated in historical grids of sex, identity, and gender. Loosely defined by Gayle Rubin as "the lesbian vernacular term for women who are more comfortable with masculine gender codes, styles, or identities than with feminine ones,"[16] butch has been qualified by Joan Nestle as "a woman who created an original style to signal to other women what she was capable of doing – taking erotic responsibility."[17] Reflecting further, Kirsten Hill claims that "butches push the limits and explore the boundaries of gender identity not because they try to be men, but because they express and display their masculinity while remaining women. Butch then, is a distinctly feminine appropriation of the masculine."[18] Rather than see butch masculine-identification as an erasure of the feminine in favor of the masculine (which leaves both gender stereotypes hardened in their fixity), Hill presents it as a strategy for resignifying femininity. The butch feminine is conceived of as that which alters and enlarges the feminine Symbolic.

The problem remains, of course, of how to evaluate the status of feminine representation within butch economies of desire: "if the butch who wouldn't be seen dead in pearls desires the femme who wears them, what is the nature of her attitude to pearls as fetish/metonym of the desirable?" Naomi Segal has queried.[19] In a similar vein, Tania Modleski has quoted a lesbian sadomasochist "trying to account for her attraction to clothes she 'would never, *ever* wear' of her own accord.'"[20] One way this issue has been approached is through recourse to the logic of the fetish: the butch desires elsewhere that which is personally foreclosed; in loving high heels and frilly lingerie in another she enjoys (and masters) what she "loves to hate." The detachable, fetishizable femme sign retains its sex appeal as long as it is displaced to a lesbian erotic economy designating what heterosexual culture has lost, or what lesbian fetishism has recovered – a queered erotic object.

For Tania Modleski, this kind of lesbian fetishism risks sheltering or legitimating the "phobic logic" of male fetishism, a logic understood to be in collusion with misogynist theories of castration anxiety:

> Given that fetishistic disavowal in the male is the means by
> which the psyche avoids facing the fact of the woman's
> difference, the fact of her *being* a woman, the feminist anti-
> essentialist, with her fears of being decapitated by her
> "essentialist" sisters, might be confirming the very horror that
> is at the root of male castration anxiety and the dread of
> woman.[21]

In its denial of sexual difference, male fetishism houses a death-threat to feminine identity according to this view; women who dally in its appropriation risk falling into the larger trap of what Modleski critically thematizes as "feminism without women." The problem here however, is that Modleski implies that "woman" must at all costs remain vigilant in protecting the carapace of her identity against the onslaught of masculine negation.[22] This position, in addition to abetting paranoia, seems to disallow a woman's desire to dismantle "woman." Perverse as it may seem, I would argue that, not unlike her male counterparts, a woman may equally well (though perhaps for significantly different reasons and stakes), comprehend femininity as an object of dread.

In the context of reciprocal theoretical exchanges between the early twentieth century and the present, Natalie Clifford Barney's *Pensées d'une Amazone* (1920) and its sequel *Nouvelles Pensées de l'Amazone* (1939) are worth exhuming today not just as witty aphorisms of early French feminism (a version of the venerable French tradition of the maxim, champi-

oned by the "masters" from Pascal and La Rochefoucauld to Gide and
Cioran), but more tendentiously as a philosophy of gynophobia offering
a kind of conceptual grid of gendered negative affect.[23] The "Dédicace" of
Pensées d'une Amazone consists of a long list of people and groups for
whom the book is written, but a negative phrase protrudes: "Pas à ceux
qui m'appellent: Miss" ("Not dedicated to those who call me: Miss").[24]
Long before this feminine appellation was scalpeled into the euphemistic
"Ms" Barney understood its charge as a synecdoche of oppressive femininity. Terms such as "Miss" or "Lady" were pilloried as concentrates of
what is most feminine in feminine culture; for Barney, the "lady" was an
"expurgated woman" (PA, 131). Though not averse to "playing the
femme" she figured femininity, in *Traits et Portraits* as a decadent chrysalis to be sloughed off by women of the future; parthenogenesis would
reveal the new androgyne: "In the beginning there was the androgyne, and
he will be there again at the end of time."[25]

Such utopian aspirations lay beneath Barney's maternophobia and cas-
tigation of the institution of marriage. Marriage and family certainly came
under her knife, much as they had in André Gide's paean to gay nomad-
ism, *Les Nourritures terrestres* (1897) – in which he launched the famous
"Familles, je vous hair" – and much as they had in Rachilde's equally
pitiless polemic, *Pourquoi je ne suis pas féministe* (1927): "I never trusted
women since I was first deceived by the eternal feminine under the maternal mask and I don't trust myself anymore."[26] In the *Pensées* Barney made
comparable pronouncements: "Marriage, a false value" (PA, 2); and "Maternity? The child limits the woman to himself – and then leaves her" (PA,
2). But her assertion that "there would be no more marriages" sets the
terms for an anticonjugal utopia of "associations of tenderness and passion." Fidelity, "the death-knell to union," would be replaced with open
relationships: "To be neither alone, nor together" (TP, 31). Barney even
rebaptized kinship terminology in order to configure a new queer family:
"We will be better than the wife, mother or sister of man, we will be man's
feminine brother" (PA, 9).

Undermining essentialist myths by *endorsing* them – a distinctly
gynophobic move that set her off from other feminists who saw patriarchal culture as the root cause of women's evils – Barney used her explosive, pithy utterances in *Pensées d'une Amazone* to express exasperation
and contempt toward female nature:

That catastrophe: To be a woman.
Fabricating sentiment: "women's work."
It is a good idea to believe in the mystery of woman, that will
   give her some.

If woman had reason, she would realize she has none.
I speak for her, but it's he who understands. (PA, 1, 128, 133,
136)

Though Barney could occasionally show compassion toward her sex,
lamenting bodies maimed by abortions, or haplessly clothed in male
costume, she directed the brunt of her ire at women. In the *Nouvelles
Pensées de l'Amazone* (1939) the gynophobic strain in her thought
continued:

> Woman is conservative to the point of death.
> Her femininity puts up a good front against her perilous inner
>   life.
> Their flesh: a ruin of roses.
> The female saints – and there are some – will be the only
>   women eligible to become feminists because they triumph
>   over their femininity, rather than because of it.[27]

If it is tempting to dismiss the antifeminine streak in Barney's writings as
self-hate or bad feminism, there is something strangely compelling in the
force of her negation. Femininity is violently abjected: held up, publicly
humiliated, devoured, and flushed out. "Their flesh: a ruin of roses" –
Barney's gloss on a line of Sappho's poetry translated by Renée Vivien –
evokes the pathos of abjected femininity, with its failed masquerade,
shattered ego ideal, and body image in ruins.

On a superficial level, such feminist antifemininity shares disturbing
similarities with Barney's male misogynist contemporaries – men like
Charles Maurras and Maurice Barrés. In the twenties, the right-wing
ideologue, Maurras, devoted a work on "Feminine Romanticism" to a
superficially friendly assessment of *belle époque* women writers: Renée
Vivien, Madame de Régnier, Lucie Delarue-Mardrus, and the Countess
Anna de Noailles. Subtitled "Allegory of Disordered Sentiment,"
Maurras' book evoked a supra-feminine aesthetic comprised of utopian
yearnings and expressive flights toward the unsayable. He praised the
poetry of Renée Vivien on the grounds that, in the manner of Baudelaire,
it preserved a sense of "moral evil." Of her dreamlike chains of thought, he
noted: "they are not false, they are *feminine*" (his emphasis): woman-
thought, for Maurras, was flawed but redeemable as a pure expression of
essentialism; suffused with a "maternal instinct that constructs the universe in the form of a cradle."[28] If at times he seemed indulgent toward
clichés of womanliness, by the text's conclusion he had reverted to the
mode of rhetorical denigration for which he was famous in his antisemitic
texts. He deplored the "barbarous," "foreign," "perverse," "profane," and
"arid" qualities of feminine poetics as symptoms of cultural devirilization.

Maurras' anomalous engagement with women's literature forms a piece with Maurice Barrès' obsession with the novels of Rachilde (Marguerite Eymery). Rachilde's *Monsieur Vénus*, the male concubine of the sexually voracious New Woman, Raoule de Vénérande, was read by Barrès as a "symptom" of a libidinally enervated masculine culture, a case history of deformity in love, a grand example of "la maladie du siècle" in which "male force" and "feminine grace" compete with each other as phobic objects.[29] What emerges from a consideration of Maurras and Barrès side by side with Barney is the sense that male misogyny has made common cause with feminist gynophobia in condemning the feminine "cause" of fin-de-siècle decadence.

In the present fin de siècle there may be a comparable alliance between misogyny and gynophobia based on shared aversion to mainstream feminisms. Leo Bersani's controversial book, *Homos*, explores the implications of such antifeminism while outing gay misogyny:

> The relation of gay men to feminism is bound to be more
> problematic than anyone wants to admit. . . . In his desires, the
> gay man always runs the risk of identifying with culturally
> dominant images of misogynist maleness. For the sexual drives
> of gay men do, after all, extend beyond the rather narrow circle
> of other politically correct gay men. A more or less secret
> sympathy with heterosexual male misogyny carries with it the
> narcissistically gratifying reward of confirming our membership
> in (and not simply our erotic appetite for) the privileged male
> society.[30]

Though Bersani's acknowledgment of a misogynist homosociality complicitously shared by gay and straight men avoids fully confronting the status of the confession itself (is Bersani simply accepting misogyny as a fact of homo life?), he nonetheless points to an intriguing "new genre of heterosexual desire" revolving around a curious oxymoron: the desire "of a gay man for a woman he can *count on* not to desire him, of a lesbian for a man she can *count on* not to desire her"[31] Although this new form of desire may look less like desire and more like *aphanisis* – that total disappearance of sexual desire, which, according to Ernest Jones was more frightening to both sexes than the fear of castration – Bersani's queerly heterosexual genre may in fact provide a space for feminist gynophobia and gay effeminophobia to come together in such a way that they redefine the love of masculinity without endorsing misogyny.

For many feminists, femininity's only tangible property is its own masquerade. Paradoxically, it is often *masculine* drag performance or newly configured lesbian *femme* positions that have given this masquerade a revived *raison d'être*. Camp womanliness clearly engages a critical sensibility that alters the status of femininity "as we know it," rendering it obsolete as a natural sign, doubling it up as a signifier of an imitation of an imitation, and rehousing it under the rubric of gay and lesbian female impersonation. In the Australian film *Priscilla Queen of the Desert*, femme-ness within drag is given its fullest tribute in the luxuriant visual inventiveness of costumes and cabaret numbers, and in the ennobled pathological narcissism of its leading lady, Bernadette. Here gynophilia may be interpreted as the cross three queens must bear, or as an example of misogyny hiding behind apparently gynophilic drag, or as a sartorial feast of trash and glitz made into art, vanquishing, even if only momentarily, the reflexes of a misogynist and homophobic public. High heels, feathers, sequins, lipstick, falsies, wigs – these girl-things, strewn across the desertscape, spawn a fantasy of unlimited object-choices. The family romance of heterosexual difference (preserved in the film's subplot of marriage and paternity) recedes before the spectacle of polymorphously perverse regalia – the real "heroines" of the picture are queer object-choices that consecrate the feminine masquerade with mirth and pleasure.

It may be that queer effeminacy, in naturalizing feminine artifice and in substituting a gorgeous prosthetics of being for the obelisk of phallocentric power, provides the only life-world in which a feminist gynophobe can freely indulge in gynophilia. Or is this just another round of feminine imitations of male imitations of femininity? For the contemporary artist and theorist Mary Kelly, exploring in her latest projects the way in which the relatively recent social phenomenon of women in the military regenders psychic models of defense, the problem of resignified manliness is now on the agenda:

> For the woman, display provides a form of protection against her social subordination, but it is also problematic. In the case of display, not only, as Lacan says, on the part of the male animal, but also the "female animal," entering the play of combat means covering her vulnerability with a peculiar psychic armor, one that separates her, finally, from other women. While a certain form of precocious femininity has been exorcised, and I would not want to revalorize it here, women may have overidentified with the kind of agency ascribed to men. In effect, the internalization of that ideal has supported the unconscious alignment of the feminine with derogation and abjection. In the historical perspective of sexual politics, Joan Riviere's influential observation of the woman's crisis has been

reversed. Now it seems that "manliness" is her defense and on her narcissistic shield, the icons of hysterics have been painted over with emblems of the master. To address that critically would mean acknowledging that one of feminism's monumental paradigms – the masquerade, has shifted.[32]

Inadvertently, Kelly evokes a kind of two-pronged gynophobia focusing on the "exorcism of precocious femininity," and the erection *by* women of psychic blockades *between* women (a "smart" technology of the feminine subject permitting "overidentification with the kind of agency ascribed to men"). Kelly's insight into the new "womanliness as manliness" is ingenious but leaves us wondering: are we simply ricocheting again between disavowed and abjected gender stereotypes? Or is this newly configured gynophobia part of some larger epistemic transformation whereby masculinity and femininity are profoundly altered as internalized ego ideals?

In light of recent efforts to rehabilitate or reinvent the "femme" or "femme-inist,"[33] it would seem that binarism will endure, with sex and gender stereotypes endlessly re-tuning themselves to accommodate "queered" desires. Thus, just as Mary Kelly puts the masquerade of manliness in the place of feminine masquerade, so concomitantly, a new generation of femmes makes the case that femmes have revalorized the masquerade of womanliness.[34] As Kirsten Hill remarks, "The current challenge and achievement of femmes has been to validate a greater variety of expressions of femininity as sources of power, and to disentangle that identification from notions of weakness, passivity and vulnerability."[35]

Despite the persuasiveness of these resignification arguments, the feminine mystique persists. Does camping femininity sufficiently convert it into an ontologically liberating feminist semiotics? Having dislodged femininity from its socially rewarded referential foundations, are its institutions worth conserving? Or is the desire to transcend femininity and the somewhat exhausted gender/sex discourses that surround it simply utopian?[36]

For the moment, queerness and queer studies seem to promise an alternative thirdness, a serious displacement of masculine and feminine. In revealing the heterosexist bias within much feminist theory, gay, lesbian and queer studies has not only come out (from under?) feminism, it has also begun to move away from feminism altogether to an elsewhere of provisionally marked sexualities, spaces, and dialogues. The tangible queering of feminist theory has helped give rise to queer-envy in multiple disciplines in the humanities and social sciences.

Gay, lesbian, and queer studies may well have upstaged feminist theory in rewriting the history of sexuality, institutions, and the law, and in dealing urgently with the politics of identity. Mortal survival in the age of AIDS, technologies of transgender, the blurring of identification and desire in theories of subject formation, the role of aesthetic and subcultural practices (opera, ballet, drag performance, theater, musicals, fashion shows, fanzines, etc.), in "outing" the subject to him or herself, and the desanctification of the "heteronormative" family – these stand out as compelling recent developments in queer studies.[37] By contrast, "late" feminism has embarked on a phase of healthy yet intellectually inhibiting self-criticism, aggravated by the postponed recognition that as a historic movement it was too straight, Eurocentric, and middle class; too oblivious to racial and ethnic differences; too smug about assumptions of consensus; too generationally rivalrous. This is not to suggest that once-upon-a-time there was a prelapsarian feminism basking in the full flush of community; but certainly as it has become more institutionally recognized, women's studies has been increasingly riven by incompatible intellectual tendencies.

It is perhaps by admitting issues such as gynophobia – a nexus of symptoms common to feminism and queer studies alike – that we might avoid a tendency toward reactive, separatist triage in the determination of gender/sex identities. A more complete mapping of gynophobia would explore its implications as a force within feminism driving sapphic antifemininity, lesbian antifeminism, butch antifemme positions, misogyny that masks itself behind gynophilic drag performance, so-called puritanical feminism, phobias centering on the fantasm of the desiring mother, queer-envy on the part of straight women, and finally (though not exhaustively), the quest for philosophical categories of feminine subjectivity that critique theories based on Freudian models of castration and sexual difference, that is, theories of fetishism, masquerade, and performative mimesis.

Underlying such an investigation of gynophobia would be the sense that feminism itself is no longer "at home" with feminism, not because it is "postfeminist" (in the historicist, conservative sense of that word), nor because it disagrees with the long-term political goals of a range of women's movements, but rather, because, as its name suggests, feminism embalms nostalgic constructs of "femininity," "femme-ness," and "woman" even as it disowns these terms through sophisticated theoretical revisions.[38] While it would be no doubt morally suspect and tactically inadvisable for feminists to relinquish the readily understood lexicon of their identity politics, it may be time now to classify femininity as an enduring anachronism on its way to gradual depletion as a signifier.

My purpose here has been neither to review "dykotomies" (Alisa Solomon's term), nor to bemoan femininity's definitive passing (one has only to look at the fashion industry, the beauty market, and the Hollywood star system to ascertain that commodified femininity is alive and well).[39] Rather, I have been interested in framing a discussion around a concept referring first, and most generally, to an age-old allergy to mass-marketed images of "classic" femininity, and second, to the challenges posed by feminist theory from the 1930s to the present, to psychoanalytic paradigms of phallic lack, egoic deficiency, preoedipal infantilization, passivity, hysteria, penis-envy, compensatory narcissism, hyper-defensiveness, performative masquerade, cosmetic fetishism, reified motherhood, the theory of a feminine *jouissance* beyond representation, and the exclusion of female signifieds from the Symbolic order. Certainly the work of Michèle Montrelay, Catherine Millot, Luce Irigaray, Jacqueline Rose, Juliet Mitchell, Jane Gallop, and Judith Butler has been particularly significant in challenging misogynist, (hetero) sexist assumptions within Freudian and Lacanian psychoanalytic models. The future of feminist psychoanalytic inquiry remains, however, uncertain, in the thrall, perhaps, of a phobia of itself: wary of its stake in fictions of feminine character that no longer signify in the next round of debate around the gendered character of the subject; wary too, of the possibility that self-subjection may be part of the hidden cost of subjectification. This last phrase reprises Denise Riley's caveat: "The dangerous intimacy between subjectification and subjection needs careful calibration." Riley is alluding here to how "the risky elements to the processes of alignment in sexed ranks are never far away, and the very collectivity which distinguishes you may also be wielded, even unintentionally, against you."[40] Riley's concerns point to how the salutary process of coming-to-subjecthood can potentially backfire in enhancing awareness of subjectivity's vulnerability to auto-negation.

"What 'Negation' offers is a way of theorizing a subject who comes into being on the back of a repudiation, who exists in direct proportion of what it cannot *let be*," Jacqueline Rose observes in her discussion of the influence of Freud's 1925 *Verneinung* essay on the concept of negativity upon Lacan and Melanie Klein.[47] Gynophobia can perhaps best be understood as a subjectivity that "comes into being on the back of a repudiation." It "is" insofar as it "cannot *let be*" (in the sense of allow to exist, leave intact or leave to its own devices), an *a priori* metaphysic of gender identity. A differential account of selfhood, forged out of foreclosure and flight, gynophobia speaks to a feminism that remains faithful to a radical, relentless criticality, coincident, perhaps, with the dark side of Kleinianism (i.e.

that portion of Melanie Klein's work that tracks the path of libidinal frustration on a regressive course of self-wreckage, social demolition, persecutory anxiety and depression). Dubbed the "high priestess of psychic negativity,"[42] Klein, together with her disciple Joan Riviere, deployed a logic of negation and interiorized anxiety that in many ways seems crucial to understanding the complex motivations of femininity's turn away from itself. Persecutory anxiety was interpreted as an expression of the ego's fear for itself by Klein and Riviere,[43] and I would maintain that this notion of "fearing for the ego" may be read in the context of gynophobia as a reparative strategy for preserving and protecting an ideal ego no longer dependent on the metaphysical scaffolding of femininity. Pain is mined for its access to an as yet "unhurt" love object (an undamaged gender ideal?), and the motion of "flight" is similarly mobilized as a force of affirmative negation. In an essay on "Hate, Greed and Aggression" (1937), Riviere writes: "Now flight is essentially and invariably a safety device; and we must consider what it is that is *saved* by rejection."[44] Pleasure, personal safety, and life itself are secured by flight according to Riviere. At the risk of making redemptive extrapolations, I would suggest that the gynophobic subject expresses a life-preserving "aversivity" in rendering femininity the phobic object. As Jacqueline Rose has argued: "Object-relations are 'improvements on' and 'protections against' primordial narcissistic anxiety; distrust of the object is better than despair."[45] In distrusting femininity, even to the point of brooking gynocide, gynophobia assumes responsibility for what Tania Modleski has cautioned against: namely, the project of "unbecoming women."[46]

Notes

A profound debt of thanks go to Naomi Segal and Mandy Merck. Their criticisms and suggestions have been invaluable in shaping what proved to be, for the author, an anxiety-provoking essay.

1   Though I am suggesting that gynophobia has been under-addressed in feminist critique, there have been important discussions of variously defined forms of it. Denise Riley's "Am I That Name?" in *Feminism and the Category of "Women" in History* (Minneapolis: University of Minnesota Press, 1988), Susan Gubar's "Feminist Misogyny: Mary Wollstonecraft and the Paradox of 'It Takes One to Know One,'" in *Feminist Studies* 20, 3 (Fall 1994): 453–73, and Tania Modleski's *Feminism Without Women: Culture and Criticism in a "Postfeminist" Age* (New York: Routledge, 1991) each explore sig-

nificant aspects of the problem. For an interesting treatment of Willa Cather's lesbian effeminophobia (her denunciation of Oscar Wilde's so-called effeminacy) see Eve Kosovsky Sedgwick's chapter "Willa Cather and Others" in *Tendencies* (Durham: Duck University Press, 1993), pp. 167–76.

2   Judith Butler, *Gender Trouble: Feminism and the Subversion of Identity* (New York: Routledge, 1990), p. 142.

3   Judith Butler argues in her introductory essay to the special issue of *differences* ("Against Proper Objects"), "If gender is said to belong to feminism, and sexuality in the hands of lesbian and gay studies is conceived as liberated from gender, then the sexuality that is 'liberated' from feminism will be one which suspends the reference to masculine and feminine, reenforcing the refusal to mark that difference, which is the conventional way in which the masculine has achieved the status of the 'sex' which is one." *differences* 6 (Summer–Fall 1994), p. 20.

4   Biddy Martin, "Extraordinary Homosexuals and the Fear of Being Ordinary," in *differences* 6 (Summer–Fall 1994), p. 101.

5   Denise Riley, "Am I That Name?" in Feminism and the Category of "Women" in *History*, p. 6.

6   Ibid., p. 17.

7   In her essay "Feminist Misogyny: Mary Wollstonecraft and the Paradox of 'It Takes One to Know One'" (p. 460), Susan Gubar reviews the biographical case for Wollstonecraft's "self-revulsion of a woman who knew herself to be constructed as feminine" (that is, according to Gubar's interpretation, too vulnerable to her own sexual appetites, a slave to the will of her lover). My thanks to Anne Mellor for signaling Gubar's illuminating article.

8   Sigmund Freud, "Anxiety" in *Introductory Lectures on Psychoanalysis*, ed. and trans. James Strachey (New York: W. W. Norton & Co. 1977), pp. 404, 405.

9   Mary Wollstonecraft, *A Vindication of the Rights of Woman*, ed. Carol H. Poston (New York: W. W. Norton & Co.), p. 8. My thanks to Mandy Merck for reminding me of Wollstonecraft's crucial importance to discussions of gynophobia.

10 Biddy Martin paraphrasing Elisabeth Bronfen's *Over Her Dead Body: Death, Femininity and the Aesthetic* (New York: Routledge, 1992) in her essay "Extraordinary Homosexuals and the Fear of Being Ordinary," *differences* 6 (Summer–Fall 1994), p. 103.

11 Mina Loy, "Feminist Manifesto" in *The Last Lunar Baedeker*, ed. and introduced by Roger Conover (Highlands: The Jargon Society, 1982), pp. 269–71.

12 Djuna Barnes, *Ladies Almanack* (Elmwood Park, IL: Dalkey Press, 1992), pp. 11, 12.
13 Radclyffe Hall's gynophobe was anchored in the mythic typologies of the tomboy/butch. In *Miss Ogilvy Finds Herself* (in Joan Nestle, ed., *The Persistent Desire: A Femme-Butch Reader* (Boston: Alyson Publications Inc., 1992), pp. 26–7), Hall fictively portrayed herself as a "queer little girl ... whose instinct made her like and trust men":

> She saw herself as a queer little girl, aggressive and
> awkward because of her shyness: a queer little girl who
> loathed sisters and dolls, preferring the stable-boys as
> companions, preferring to play with footballs and topos,
> and occasional catapults. [...] Miss Ogilvy's instinct made
> her like and trust men for whom she had a pronounced
> fellow-feeling; she would always have chosen them as her
> friends and companions in preference to girls or women;
> she would dearly have loved to share in their sports, their
> business, their ideals, and their wide-flung interests. [...]
> Towards young girls and women she was shy and
> respectful, apologetic and sometimes admiring. But their
> fads and their foibles, none of which she could share, while
> amusing her very often in secret, set her outside the sphere
> of their intimate lives, so that in the end she must blaze a
> lone trail through the difficulties of her nature.

14 Colette, *The Pure and the Impure* (New York: Farrar, Straus, and Giroux, 1967), pp. 67–9. This citation is made by Gayle Rubin in her introduction to Renée Vivien, *A Woman Appeared to Me*, trans. Jeannette H. Foster (USA: Naiad Press, 1976), p. vii. Rubin wrote this introduction early in her career, consulting Vivien and Barney archives that had attracted little notice by critics at the time. Her interest is in establishing Vivien, and other members of the Barney circle as important forerunners of seventies lesbian consciousness. The footnotes in this introduction are especially rich. In 1988, Elaine Marks wrote a piece entitled " 'Sappho 1990': Imaginary Renée Viviens and the Rear of the Belle Epoque" for a special issue of *Yale French Studies* 75 ("The Politics of Tradition: Placing Women in French Literature," ed. Joan Dejean and Nancy K. Miller), in which she takes Rubin to task (along with the right-wing ideologue, Charles Maurras, author of *Le Romantisme féminin*), for reading Vivien's work tendentiously; that is, for focusing on Vivien as an avatar of

lesbian community. Marks wants to widen lesbian gender parameters and contexts; de-restricting roles and "differently" marked identities. While I appreciate Marks's call for nuanced reading ("It is not Renée Vivien's place in French or lesbian literature that it is important to determine but the multiple discursive contexts of the *belle époque* that traverse her texts" she concludes [p. 189]), I still think it is permissible to develop a singular angle in literary interpretation – for my own purposes here, what strikes me most perusing Vivien's 1904 novel, *Une femme m'apparut*, is that it begs to be read as a classic (if egregiously stereotyped) "femme" text.

15   Liane de Pougy, *Mes Cahiers bleus* (Paris: Plon, 1927).

16   Gayle Rubin, "Of Catamites and Kings: Reflections on Butch, Gender and Boundaries" in Nestle, ed., *The Persistent Desire: A Femme-Butch Reader*, p. 467.

17   Joan Nestle, "The Femme Question" in *The Persistent Desire: A Femme-Butch Reader*, p. 141.

18   Kirsten Hill, "Butch-Femme vs. the Hetero-patriarchy and Lesbian-Feminism," unpublished paper.

19   Naomi Segal in written comments on a draft of this essay, which owes an enormous debt to her detailed criticisms and suggestions.

20   Tania Modleski, *Feminism without Women: Culture and Criticism in a "Postfeminist" Age*, p. 156.

21   Ibid., p. 22.

22   For attempts to theorize a lesbian fetishism devoid of gynophobia, see Elizabeth Grosz ("Lesbian Fetishism?," *differences* no. 3 (Summer 1991), p. 51) and Teresa de Lauretis (*The Practice of Love: Lesbian Sexuality and Perverse Desire* [Bloomington: Indiana University Press, 1994]). In Grosz's original argument the "masculine" lesbian disavows her castration and therefore, unlike the narcissist and the hysteric, does not fetishize her own body, but that of her female love-object. But rather than speculating on the possible gynophobia in this disavowal, Grosz argues that the butch's "fetish is not the result of a fear of femininity but a love of it." In *The Practice of Love*, Teresa de Lauretis takes up the other pathway traced by Grosz, that of the femme who accepts her castrated status and seeks out a "phallic" woman, to reply that it is not the phallus which the femme recognizes and desires in the insignia of the butch, but a non-phallic fetish (albeit one of "masculinity") which both represents and makes good the "loss of the female body itself, and the prohibition of access to it" (p. 243). Finally, in a review of this book entitled "The Labors of Love. Analyzing Perverse Desire," *differences* 6 (Summer–Fall 1994), Grosz comes to reject a specifically "lesbian psychology"

to argue instead "for the apparent mobility of (perverse) desire" (p. 291). She notes that de Lauretis may be developing a notion of lesbian attraction rather than desire; a notion, moreover, that need not apply exclusively to lesbians:

> The fetish is a displacement of the bodily dispossession that constitutes the castration that the girl suffers. This fetish cannot be identified with the object of lesbian desire (the woman) but is the subject's means of access to and mode of attraction for the love-object. No doubt there is a potentially infinite number of signs, traits, gestures, mannerisms that pose the lure Lacan attributed to the *objet petit a*. These "strange attractors" which signal the inducements of the erotic object to a desiring subject are those special details that attract a woman to a woman. (Grosz 1994, p. 285)

23 Barney's biography has consistently eclipsed her literary oeuvre. Her *Pensées d'une Amazone* and its sequel are still only available in French and have yet to be reissued in a modern edition.

24 Natalie Clifford Barney, *Pensées d'une Amazone* (Paris: Emile-Paul, 1920), p. vii. All further references to this work will appear in the text abbreviated PA.

25 Natalie Clifford Barney, *Traits et Portraits* (Paris: Mercure de France, 1963), p. 208–9. Further references to this work will appear in the text abbreviated TP.

26 Rachilde (Marguerite Eymery), *Pourquoi je ne suis pas féministe* (Paris: Edition de France, 1928), p. 6; as cited by and translated by Maryline Lukacher, *Maternal Fictions: Stendhal, Sand, Rachilde and Bataille* (Durham: Duke University Press, 1994), p. 110.

27 Natalie Clifford Barney, *Nouvelles Pensées de l'Amazone* (Paris: Mercure de France, 1939), pp. 50, 51, 52, 55. Further references to this work will appear in the text abbreviated NP.

28 Charles Maurras, *L'Avenir de l'intelligence* (Paris: Ernest Flammarion Editeurs, 1927), p. 166.

29 Maurice Barrès, "Complications d'amour," Preface to Rachilde, *Monsieur Vénus* (Paris: Flammarion, 1977), pp. 14, 19.

30 Leo Bersani, *Homos* (Cambridge: Harvard University Press, 1995), p. 63.

31 Ibid., p. 65.

32 Mary Kelly, "Miming the Master: Boy-Things, Bad Girls and Femmes Vitales," cited from manuscript. Also in *Imaging Desire*,

Mary Kelly: Selected Writings (Cambridge, MA: MIT Press, 1996), p. 226.

33 See, Paula Austin, "Femme-inism" in *The Persistent Desire: A Femme-Butch Reader*, pp. 362–6.

34 The argument about changing the definition of masculinity and femininity by feminizing the former and masculinizing the latter, harks back to the androgynous femme aesthetic associated with Natalie Barney. According to Shari Benstock, *Women of the Left Bank. Paris 1900–1940.* (Austin: University of Texas Press, 1986), Barney eroticized and feminized "the very bodily features (lithe limbs and small breasts) that marked for male artists of the period a castrated and ambiguous sexual identity" (p. 303).

35 Kirsten Hill.

36 In a recent lecture on paranoia, Eve Kosovsky Sedgwick questions the "hermeneutic suspicion" (in the phrase of Paul Ricoeur) that queer theory has habitually brought to the critique of gender identity. She sees the urge to "expose" gender performance (through heuristic moves to demystify, destabilize, deconstruct or decenter covert ideologies of the subject) as symptomatic of paranoid reading practices that, in their turn, risk overlooking "real" or highly visible political threats to the civil and sexual rights of minorities. Sedgwick's argument prompts reexamination of feminism and queer theory in terms of the focus of their anxieties: has the interpretation of the precariousness of identity created a cocoon that shields us from the harshness of *Realpolitik*?

37 See Michael Warner's section on "Heteronormativity in Social Theory" in his preface to *Fear of a Queer Nation: Queer Politics and Social Theory*, ed. Michael Warner (Minneapolis: University of Minnesota Press, 1993), pp. xxi–xxviii. On the issue of queered parenting, see in the same volume, Eve Kosovsky Sedgwick's essay, "How to Bring Your Kids up Gay," pp. 69–81.

38 Cora Kaplan makes a similar point (stated over-categorically, as is my own): "All feminisms give some ideological hostage to femininities and are constructed through the gender sexuality of their day as well as standing in opposition to them" ("Pandora's Box: Subjectivity, Class, and Sexuality in Socialist Feminist Criticism" in *Making a Difference: Feminist Literary Criticism*, ed. Gayle Greene and Coppélia Kahn (London: Methuen, 1985), pp. 157–60).

39 See Alicia Solomon, "Dykotomies" in *Unleashing Feminism: Critiquing Lesbian Sadomasochism in the Gay Nineties*, ed. Irene Reti (Santa Cruz, CA: HerBooks, 1993).

40 Riley, p. 17.

41   Jacqueline Rose, "Negativity in the Work of Melanie Klein" in *Why War? Psychoanalysis, Politics, and the Return to Melanie Klein* (Oxford: Blackwell, 1993), p. 153.

42   Ibid., p. 138.

43   Joan Riviere, General Introduction to Melanie Klein, Paula Heimann, Susan Isaacs, and Joan Riviere, eds, *Developments in Psycho-Analysis* (1952) republished in *The Inner World and Joan Riviere*, Ed. Athol Hughes. London and New York: Karnac Books (1991), pp. 262–3. Glossing Klein, Riviere writes:

> persecutory anxiety is the ego's *fear for itself*; while damage and destruction to the good object (loss of it) are denied; depression and mourning are predominantly the ego's reaction to its *fear for the loved object* which is destroyed and lost; in this reaction is included fear for the ego. Pain must surely enter into both these, but if we could conceive of pure pain unmixed with grief or fear, we might say it would arise from the *loss* of a loved object which was still unhurt.

44   Riviere, "Love Hate and Aggression" in *The Inner World and Joan Riviere*, p. 182. Riviere's essay originally appeared in a book co-edited with Melanie Klein entitled *Love, Hate and Reparation* (London: Hogarth Press, 1937).

45   Jacqueline Rose, *Why War?*, p. 152.

46   Modleski, *Feminism without Women*, p. 13.

Chapter 5

Mother, Don't You See I'm Burning? Between Female Homosexuality and Homosociality in Radclyffe Hall's *The Unlit Lamp*

Trevor Hope

In her essay "The Mythic Mannish Lesbian: Radclyffe Hall and the New Woman," Esther Newton has powerfully articulated the ambivalence of the works of Radclyffe Hall (but especially of *The Well of Loneliness*) for lesbians and feminists:

> Unable to wish Radclyffe Hall away, sometimes even hoping to reclaim her, our feminist scholars have lectured, excused, or patronized her. Radclyffe Hall, they declare, was an unwitting dupe of the misogynist doctors' attack on feminist romantic friendships. Or, cursed with a pessimistic temperament and brainwashed by Catholicism, Hall parroted society's condemnation of lesbians. The "real" Radclyffe Hall lesbian novel, this argument frequently continues, the one that *ought* to have been famous, is her first, *The Unlit Lamp* (1924). Better yet, Virginia Woolf's *Orlando* (1928) should have been the definitive lesbian novel. Or Natalie Barney's work, or anything but *The Well*. (Newton 1985, 9)

Implied in this passage, I believe, as indeed in the history of feminist and lesbian critical reception of Hall's work more generally, are several rather densely overinscribed ambivalences: ambivalences which, to evoke the title of the Hall novel that is the focus for this essay, may be simultaneously enlightening and obfuscating. Critical encounters take place in the reading of Hall's work in ways which map several discursive cruces and crises: between feminism and lesbianism, between romantic friendship and lesbian pathology, homosocial continuity and the dialectics of desire; between woman-identification and gender transgression, gender-normativity and congenital inversion; between sociological and medical, or psychical and somatic readings of lesbianism; between social-contructionist and biologically essentialist forms of critical and political practice; between optimism and pessimism, health and disease, inclusion and outlawry, sociality and criminality; between *The Unlit Lamp* and *The Well of Loneliness*.

To spell out such a list of dualities is patently to assume the hackneyed critical duty – or heroic deconstructive quest? – of demonstrating that each pair of terms is fictional and/or mutually constitutive, and yet my intention here is not swiftly to transcend and displace these oppositions – or structural ambivalences, as I shall persist in considering them – but rather to linger with them, in the context of a reading of *The Unlit Lamp*, in order to begin to expose how, in their very volatility and mobility, they continue productively to drive debates in lesbian and feminist theory. While to maintain that the elements that form these pairs are radically disjoint is absurd – amongst other things this would imply that one was *either* a feminist *or* a lesbian, *either* a culturalist *or* a full-blown biological determinist, and *if* a feminist *then* a culturalist, etc., etc. – these alignments and oppositions *are* legible and rhetorically operative both specifically within the corpus of Hall criticism and within broader contemporary accounts of the relationship between (to linger again for a moment with the fantasy of a possible dichotomization) gender "and" sexuality, feminist "and" lesbian theory.

Lillian Faderman's reading of *The Well of Loneliness* in *Surpassing the Love of Men* is vulnerable to the critique that Esther Newton offers of a certain school of lesbian-feminist interpretation. Faderman presents Hall's motives in portraying Stephen Gordon, the novel's protagonist, as a congenital invert as stemming from the immediate influence of the sexologists – "Her authorities were all Krafft-Ebing disciples such as Havelock Ellis, Iwan Bloch, and Magnus Hirschfeld" – and from political contingency:

> Hall believed that her novel would provide lesbians with a
> moral and medical defense against a society which viewed

same-sex love as immoral or curable. If a female argued that she *chose* to center her life on another female, she laid herself open to accusations of immorality, she willfully flew in the face of the conventions of her day. If she accepted the psychoanalytical theory that something has happened to her in childhood to cause her aberration, she had no excuse not to seek a cure which would undo the trauma and set her straight. But if she maintained that she was born with her "condition," although some might consider her a freak she could insist, as Hall actually did, that God created her that way, that she had a purpose in God's scheme of things even if she was a freak. (Faderman 1981, 317–18)[1]

Faderman reads Hall's recourse to congenital inversion as an unfortunate foreclosure of the political possibilities articulated in the earlier novel:

> While *The Unlit Lamp* gives some vague Freudian explanation for Joan's and Elizabeth's interest in each other, it does not suggest that they suffer from a congenital problem. In fact, in this book the choice of another female as love object seems to have its roots primarily in feminism and in a rejection of the sexist and heterosexist values of society. Love between women and feminist consciousness seem to be as inextricably bound together in this early novel as they are for contemporary feminists. (Faderman 1981, 318)

These statements by Faderman do indeed seem to uphold a certain dichotomization that aligns the "good" Hall with a view of lesbianism as an expression of feminist politics and as such voluntary, "canny," and healthy, while the "bad" Hall tends to become a site for the projection of non-, if not anti-feminist values associated with a pathetic, aberrant and unhealthy somatism. While I shall have space here only for a consideration of one of these two novels, I hope it will be clear from my reading of *The Unlit Lamp* that the distinctions drawn between the two works have been overstated, perhaps as a symptom of those ambivalences that drive the critical imbrications of lesbianism and feminism. While there are significant differences between the novels in their conception of community, politics, female homosociality and homosexuality, and the lesbian body, a careful reading might concentrate rather on the persistence of ambivalences *across* the two works that an overly hasty comparison occludes. This ambivalence, I will argue, inheres in the ways lesbian sexuality and the lesbian body address themselves to the social gaze – and articulate themselves within and *against* the social body – of a modernity marked by the asymmetric economy of sexual difference.[2]

One point that deserves immediate attention is the fact that lesbianism is never narratively realized in *The Unlit Lamp*. Whilst it is realized, however tragically, in *The Well*, lesbianism in the earlier novel is constantly frustrated by a disciplinary female homosociality against which it struggles, ultimately in vain, to articulate itself. "The novel," for Newton, "portrays a devouring mother using the kinship claims of the female world to crush her daughter's legitimate bid for autonomy" (Newton 1985, 12).[3] Whilst the political implications of this view will require further consideration, it should at least be clear that Hall's portrayal of female homosociality (the "love between women" and "feminist consciousness" that Faderman reads as "inextricably bound" in *The Unlit Lamp*) is far from univocally idyllic, emphasizing, as it does, in the form of a pathological bonding of mother and daughter, the foreclosure of symbolic possibilities to women, including both same-sex desire and professional achievement.

Not surprisingly, the questions of *stigma* and *pathos* become central to the ambivalence over lesbian ontology and lesbian politics in the reading of Hall. Stigmatization plays a fraught role in the articulation of lesbianism within the *polis* insofar as it is surely a prerequisite of this articulation that the *significance* of lesbianism should be visibly objectified upon the social body. Stigmatization might be seen as the price of a lesbian ontology that articulates itself against patriarchal Law. At the same time, it contravenes the no less patriarchally regulatory phantasm of that unarticulated female "homofusionality" required to support the male imaginary yet denied access to symbolic articulation. There is, here, an important double bind for lesbian, and all feminist, interventions in the imaginary economy of patriarchy. How does an "entre-femmes," which sustains difference and desire, emerge from – *come out of* – the impoverished version of female solidarity conceived within the patriarchal imaginary without simply repeating the ritualized abjection of the feminine? And, given the anchoring of the male imaginary in a specifically *maternal* support, how, in particular, can an entre-femmes that sustains female homosexual desire be *birthed* from female homosociality in such a manner as not to "leave behind" the relation to the maternal?[4]

Put another way, we need, perhaps, confronted with Hall's work, to ask ourselves to what extent a disciplinary female homosociality, represented alternately by the "kinship claims of the female world," by a "devouring mother," or by feminism itself, to invoke the suggestive title of this anthology, has the potential to become a closet of normativity out of which lesbianism has to emerge at the expense, precisely, of those emotional and political bonds, and at the cost of a corrosive, freakish symptomaticity. Is the lesbian continuum imagined by a certain tradition of lesbian feminism itself potentially a blanket term, perhaps even a fire blanket, that threatens to extinguish the lamp – the heat and light – of lesbian desire, or does the very notion of such a continuum perhaps represent a failure on the part of such theorizations to shed light on the complexity of female homosocial desire operative within the personal and political affiliation of women?[5]

Inversion, Degeneracy, and the Social Symptom

Both *The Unlit Lamp* and *The Well of Loneliness* are explicitly concerned with discourses of disease and symptomaticity. In each case we find the typical modern concern with the symptom as a melancholic inscription bespeaking the pathos of familial descent (as the insertion of the embodied individual within the economic and biological nexus of inheritance) and the sense of an archaic and originary taint.[6] The symptom, then, asserts itself ambivalently within the question of legitimacy, legitimation, filiation, and perversion. On the one hand this symptom expresses the accident of a biological deviation or "swerve" from legitimate genetic filiation apparently stemming from a weakened legitimation of the Name of the Father. On the other hand, in the guise of the "throwback," it somehow also figures as the uncanny revelation of an essential, indeed founding (illegitimate) Truth that has always already recast the heroics of filiation as a unidirectionally tragi-farcical descent.[7]

The thematics of disease in both *The Unlit Lamp* and *The Well* is quite explicitly linked to the question of familial descent and degeneracy. The melancholics of patriarchy is clearly evident in the fact that the father of each of the protagonists – Joan Ogden and Stephen Gordon – dies early in the plot, some time during the young woman's adolescence. In *The Unlit Lamp*, however, the paternal lineage has been eclipsed in favor of Mrs Ogden's debased and economically eroded yet romanticized inheritance:

> [Mrs Ogden] had been a Routledge before her marriage, a fact
> which haunted her day and night. "Poor as rats, and silly proud
> as peacocks," someone had once described them. "We
> Routledges" – "The Routledges never do that" – "The
> Routledges never do this"! (Hall 1981, 16)

According to that most symptomatic of degenerative tropes, the portrait of the paradoxically esteemed yet perversely tainted ancestor oversees his lineage of *descent*, and modernity's logic of melancholic wounding is amply suggested by the family's anachronistic clinging to aristocratic vigour and warrior valour even as his essential taint rematerializes as corporal symptomaticity and the endless exhaustion of (social-symbolic and economic) capital:

> Round and round like squirrels in a cage, treading the wheel
> of their useless tradition, living beyond their limited means,
> occasionally stooping to accept a Government job, but usually
> finding all work *infra dig*. Living on their friends, which
> somehow was not *infra dig.*, soothing their pride by recounting
> among themselves and to all who would listen the deeds of
> valour of one Admiral Sir William Routledge said to have been
> Nelson's darling – hanging their admiral's picture with laurel
> wreaths on the anniversary of some bygone battle and never
> failing to ask their friends to tea on that occasion – such were
> the Routledges of Chesham, and such, in spite of many
> reverses, had Mary Ogden remained. (Hall 1981, 16)

The hemorrhaging of the capital of patronymic legitimacy is figured through the occlusion of the Name of the Father that results from the very literal dying off of the male lineage, rendering the mantra of "We Routledges" as hollowly, melancholically *symbolic* as, of course, it was always destined to be. The logic of its iterative evocation of an ever-eclipsed authorial legitimacy is as cruelly parodic as the ancestral portrait in the age of mechanical reproduction:

> True, Chesham had been sold up, and the admiral's portrait by
> Romney bought by the docile Bishop of Blumfield at the
> request of his wife Ann. True, Ann and Mary had been left
> penniless when their father, Captain Routledge, died of lung
> hæmorrhage in India. True, Ann had been glad enough to
> marry her bishop, then a humble chaplain, while Mary
> followed suit with Major Ogden of the Buffs. True, their
> brother Henry had failed to distinguish himself in any way and
> had bequeathed nothing to his family but heavy liabilities when
> his hæmorrhage removed him in the nick of time – true, all
> true, and more than true, but they were still Routledges! And
> Admiral Sir William still got his laurel wreaths on the
> anniversary of the battle. He had moved from the decaying
> walls of Chesham to the substantial walls of the bishop's
> palace, and perhaps he secretly liked the change – Ann his
> descendant did. In the humbler drawing-room at Leaside he
> received like homage; for there, in a conspicuous position, hung
> a print of the famous portrait, and every year when the great
> day came round, Mary, his other descendant, dutifully placed

her smaller laurel wreath round the frame, and asked her
friends to tea as t'radition demanded. (Hall 1981, 16)

The economics of sanguinity that, for Foucault, grounds the modern
epistemological regime of race in its intrication into the operations of
sexuality is figured in the staging of paternal haemorrhaging in the colonial
context: the *ethnos* of Englishness, and the very discourse of ethnicity that
underpins Hall's conception of inverts as an outcast race is thus, again
melancholically, pinned to the pathos of colonial exhaustion.[8]

The father's study (so mercilessly revealed as the pretension of a dining
room!) figures prominently in *The Unlit Lamp*, implying the eclipse
of cognitive expertise, a lost geometric singularity of canny significan-
tory authority that phantasmatically haunts the small-mindedness and
willful anti-cognition of a disseminated and corporally encrypted signification: the symptom arises in the place where knowledge (never) was.[9] The
novel, that is, seems to proclaim the triumph of the regime of what Lacan
has called the *patheme* over that of the *episteme*. The "seat" of learning is
eloquent according to the ghostly testimony of the *trace*:

> The dining room at Leaside was also Colonel Ogden's Study.
> It contained, in addition to the mahogany sideboard with
> ornamental brackets at the back, the three-tier dumb waiter and
> the dining room table with chairs *en suite*, a large roll-top desk
> much battered and ink-stained, and bleached by the suns of
> many Indian summers. There was also a leather arm-chair with
> a depression in the seat, a pipe-rack and some tins of tobacco.
> All of which gave one to understand that the presence of the
> master of the house brooded continually over the family meals
> and over the room itself in the intervals between. And lest this
> should be doubted, there was Colonel Ogden's photograph in
> uniform that hung over the fireplace; an enlargement showing
> the colonel seated at his writing-table, his native servant at his
> elbow. (Hall 1981, 9)

Again, colonial exhaustion – the bleaching and battering that has
ostensibly undermined (but surely also "justified"?) the project of
bureaucratic authority and national self-legitimation – is also part of a
narrative that anchors the familial pathology to national degeneration, and
the scene of writing, of subjectivity within the symbolic, is imperially
dis-placed:

> In 1880 the Ogdens had left India hurriedly on account of
> Colonel Ogden's health. When Milly was a baby and Joan
> three years old, the family had turned their backs on the

pleasant luxury of Indian life. Home they had come to England
and a pension, Colonel Ogden morose and chafing at the
useless years ahead; Mrs. Ogden a pretty woman, wide-eyed
and melancholy after all the partings, especially after one
parting which her virtue would have rendered inevitable in any
case. (Hall 1981, 15)

If the familial symptom is now what occupies the structurally empty
place of the Name of the Father, the political economics of its current
valency and circulation becomes feminine and domestic:

Mrs. Ogden put her hand up to her head wearily, glancing at
Joan as she did so. Joan was so quick to respond to the appeal
of illness. Mrs. Ogden would not have admitted to herself how
much she longed for this quick response and sympathy. She,
who for years had been the giver, she who had ministered to a
man with heart disease, who had become a veritable reservoir
of soothing phrases, solicitous actions, tabloids, hot soups and
general restoratives. There were times, growing more frequent
of late, when she longed, yes, longed, to break down utterly, to
become bedridden, to be waited upon hand and foot, to have
arresting symptoms of her own, any number of them. (Hall
1981, 12)

While the labor of caretaking – as an effect of the division of labor in the
reproduction of the flesh – has, of course, devolved upon women as an
effect of patriarchal power, I think that *The Unlit Lamp* implies that it
also operates as an insidious ruse of disciplinarity when wielded (consciously or not – or perhaps specifically not, regardless of the novel's
frequent assertions of the artfulness of invalidity, since this is a form of
power that has less to do with the will of a subject than the "obscene"
demands of a body) by a woman. In this manner, Hall's novel seems to
bespeak what might now be termed codependency (the "quick response"
of the projective operations of *sympathy*) raised to a principle of social and
political theory:

Mrs. Ogden was a strong woman. She did not look robust,
however; this she knew and appreciated. Her pathetic eyes were
sunken and somewhat dim, her nose, short and straight like
Joan's, looked pinched, and her drooping mouth was pale. All
this Mrs. Ogden knew, and she used it as her stock-in-trade
with her elder daughter. There were days when the desire to

produce an effect upon someone became a positive craving. She
would listen for Joan's footsteps on the stairs, and then assume
an attitude, head back against the couch, hand pressed to eyes.
Sometimes there were silent tears hastily hidden after Joan had
seen, or the short, dry cough so like her brother Henry's.
Henry had died of consumption. (Hall 1981, 12–13)

Symbolic power is eclipsed in *The Unlit Lamp* by a contagion of sympathy that addresses and initiates its victims not as subjects or even objects
but rather as abjects: as corporal surfaces ripe for an acephalic symptomatic inscription. Of course, the tragedy of the novel is how such
contagious inscription seems unavoidable.

Joan spends her life trying to escape Seabourne with her long-suffering
governess and beloved friend, Elizabeth. Her plans are repeatedly foiled
by the intricated narratives of illness and mismanaged finances. Her sister
Milly does escape to London, only to succumb to her "sociobiological"
Fate of tuberculosis. According to the trajectory of infection, by the
end of the novel Joan has – in psychoanalytic terms, through the
de-subjectivizing force of a "projective identification" – assumed her
mother's symptoms: "Her head ached badly, as it did pretty often these
days . . . She had taken to thinking a great deal about her health lately, not
because she wanted to, but rather because she was constantly assailed by
small, annoying symptoms, all different and all equally unpleasant." Joan's
old friend Richard summarizes this tragic logic late in life, but before she
finally is forced to assume the position of live-in nurse for a retarded
relative:[10]

> "I tell you, Joan, the sin of it lies at the door of that old woman
> [her mother] in Lynton; that mild, always ailing, cruelly gentle
> creature who's taken everything and given nothing and
> battened on you year by year. She's like an octopus who's
> drained you dry. You struggled to get free, you nearly
> succeeded, but as quickly as you cut through one tentacle,
> another shot out and fixed on you.
>
> "Good God! How clearly one sees it all! In your family it
> was your father who began it, by preying first on her, and in a
> kind of horrid retaliation she turned and preyed on *you*. Milly
> escaped, but only for a time; she came home in the end; then
> she preyed in her turn. She gripped you through her physical
> weakness, and then there were two of them! Two of them?
> Why, the whole world's full of them! Not a Seabourne
> anywhere but has its army of octupi; they thrive and grow fat

in such places . . . Look at Elizabeth: do you think she's really
happy? Well, I'm going to tell you now what I kept from you
the other day. Elizabeth got free, but not quite soon enough;
she's never been able to make up for the blood she lost in all
those years at Seabourne. She's just had enough vitality left to
patch her life together somehow, and make my brother think
that all is very well with her. But she couldn't deceive me, and
she knew it; I saw the ache in her for the thing she might have
been . . . I suppose I ought to hate Elizabeth, but I can't help
knowing that when she broke away there was one tentacle
more tenacious than all the rest; it clung to her until she cut it
through, and that was *you*, who were trying unconsciously to
make her a victim of your own circumstances.

"Joan, the thing is infectious, I tell you; it's a pestilence that
infects people one after another . . ." (Hall 1981, 300–1)

The hypothetical temporality caught in the aching for what *might have
been*, feeds directly into the question of an ever-imminent obscenity in the
novel. The fact that the symptom most frequently takes the form of a
*head*ache seems equally to suggest something "anticephalic" in its operations, as if it represents a case of the soma encroaching upon the symbolic
space of the psyche. The collapsing of symbolic space in corporal exchange is morbidly suggested by the oblique references to vampirism in
this passage.[11] It seems to me that the pathos of Hall's narrative tends to
confirm Richard's analysis. (Hall apparently originally intended to call the
novel "The Octopus.") Although there is clearly a broader social logic
behind these operations of power, they are so insistently associated, in
Richard's rendition, with femininity and female homosociality as to
render these essentially abject.

Mother/Daughter Bonds

There are hints of the manner in which the contagious antisubjectivity of
compulsory female homofusionality in the novel relates to the possibility
of lesbian eroticism and female autonomy. Joan's short hair (the highly
meaning-laden hair of the New Woman) seems to be an attempt on her
part to position herself as the subject of a symptom: "They had cut her
thick hair during scarlet fever, and Joan refused to allow it to grow" (Hall
1981, 11). There is, in this, the acknowledgment of the possibility of
assuming the stigma and inhabiting it as a mode of symbolic address. The
same logic of the redeployment of the symptom to significatory purposes
might be seen as the motivation behind Joan's specific ambition: to be-

come a doctor – to *read* the symptom, then, from the privileged position of alienation that frees one from engulfment in its opacity.[12] Being the canny decoder of the symptom appears, in other words, to save one from the burden of being or housing the encrypted symptom. But, of course, her father and mother thwart Joan's ambition through the appeal to gender- and class-conformity. Her father:

> "You must be mad," he told her. "It's positively indecent – an unsexing, indecent profession for any woman, and any woman who takes it up is indecent and unsexed. I say it without hesitation – indecent, positively immodest!" (Hall 1981, 110)

And her mother:

> "If you were a boy I would say this to you, and since you seem to have chosen to assume an altogether ridiculous masculine role, listen to me. There are things that a gentleman can do and things he cannot; no gentleman can enter the medical profession, no Routledge has ever been known to do such a thing. Our men have served their country; they have served it gloriously, but a Routledge does not enter a middle-class profession . . ." (Hall 1981, 110)

The *indecency* and *immodesty* of the career ambition surely stem from the threat that Joan poses to the ocular regime: the *voyure*. She would shake the securely melancholic onto-logic of the symptom to articulate its pregnant meaning and render it visible and significant within the social *voyure*. It is the attempt to orient the stigma to the social, to "decrypt" it in such a manner as to make blatant its significatory potential, that renders it obscene.

Not surprisingly, then, the in/visibility of the symptom within the social is also at the heart of the ambivalent erotics and the dense nexus of female homosexuality and homosexuality in the novel. The symptom and its effects of sympathy bind mother and daughter in an eroticized conspiracy of secrecy:

> Then as Joan's eyes would grow troubled, and the quick: "Oh, Mother darling, aren't you well?" would burst from her lips, Mrs. Ogden's conscience would smite her. But in spite of herself she would invariably answer: "It's nothing, dearest; only my cough," or "It's only my head, Joan; it's been very painful lately."
>
> Then Joan's strong, young arms would comfort and soothe, and her firm lips grope until they found her mother's; and Mrs.

Ogden would feel mean and ashamed but guiltily happy, as if a
lover held her. . . .
    "But you're ill, too, and father's heart isn't always as bad as
he makes out. This morning —— "
    "Hush, Joan, you mustn't. I know I'm not strong, but we must
never let him know that I sometimes feel ill." (Hall 1981, 13)

The mother binds her daughter to her in the "hushed" opacity of the
unarticulated symptom. It is the obscene threat of this symptomatic bond
being socialized and symbolized that surely enables us to understand an
otherwise totally opaque aspect of Mrs Ogden's response to Joan's career
aspirations:

Elizabeth might think that women could fill men's posts, but
she knew better. Yet, after all, Joan was so like a boy – one felt
that she was a son sometimes . . . And Joan – Joan was moving
away, not very far, only a little way. Joan was becoming a
spectator, and Joan as an audience might be dangerous. (Hall
1981, 55)

This passage surely only makes sense insofar as it implies the possibility
that Joan's symbolic alienation from the imaginarily constituted bond of
mother–daughter fusionality has the potential to cast a retrospective *light*
upon the unarticulated possibility of a mother–daughter lesbian desire. It
is the perpetuation of this stubbornly un-enlightened inarticulation that
surely gives meaning to the title of the novel. The lamp, as when Mrs
Ogden is making preparations for the annual Admiral's day, must remain
unlit:

But what a pity that it would be too light to light the lamp;
still, the shade certainly caught the eye, she was pleased that she
had taken the plunge and bought it at the sale. (Hall 1981, 32)

Newton discusses the question of mother–daughter eroticism in Hall's
work, and in lesbian sexuality more broadly. She cites this passage from
The Unlit Lamp:

The mother and daughter found very little to say to each other;
when they were together their endearments were strained like
those of people with a guilty secret . . . Joan knew that they
never found what they sought and never would find it now,
any more . . . She wanted to love Mrs. Ogden, she felt empty
and disconsolate without that love. She longed to feel the old
quick response when her mother bent towards her, the old

perpetual romance of her vicinity. She was like a drug-taker
from whom all stimulant has been suddenly removed; the
craving was unendurable, dangerous alike to body and mind.[13]

Newton comments thus:

> In this respect only, *The Lamp* is a "closet" novel. Hall, hiding
> in the old language, describes what is, I believe, a central
> component of lesbian sexuality – mother/daughter eroticism. I
> write "eroticism" because sexual desire is distinct from either
> "identification" or "bonding." A woman can be close to her
> mother ("bond," "identify") in many ways and yet eroticize
> only men. Conversely, one can hate one's mother and have
> little in common with her, as did Radclyffe Hall, and yet desire
> her fiercely in the image of other women. In my view, feminist
> psychology has not yet solved the riddle of sexual orientation.
> (Newton 1985, 21)

Neither, apparently, will Newton solve the riddle, since it is not clear
whether she uses the term "eroticism" to distinguish this mother–
daughter relation from identification or from desire. We are back, here, to
the never quite explicit connection that Adrienne Rich implies between
motherhood and lesbianism in "Compulsory Heterosexuality and Lesbian Existence." The problem, as I see it, is that the tendency in psychoanalytic thought and in a certain strand of lesbian-feminism has been to
understand lesbian eroticism as modeled upon the mother–daughter bond
read as imaginary and identificatory. What I feel Hall's work implies is
that lesbian desire has a particular relation to the disciplinarily suppressed
potential for the *symbolic* articulation of this bond. It is the undecidability
of this fraught imaginary–symbolic nexus that threatens Joan's relationship to her mother with an ever-imminent obscenity. The mother–
daughter bond is both sustained and threatened by the symbolic sanction
against lesbianism and incest. It is imaginarily sustained, but refused access
to the symbolic by the threat of stigmatization within the *voyure*. I think
it is also this ambivalence that saturates the almost apocalyptic (and perhaps desired) communicational impasses that confronts Joan when her
mother asks her directly to state her love for her:

> "Joan, do you love me, dearest?" It had come. This was the
> thing Joan had been dreading for weeks, perhaps it was all her
> life that she had been dreading it. She felt that time had ceased
> to exist, there were no clear demarcations; past, present and
> future were all one, welded together in the furnace of her

horrible doubt. Did she love her mother, did she – did she?
Her mother was waiting; she had always been waiting just like
this, and she would always wait, a little breathlessly, a little
afraid. She stared out desperately into the darkness – the
answer, it must be found quickly, but where – how? (Hall
1981, 66)

Mother and daughter are locked within the timelessness and cognitive
darkness of that tremulous waiting. The thetic break that would at least
articulate the "desire" (a not-yet desire, or a desire held under erasure)
between mother and daughter within the temporal dis-locations of the
differential pursuit of the lost object is seemingly impossible, for the
mother and the daughter are monstrously present to one another, locked
in their anticommunicational secrecy. The monstrosity of the impossible
avowal is matched by the equally impossible absoluteness of the unarticulated negation:

Deception; was it ever justifiable to deceive, was it justifiable
now? And yet, even if she were sure that she did not love her,
could she find the courage to push her away? To say: "I don't
love you, I don't want to touch you, I dislike the feel of you –
I dislike above all else the *feel* of you!" How terrible to say
such a thing to any loving creature, and how more terrible to
say it to her mother! The hydra had grown another head; what
would her mother do if she knew Joan loved her less? (Hall
1981, 67)

Finally, the bond to the mother is rendered compulsory not only by the
sense that it would *itself* be rendered obscene were it ever to dis-articulate
itself from imaginary fusionality but also by the threat that such a
dis-articulation would render other homosocial relations dangerously
articulate:

Why was she terrified? She was terrified because she feared that
she did not love her mother, and one night she knew that she was
terrified because, if she could not love her mother, she might
grow to love someone else instead – Elizabeth for instance. The
hydra grew another head that night. (Hall 1981, 68)

It is, I hope, quite clear that I do not share the pessimism of *The Unlit
Lamp*. I find it astonishingly and viscerally wrenching in its evocation of
the pathology of a female homosociality forever locked within the suffo-

cating spatio-temporal unicity of the imaginary, just as similar evocations of mother–daughter dystopia in psychoanalytic accounts are also unfathomably disturbing. But I do not believe that the disciplinary workings of a patriarchal symbolic that attempts to impoverish the social and symbolic mediation of relations between women – including desire – can ever succeed in creating such an unspaced space, a point to which I shall return.

The Incandescent Symptom

If the anticommunicational symptom of mother–daughter love remains stubbornly "unlit," however, there is another nexus of symptomaticity in the text that becomes flagrantly luminescent:

> Surely the last place in the world where anyone would have expected to meet a tragedy was in the High Street of Seabourne. There never was a street so genteel and so lacking in emotion; it was almost an indecency [!] to associate emotion with it, and yet it was in the High [S]treet that a thing happened which was to make a lasting impression on Joan. . . .
> . . . Then someone screamed, not once but many times. It was an ungainly sound, crude with terror. The screams appeared to be coming from Mrs. Jenkin's, the draper's shop, whither Elizabeth was bent; and then before any of them realized what was happening, a woman had rushed into the street covered in flames. The spectacle she made, horrible in itself, was still more horrible because this was the sort of thing that one heard of or read of but never expected to see. Through the fire which seemed to engulf her, her arms were waving and flapping in the air. Joan noticed that her hair, which had come down, streamed out in the wind, a mass of flame. The woman, still screaming, turned and ran towards them, and as she ran the wind fanned the flames. Then Elizabeth did a very brave thing. She tore off the long tweed coat she was wearing, and running forward managed somehow to wrap it round the terrified creature. It seemed to Joan as if she caught the woman and pressed her against herself, but it was all too sudden and too terrible for the girl to know with any certainty what happened; she was conscious only of an overwhelming fear for Elizabeth, and found herself tearing at her back, trying to pull her away; and then suddenly something, a mass of something, was lying on the pavement with Elizabeth bending over it. (Hall 1981, 95–6)

The painfulness of this description is surely only increased by the number of ambivalences that it conjures up. On the one hand, of course, we are entitled to read Elizabeth's act as one of female courage in rescuing the victim from consumption within the communitarian focal point of the High Street. On the other hand, the imagery of the novel that links this woman's incandescent spectacle to both female self-determination and lesbian eroticism makes the act of smothering and extinguishing her within an embrace resonate once again with the contagion of the female censorship of social and erotic visibility. The High Street spectacle metonymically links this woman's inflammatory passage to the ambulatory aristocratic feminism of Lady Loo, another fleeting character:

> For Lady Loo, once the best woman to hounds in a hard riding hunt, had begun to find life too restful at Moor Park. She had awakened one day filled with the consciousness of a kind of Indian summer [!] into which she had drifted. Some stray gleam of youth had shot through her, filling her with a spurious vitality that would not for the moment be denied. And since the old physical activity was no longer available, she turned in self-defence to mental interest, and took up the Feminist Movement with all the courage, vigour and disregard of consequences that had characterized her in the hunting-field. It was a nine-days' wonder to see Lady Loo pushing her bicycle through the High Street of Seabourne, clad in bloomers and a Norfolk jacket, a boat-shaped hat set jauntily on her grey head. (Hall 1981, 117)

The woman's fleeting incandescence also casts a light on the hunger – we must presume a hunger for her consumption as much as for the pure obscenity of the event – of the good High Street citizens:

> A few moments ago the street had been practically empty, but now quite a throng of people were pressing forward towards Elizabeth. Joan shouldered her way through them; half-unconsciously she noticed their eager eyes, and the tense, greedy look on their faces. There were faces that she had known nearly all her life, respectable middle-class faces, the faces of Seabourne tradespeople, but now somehow they looked different; it was as though a curtain had been drawn aside and something primitive and unfamiliar revealed. (Hall 1981, 96)[14]

As Joan and Elizabeth work to pare the woman away from the shroud – of what? of skin? of clothes? of femininity? feminism? burgerdom?

ignorance? of incandescence? – that has welded itself so tightly, so symptomatically, to her burnt body (precisely, of course, in order to re*dress* her), Joan investigates the ambivalent nature of their ministration: "The poor thing's suffering horribly, she's probably going to die before the doctor comes, and not one of us really knows how to help her; how humiliating." And in its turn, before the "greedy" expert interpretive gaze of the male doctor, the shared corporality of female humiliation is condensed upon Elizabeth as yet another surface of symptomatic spectacle:

> Elizabeth nodded, her mouth was drawn down at the corners
> and her arms hung limply at her sides. Something in her face
> attracted the doctor's attention and his glance fell to her hands.
> "Let me look at your hands," he said.
> "It's nothing," Elizabeth assured him, but her voice sounded
> far away.
> "I'm afraid I disagree with you; your hands are badly burnt,
> you must let me dress them." . . .
> "Anywhere else?" the doctor demanded.
> "Nowhere else," Elizabeth assured him. "I think my hands
> must have got burnt when I wrapped my coat around her."
> The doctor stared. "It's a mystery to me," he said, "how you
> managed to do all you did with a pair of hands like that." (Hall
> 1981, 98)

Given the importance of the trope of the lesbian's hands – specifically their pathological largeness and awkwardly obvious visibility and clumsiness – in Hall's work, the doctor's diagnosis here takes on a special significance in relation to female symptomaticity, female ignorance, feminine dexterity and nurturance, unsexing medical competence and lesbian manual *in*competence.[15] The ocular impression of this new symptom does, however, stoke the fire of Joan's erotic interest:

> She held out her hands obediently, and Joan noticed for the
> first time that they were injured. The realization that Elizabeth
> was hurt overwhelmed her; she forgot the woman on the bed,
> forgot everything but the burnt hands. With a great effort she
> pulled herself together, forcing herself to hold the dressings,
> watching with barely concealed apprehension lest the doctor
> should inflict pain. She had thought him so deft a few minutes
> ago, yet now he seemed indescribably clumsy. But if he did
> hurt it was not reflected on Elizabeth's face; her lips tightened a
> little, that was all. (Hall 1981, 98)

The trope of the eroticized wound and Joan's anxiety about (or for?) Elizabeth's pain and, surely, identification with the *doctor's* clumsy hands, brings us back to the sudden vacillation between nurturance and sadism that afflicts lesbianism when it is conceived theoretically as incapable of symbolic articulation: trapped in the violent proximity of the imaginary.[16] At first Joan reads the symptom as a sign of irreducible difference: "Joan felt lonely; something in what had happened seemed to have put Elizabeth very far away from her; perhaps it was because she could not share her pain." Finally, though, Joan with latch onto the possibilities of a sadistic and annihilating maternal nurturance: "Joan realized that whatever there was to do must be done by her; that Elizabeth the dominating, the practical, was now as helpless as a baby. The thought thrilled her" (Hall 1981, 99).

Yet the wounded hands also motivate Joan's interest in becoming a doctor – as her mother is uncannily quick to realize. Again they represent the imminent possibility of the emergence of a symbolic significance at the same time as the shame and jealousy that this provokes always immediately refigures that potential meaning within the possessive corporal rivalry of the female homosocial imaginary:

> "Is *that* where you've been all these hours? I see, you've been
> home with Elizabeth and never let me know!"
> "I couldn't, Mother, there was no one to send."
> "Then why didn't you come yourself? You must have
> known that I'd be crazy with anxiety!"
> Joan collapsed on a chair and dropped her head on her hand.
> She felt utterly incapable of continuing the quarrel, it seemed
> too futile and ridiculous. How could her mother have expected
> her to leave Elizabeth; she felt that she should not have come
> home even now, she should have stayed by her friend and
> refused to be driven away. She looked up and something in her
> tired young eyes smote her mother's heart; she knelt down
> beside her and folded her in her arms.
> "Oh my Joan, my darling", she whispered, pressing the girl's
> head down on her shoulder. "It's only because I was so
> anxious, my dearest – I love you too much, Joan."
> Joan submitted to the embrace quietly with her eyes closed;
> neither of them spoke for some minutes. Mrs. Ogden stretched
> out her hand and stroked the short, black hair with tremulous
> fingers. Her heart beat very fast, she could feel it in her throat.
> Joan stirred; the gripping arm was pressing her painfully.
> Mrs. Ogden controlled herself with an effort; there was so
> much that she felt she must say to Joan at that moment; the

words tingled through her, longing to become articulate. She
wanted to cry out like a primitive creature; to scream words of
entreaty, of reproach, of tenderness. She longed to humble
herself to this child, beseeching her to love her and her only,
and above all not to let Elizabeth come between them. But even
as the words formed themselves in her brain she crushed them
down, ashamed of her folly. (Hall 1981, 102).

My reading of *The Unlit Lamp* has detected an extremely negative
narrative, or antinarrative, of female proximity. If *The Well of Loneliness*
is, in some senses, the classic lesbian *Bildungsroman*, we might almost be
justified in describing the narrative of *The Unlit Lamp* as one of "anti-
Bildung." This confounds those readings which would find in it a positive
model of lesbianism as the site of the seamless suturing of the erotic,
emotional, and political solidarities of a congruent and coextensive
homosocial–homosexual continuum. I do not, however, wish to enact
the very tempting move of offering the other narrative, the *belated* one, as
the compensatory *telos* of Hall's writing and of lesbian and feminist
critical practices. For, as a narrative of *Bildung*, and more specifically as a
Künstlerroman, *The Well* stages and enacts its protagonist's insertion into
the symbolic and scopic economies of sociality on disturbingly conventional terms. Specifically, this insertion depends on the escape from what
is again conceived as the timeless proximity of mother–daughter bonding,
and this, it seems to me, is achieved at the traditional price of the mother's
narrative abjection. Stephen's escape into an alternative "bioeconomy"
within which, however outcast, she nonetheless *has* a canny symbolic
function (tending to others' injured bodies, not to say intervening in the
politics of the *national* body, intervening in the significatory regime of
symptomaticity), involves her departure from the terrain of maternity
("these Malvern Hills [which] in their beauty, and their swelling slopes
seemed to hold a new meaning. They were pregnant women, full-
bosomed, courageous, great green-girdled mothers of splendid sons,"
(Hall 1982, 8)) The strategy of turning to *The Well*, while I find it very
powerful, disturbs me also, although I do feel that in many ways it offers
a more positive rendition of lesbianism. *The Well* does after all refuse to
shun the lesbian symptom, reorienting it as a stigma towards a social
voyure into which it refuses, nonetheless, hygienically to dissolve itself.

Yet perhaps *The Unlit Lamp* is itself rather canny about the problems of
this redemptive vision. It is Richard – significantly, and perhaps, in Hall's
odd hierarchy of readerly competence inevitably, a male and inverted
spectator – who appears to detect the redemptive future signification in
the sheer symptomatic corporality of Joan's presence:

He found her adorable, with her black, cropped hair, her
beautiful mouth, and her queer, gruff voice. Her flanks were
lean and strong like a boy's; they suggested splendid, unfettered
movement. She looked all wrong in evening dress, almost
grotesque; but to Richard she appeared beautiful because
symbolic of some future state – a forerunner. As he looked at
her he seemed to see a vast army of women like herself, fine,
splendid and fiercely virginal; strong, too, capable of gripping
life and holding it against odds – the women of the future.
They fascinated him, these as yet unborn women, stimulating
his imagination, challenging his intellect, demanding of him an
explanation of themselves. (Hall 1981, 209)

Interesting that this demand for social signification addresses itself to the
male subject. Interesting too, surely, that Richard – the "unmanly man" –
is the place marker for my own invertedly male critical interpellation
within the cognitive economy of the text. But the problem of this future-
and symbolic-oriented reading offered by the male invert is also clear from
this passage. The vision of a new biopolitical order founded in the "fierce
virginity" of these immaculately *unborn* women suggests again that symbolic recuperation comes at the price of the abjection of maternity. This
abjection constitutes the disciplinary bind of *The Unlit Lamp*. In the
terms of the novel, in which symbolic distance between women is negated
as they are shown to be fused within a symbiosis of imaginary female
homosociality, symbolic distance must necessarily imply the ritual der-
eliction of the mother. Redemption *on these grounds* (and I shall assert
again that I do *not* mean to imply that the novel exhausts the limits of
female homosociality's discursive terrain) implies the abjection of what
has been theorized as the maternal-feminine.

In a timely and thought-provoking essay on recent developments
within queer theory which tend to sunder sexuality from gender in the
attempt to wield lesbian desire apotropaically against the depressing stereotype of female homosociality as dedifferentiated morass, Biddy Martin
has indicated the dangers of precisely such a move:

Given the culture in which we live, it is no surprise that queer
theorists, too, would repeat the age-old gesture of figuring
lesbian desire in phallic terms in order to distinguish it from
what then appears to be the fixed ground or maternal swamp of
woman-identification. But making "lesbian" signify desire and
difference between women too often leaves femininity's
traditional association with attachment, enmeshment, and home
intact, fails to reconceptualize homosocial relations among

women, and damages feminist and queer projects. (Martin 1994, 100–1)

The phallic critical wedge that would hew lesbianism from the imagined and imaginary formlessness of the female homosocial continuum threatens also to splinter the theoretical affiliations between feminism and queer sexuality in such a way that gender, and specifically gender as assumed to be cryptically embodied in and borne by the maternal-feminine, becomes something to be fled, left at home, repudiated within the privacy and specular privations of the domestic realm, abjected from the symbolic. How, then, might Hall teach us to begin to undo theoretically the temporal bind whereby the belated narrative emerges at the expense of what is ever more insistently "retro-jected" to the symbolically encrypted, atavistic prehistory of symptomatic fusionality? I *do* indeed want to suggest that we retain *"lesbian"* as *a* privileged signifier in the articulation of the symbolic possibilities of femininity. Obviously, I wish to do so, however, in a manner which *neither* conceives female homosexuality as the crushingly binding, "octupial," force of identity conceived as the primeval, unspaced ground of an unarticulated homogeneity *nor* deploys it as the propulsive movement of a disidentificatory symbolic trajectory. I want to propose that, against the visions of identification as fusionality and of desire as radical disjunction we might begin to read lesbianism as that which might, which *promises* to, fold and pleat the fabric of femininity in such a manner as to rescue it from the drastically impoverishing scopic economy of a patriarchal imaginary that insists on the maternal-feminine as the whole cloth from which Semblance will tear the *masculine* subject. In this articulation, lesbianism does not bind female identity within a monolithic phallomorphism of Semblance, but neither does it necessitate a revisioning, be it liberationist or pathologizing (or both!) of lesbianism as the phallic and sadistic cutting edge that severs the cord of maternal filiation in the name of a generative principle of extraordinary difference. If, in the terms of the title of this anthology, feminism is read as the generative ground of lesbian, bisexual, and gay critique, it is surely urgent that, *contra* Kristeva, we begin to imagine a relationship of filiation where the mother neither consumes her offspring nor is cannibalized by her young according to the demands of the psychoanalytic theory of perversion as alimentary-sadistic overidentification.

But what, then, of the intrication of lesbianism within a complex fleshly economy – a social-corporal economy – within which it figures as the freakish trauma of difference, as perversion and aberration? Newton beautifully portrays the conundrum within which the Law places the question of lesbian ontology. Considering the cost of Stephen Gordon's self-understanding as "flawed in the making," Newton concedes and rebuts:

A high price to pay for claiming a sexual identity, yes. But of those who condemn Hall for assuming the sexologists' model of lesbianism I ask, Just how was Hall to make the woman-loving New Woman a sexual being? For example, despite Hall's use of words like "lover" and "passion" and her references to "inversion," her lawyer actually defended *The Well* against state censorship by trying to convince the court that "the relations between women described in the book represented a normal friendship." Hall "attacked him furiously for taking this line, which appeared to her to undermine the strength of the convictions with which she had defended the case. His plea seemed to her, as her solicitor commented later, 'the unkindest cut of all' and at their luncheon together she was unable to restrain 'tears of heartbroken anguish.'" (Newton 1985, 22–3)

Both *The Well* and *The Lamp* remain – perhaps necessarily and productively – caught within the logic of symptomaticity and corporality in the biopolitical regime of modernity. To conceive of lesbianism's oppositional potential as residing *either* within the principle of female homosocial continuity *or* in a queerly antinormative vanguardism is perhaps to fall for the ruse of symptomaticity: to fail to acknowledge the extent to which the homosexual becomes the fraught nexus of temporal condensation upon which is wrought the paradox of modernity's perverse filiations. Perversion read as symptomaticity *is* the explosive articulation of an archiessential corporality and degenerate aberration within the melancholic temporality of the modern social body, and Hall's corporal response to her lawyer's attempt to disarticulate lesbianism's traumatic symptomaticity within the acceptable terms of the Law seems to represent the refusal of that "unkindest cut" that would sunder her from the body even as it would disciplinarily bind her within the suffocating proximity of a hygienically censored rendition of homosociality.

If one can identify with Radclyffe Hall's tears of frustration at the attempt to confine lesbianism to the unlit recesses of a conventionally conceived femininity, however, one can simultaneously appreciate the ambivalent responses of lesbians to the manner in which the stigmata of lesbianism are so prominently incorporated into the visual economy of *The Well*. At the same time as noting that "[t]here was probably no lesbian in the four decades between 1928 and the late 1960s capable of reading English or any of the eleven languages into which the book was translated who was unfamiliar with *The Well of Loneliness*," Lillian Faderman reveals that "[a]n American sociological study of lesbians in the 1920s and 1930s indicated that 'almost to a woman, they decried its publication,'" and "[t]hey believed that if the novel did not actually do harm to their cause, at the very least it 'put homosexuality in the wrong light'" (Faderman 1981, 322). Of course, a problem arises from the fact that sociological studies, relying as they traditionally have upon an extremely uninflected notion of identity, have been notoriously unable to grasp the complexities of the relationship between homosexuality's stigmatized difference and the articulation of identity. If, in the vacillations between body and society, cognitive resistance and epistemological luminescence, *Lamp* and *Well*, we might discover the potential for a resistance to and rearticulation of the workings of the patriarchal symbolic and scopic economy, the cognitive matrix of homosexual/homophobic knowledge nonetheless renders problematic the notion that any gaze cast upon lesbianism might fully resist the taint of the "wrong light." Hall's work does not finally, it should be clear, offer a utopian vision, and perhaps it is precisely in the space that separates these two novels that Hall demonstrates the impossibility of a simple and static reconciliation of feminism, lesbianism, and the liberal democratic scopic regime of melancholic "enlightenment" that would determine a singular focus of political vision. Perhaps, once again, however, it is the essence and virtue of the symptom to promise a futurity not already coopted by the disciplinary hygienics of the social gaze, to suggest an anticommunicative ethics that outstrips the limited possibilities conceivable within the graphic economy of the existing symbolic. An ethics of symptomaticity would perhaps rather agitate the specularized surfaces of the hegemonic bioeconomy of social corporality, inflaming its essential opacities as a reminder – a corrective vision – of its self-limiting scope.

Notes

1   The question of ontology – of the essential "nature" of sexual orientation – as it relates to a range of sociomedical terms such as "aberration," "condition," "freakishness," "trauma," and their relationship to convention and/or congenitality feeds into a much greater philosophical consideration of the de-ontological nature of the citizen-subject within the Kantian imperatives of liberal-democratic sociality and the relationship between rights and the anchoring of individual bodies within a broader economy of social corporality. I believe a more sustained reading of Hall's work along these lines would have much to contribute to contemporary debates in liberal, communitarian, and poststructuralist political theory around questions of rights and sociality. As can be seen from the debate between Newton and Faderman, the ambivalences (already to be found in Hall's work)

around biological innateness, environmental influence, and political choice (ambivalences often reductively couched as the dichotomy of essentialism versus social constructionism) are very much contemporary ones. Whilst the argument for a biological element in the etiology of a person's sexual identity in unlikely, in current debates, to depend so wholeheartedly on a notion of gender inversion, many argue that sexuality must be conceived in these terms if lesbians, bisexuals, and gay men are to make a successful argument for incorporation within a liberal matrix of rights and justice, and, indeed, many conservatives accordingly argue that, since sexuality is a matter of choice, it can not serve as the basis for legal "protection." The questions of lesbian ontology and the lesbian "symptoms" that I shall be raising her are overdetermined by the paradoxes of liberal democratic citizenship as it relates to dualities of body and mind, voluntarism and determination, the private and the public, and as it purportedly insists upon a Kantian de-ontological subjecthood transparently present to itself (according to a logic, perhaps, of "zero degree deviancy," to borrow a term from Catharine Stimpson) and to others as the precondition of entry into the *ratio* of public discourse. The historical genealogy of the concept of congenital inversion also more specifically links it to turn-of-the-century discourses of biological race, the class politics of degeneration and the articulation of a program of social hygiene that haunts the historical rearticulation of nationhood and the social body within the modern bureaucratic and bio-economic formation of the welfare state.

2   For my models of the operations of sexual difference (or its occlusion) within modernity I draw heavily on the works of Luce Irigaray, Juliet Flower MacCannell, and Rosi Braidotti. I shall use the Lacanian formulation of the *voyure* to refer to an impersonal social gaze that "pins" and "anchors" modern democratic sociality within its disciplinary hold. This is neither Rousseau's hygienic regime of scopic sovereignty, nor the antisymptomatic immediacy of the gaze in Foucauldian panopticism, although it bears an important relation to both. I use the notion of an impersonal *voyure* to foreground the *absent* seat of power in modernity within which an already anachronistic paternal figure remains effectively, yet phantasmatically, installed. It is the eclipse of this originary nexus of power that drives the proliferation of the disciplinary and discriminatory effects of a "reciprocity" which must itself be recognized as insidiously caught within a political regime of Semblance. The "legitimacy" of the exchange of policial stares between fraternal citizen-subjects depends upon a melancholic reference back to the empty throne of sovereignty that is the Lacanian Other.

3   The notion of the "kinship claims of the female world" strains in
    fascinating ways, of course, against the notion of securely legitimated
    patriarchal social Symbolic in which all power or authority stems
    immediately from the Law of the father, and there is a rich strand in
    Hall's work that maps more matriarchal operations of power onto
    a female sociality tuned to the classed communitarian note of
    "County": a power encoded in the feminine and yet still melan-
    cholically enthralled by the spectre of the dead or dying fathers in
    which her work abounds.

4   An urgent qualification here: my own rhetoric is tending dangerously
    to imply that we can simply accept motherhood as exemplary of the
    dedifferentiated ground of female sociality *against* which all desire
    between women would then articulate itself. In fact, while it is neces-
    sary to take the dangers of repeating a very real abjection of maternity
    seriously, I propose that we should simultaneously insist on reading
    maternity itself as pregnant with desire and conflict problematizing
    the notion of any primary identification not already traversed by the
    dialectics of desire (a proposal at odds with much psychoanalytic
    thought on desire and identification but also with the concept of
    primary woman-identification in lesbian-feminist thought). For a
    painful rendition of the difficulty of negotiating symbolic space be-
    tween women, see such Irigarayan essays as "Corps-à-corps avec la
    mère" and "Et l'une ne bouge pas sans l'autre." For a critique simul-
    taneously directed against Freud, Lacan, and Derrida of the exploita-
    tion of the feminine as the material "support" of the symbolic (a
    support, moreover, that is the object of a sacrifice which, while rou-
    tine, is so determinedly effaced that it is not, unlike the paternal
    sacrifice of *Totem and Taboo*, religiously memorialized); see "La
    croyance même" and "Le v(i)ol de la lettre." I am attempting to
    suggest the difficulties that arise when these critiques are brought into
    closer proximity: how do we acknowledge the impoverishment of the
    "entre-femmes" within the male imaginary without enacting a narra-
    tive of rescue/escape that perpetuates the dereliction of the mother?
    How do we account for and work to overcome the disciplinary
    "hold" of a Mrs Ogden in the name of a desire which is rightfully a
    property of maternity and yet which may also be disavowed in the
    service of the patriarchal imaginary *and* in the reclamation of the
    compensatory pleasures of a sadistic grip on the daughter? It might
    also be useful, at this point, to foreground the problematic nature of
    that "we" in whose names(s) this narrative is to be authored and the
    relationship of that narrative to my own critical voice!

5   The *locus classicus* of the concept of the "lesbian continuum" is, of
    course, Adrienne Rich's extremely important essay on "Compulsory

Heterosexuality and Lesbian Existence." I have argued elsewhere, however, that while this essay can be read as reaffirming the lyrical unicity of a female imaginary within which (woman-)identification subordinates questions of desire and difference, Rich's rhetoric does, nonetheless, entertain a significant undercurrent in which questions of disarticulation and violence coincide with the explicit rendition of lesbian desire. The paradoxical concept of homosocial desire evoked here is taken from Eve Sedgwick's theorization of a troubled nexus of *male* homosociality and -sexuality. Whilst it will be crucial to my argument here that there is *no* symmetry around the axis of sexual difference, I do follow critics, such as Terry Castle and Blakey Vermeule, who have argued that the strict contrast that Sedgwick draws between a coherent lesbian/female continuum and the complexities of simultaneous continuity and radical discontinuity that ensnare (or is it "drive"?) male homosociality, within the volatile – indeed highly combustible and even explosive – economy of male homosocial desire tends to de-eroticize and potentially scotomize lesbian specificity and lesbian desire.

6 Mikkel Borch-Jacobsen has conveyed the temporal logic of the symptom with great succinctness. "Like Freud," he writes, "Le Bon uses 'pathological' states as the key to decoding 'normalcy.' The two share a common conviction (along with the vast majority of late-nineteenth-century psychologists) that the pathological return to a previous state bears witness to the existence of a state of ontogenetic and phylogenetic development that has been surpassed (that is, integrated and by the same token recovered). 'Pathological,' in this sense, does not mean abnormal; on the contrary, it is archinormality itself, primary normality. And the origin (the essence) can thus be read in the symptom" (Borch-Jacobsen 1988, 135)

7 I feel compelled here to evoke the refreshing frustration expressed by Eve Sedgwick in her powerful essay "Tales of the Avunculate: Queer Tutelage in *The Importance of Being Earnest.*" Identifying the almost compulsory explanatory recourse to the "Name of the Father" in contemporary theory (including, notably, the work of Jonathan Dollimore and Kaja Silverman), she urges:

> You will have noted a certain impatience, in this reading of
> *Earnest*, with the concept of the Name of the Father as
> having been substantially superseded, in a process
> accelerating over the last century and a half, very
> specifically by what might be termed the Name of the
> Family – that is, the name Family. (Within this family, the

position of any father is by no means a given; there are
important purposes, including feminist ones, for which the
term "familialism" may now be substituted for
"patriarchy.") Now, the potency of any signifier is proven
and increased, over and over, by how visibly and
spectacularly it *fails* to be adequated by the various
signifieds over which it is nonetheless seen to hold sway.
So the gaping fit between on the one hand the Name of the
Family, and on the other the quite varied groupings
gathered *in* that name, can only add to the numinous
prestige of a term whose origins, histories, and uses may
have little in common with our own recognizable needs.
Redeeming the family isn't, finally, an option but a
compulsion; the question would be how to *stop* redeeming
the family. How, as well, to stop being complicit in
the process by which the name Family occludes the actual
extant relations – for many people, horrifyingly
impoverished ones; for everyone, radically changed and
unaccounted-for, indeed highly phantasmatic ones – that
mediate exchanges between the order of the individual and
the order of capital, "information," and the state.
(Sedgwick 1993, 72)

Sedgwick's historically justified negation ("Forget the Name of the
Father. Forget the Name of the Father!") is actually quite productive
in the context of this essay. Without dismissing Sedgwick's frustration and the productive theoretical and political move that it initiates,
I remain stubborn in my attention to that power that accrues to
the Name of the Father in its insistent anachronism. *Totem and
Taboo* surely suggests that even the mythic Ur-father is a strangely
"undead" character who lives on in his melancholic incorporation by
the fraternal horde: his ritual consumption at the totemic feast. I am
suggesting that patriarchy compels its subjects through precisely such
a melancholic fixation, implying, as Rosi Braidotti, for example,
has insisted, that death clings to the (post-)patriarchal symbolic.
For an attempt at a more detailed exposition of the compulsory
initiatory melancholics of the totemic feast and its relationship to a
social/sexual contract that is "necrographically" inscribed, see my
"Melancholic Modernity: the Hom(m)osexual Symptom and the
Homosocial Corpse."

8 This is another continuity that confounds that attempt to
dichotomize the political force of *The Unlit Lamp* and *The Well of*

Loneliness. Whilst the latter is more infamously evocative of the work of Havelock Ellis on the question of sexuality, both novels conduct a dangerous trade in a discourse of population and an economics of vitality that suggests an ideological proximity to the concerns of the movement for social "hygiene" in which Ellis (author of *The Problem of Race Regeneration*) played a crucial role. That movement depends upon paradoxical narratives evoking the pathos of the fragile superiority and decadent eclipse of a nationalized, classed, and raced British social body. In Volume 1 of *The History of Sexuality*, Foucault argues that the organization of race around the notion of "sanguinity" is, in fact, a remnant of an earlier aristocratic racial discourse that is to some extent superseded but also redeployed within that "racism in its modern, 'biologizing,' statist form" that he identifies from the second half of the nineteenth century, culminating in Nazi eugenics (Foucault 1981, 149).

9 The father's study also figures prominently in *The Well of Loneliness* and *A Saturday Life*, another Hall novel dealing with lesbianism in which, however, the father is already dead at the opening of the narrative.

10 The portrayal of this relative comes disturbingly close to an overt argument for eugenics, again making clear the novel's extremely ambivalent relationship to a discourse of social hygiene, that hygienic operation of the *voyure* against which the symptom stands as a moment of resistance.

11 The fact that vampires in decadent literature are a figure of "queerness" has been critically acknowledged. It strikes me that what is most powerful about this figure is the way in which it operates as an overdetermined site associating queerness with an abjected view of the symbiosis of mother and embryo in pregnancy. For a particularly dense overdetermination of vampirism of this kind, see, for example, André Gide's *L'Immoraliste*, a colonial narrative, furthermore, that links anemia, as a "pathos of sanguinity" (like the bleaching of Colonel Ogden's desk) to the melancholics of Empire and the eroticization of the stereotype of the brown-skinned "noble savage."

12 Stephen Gordon in *The Well*, we should note, receives momentary public and national recognition for her work in an ambulance team during World War I, along with the rest of the "battalion" of inverts permitted to "come out into the daylight" in order to staunch the outpouring of the national lifeblood. It is surely no surprise that this telos of a medical cognitive mastery is mapped onto the narrative telos of the *Künstlerroman*.

13 The passage appears in Hall 1981, 75.

14 This passage is also wonderfully suggestive not only in its pursuit of the symbolism of luminescence in its final image, but also in the stunning transformation whereby those who are at one moment the spectators and informed "readers" of the pyrotechnics of symptomaticity suddenly find themselves obscenely embodied as the bearers of a "primitive" symptomaticity. The appalling hunger of communitarian publicity itself becomes condensed into a repugnant somatization of social corporality. It is for its relative inability to tolerate such a radical undecidability in the relationship between the eye and the gaze, symptom and *voyure*, that I feel that we need to go beyond the Foucauldian theory of panopticism as a theory of the optic regime of modernity. For all its insistence upon reciprocity, the notion of panopticism seems to evade the question of the eye's own "embodiment." For a stunning account of the manner in which the eye itself resides within a corporality and sanguinity that sustains it – the fact, one might say, that any dialectics of vision is bloodshot – see the essays "*Kore*: Young Virgin, Pupil of the Eye" and "The Eternal Irony of the Community", both in *Speculum of the Other Woman* by Luce Irigaray, pp. 147–51 and 214–26, respectively. Suffice it here to say that where the generativity of a political regime of specularity is necessarily tied, in modernity, to an economics of fleshly reproduction within which distinctions of gender and sexuality wreak structural and profoundly asymmetrical effects, this weakness of the Foucauldian paradigm surely presents problems from the perspectives of feminist and queer inquiry.

15 A similarly fraught accretion of significance is condensed upon Stephen Gordon's hands in *The Well* when she initially contemplates her role in the national-corporal trauma of war: "She stared at her bony masculine hands, they had never been skilful when it came to illness; strong they might be, but rather inept; not hands wherewith to succour the wounded. No, assuredly her job, if job she could find, would not lie at the bedsides of the wounded. And yet, good God, one must do something!" (Hall 1982, 271). Stephen does of course staunch her country's outpouring of blood as does the eponymous heroine of Hall's short story "Miss Ogilvy Finds Herself," another saga of the "primitivist" discovery of the lesbian symptom through the unraveling of the melancholics of nation in time of war.

16 I am thinking here of the surely homophobic descriptions of lesbianism in the work of Julia Kristeva. Accounts of lesbianism as amorphous and lyrical to the point of fatality are closely juxtaposed with phantasies of a sadistic revenge wrought by lesbianism upon the site of a maternally inflected nurturant homosociality. On the one hand lesbianism in *Tales of Love* is pleasingly soft- (if not entirely *un*-!)lit:

"[A]ndrogynous paradise and, in another way, lesbian loves comprise the delightful arena of a neutralized, filtered libido, devoid of the erotic cutting edge of masculinity. Light touches, caresses, barely distinct images fading one into the other, growing dim or veiled without bright flashes into the mellowness of a dissolution, a liquefaction, a merger . . . Relaxation of consciousness, daydream, language that is neither dialectical nor rhetorical, but peace or eclipse: nirvana, intoxication, and silence" (Kristeva 1987, 81). Yet moments later this very proximics suggests a violent explosion into the scopic regime and the fatality (perhaps already suggested within the orientalizing legacy of "nirvana") of fusionality: "When such a paradise is not a sidelight of phallic eroticism, its parenthesis and its rest, when it aspires to set itself up as the absolute of a mutual relationship, the non-relationship that it is bursts into view. Two paths are then open. Either they take up again, yet more fiercely, the erotic mania along with the havoc of the "master-slave" game. Or else, and often as a consequence, death breaks into the peace one thought one had taken in. A grinding death in that belly that had previously been so protective, coaxing and neutralizing . . . lethal dissolution of psychosis, anguish on account of lost boundaries, suicidal call of the deep" (Kristeva 1987, 81). There is surely much more to be said than I can outline here about this cannibalistic inversion of motherhood in an abjected version of lesbianism in relation to the "primitivism" of psychoanalytic views of perversion and oral-anal or alimentary identification.

References

Borch-Jacobsen, Mikkel. *The Freudian Subject.* Trans. Catherine Porter. Stanford: Stanford University Press, 1988.

Braidotti, Rosi. *Patterns of Dissonance.* Cambridge: Polity, 1991.

Castle, Terry. *The Apparitional Lesbian: Female Homosexuality and Modern Culture.* New York: Columbia University Press, 1993.

Ellis, Havelock. *The Problem of Race-Regeneration.* New York: Moffat, Yard & Co., 1911.

Faderman, Lillian. *Surpassing the Love of Men: Romantic Friendship and Love Between Women from the Renaissance to the Present.* New York: William and Morrow, 1981.

Foucault, Michel. *The History of Sexuality: An Introduction.* Trans. Robert Hurley. Harmondsworth: Penguin, 1981. Vol. 1 of *The History of Sexuality.* 3 vols. 1978–86.

Gide, André. *L'Immoraliste*. Paris: Gallimard, 1972.

Hall, Radclyffe. "Miss Ogilvy Finds Herself." *Miss Ogilvy Finds Herself.* New York: Harcourt, Brace, c.1934. 2–35.

———. *A Saturday Life*. London: Virago, 1987.

———. *The Unlit Lamp*. London: Virago, 1981.

———. *The Well of Loneliness*. London: Virago, 1982.

Hope, Trevor. "Melancholic Modernity: The Hom(m)osexual Symptom and the Homosocial Corpse." *differences* 6, 2–3 (Summer–Fall 1994), 174–98.

Irigaray, Luce. *Et l'une ne bouge pas sans l'autre*. Paris: Minuit, 1979.

———. "Le corps-à-corps avec la mère," *Sexes et Parentés*. Paris: Minuit, 1987. 19–33.

———. *Speculum of the Other Woman*. Trans. Gillian C. Gill. Ithaca: Cornell University Press.

Kristeva, Julia. *Tales of Love*. Trans. Leon S. Roudiez. New York: Columbia University Press, 1987.

MacCannell, Juliet Flower. *The Regime of the Brother: After the Patriarchy*. London: Routledge, 1991.

Martin, Biddy. "Extraordinary Homosexuals and the Fear of Being Ordinary," *differences* 6, 2–3 (Summer–Fall 1994), 100–25.

Newton, Esther. "The Mythic Mannish Lesbian: Radclyffe Hall and the New Woman," in Estelle B. Freedman, Barbara C. Gelphi, Susan L. Johnson, and Kathleen M. Weston, eds. *The Lesbian Issue: Essays From Signs*. Chicago: University of Chicago Press, 1985. 7–25.

Rich, Adrienne. "Compulsory Heterosexuality and Lesbian Existence," in Ann Snitow, Christine Stansell and Sharon Thompson, eds. *Powers of Desire: The Politics of Sexuality*. New York: Monthly Review, 1983. 177–205.

Sedgwick, Eve Kosofsky. *Between Men: English Literature and Male Homosocial Desire*. New York: Columbia University Press, 1985.

———. "Tales of the Avunculate: Queer Tutelage in *The Importance of Being Earnest*," in *Tendencies*. Durham: Duke University Press, 1993. 52–72.

Stimpson, Catharine R. "Zero Degree Deviancy: The Lesbian Novel In English," in Elizabeth Abel, ed. *Writing and Sexual Difference*. Brighton: Harvester, 1982. 243–59.

Vermeule, Blakey. "Is There a Sedgwick School for Girls?" *Qui Parle?* 5, 1 (Fall–Winter 1991), 53–72.

Chapter 6

Desiring Machines: Queer Re-visions of Feminist Film Theory

Carol-Anne Tyler

It is by now a critical commonplace to write of a crisis in the theorization of spectatorship, which according to any number of film and television scholars has resulted in a certain myopia, an inability to make out the differences in or heterogeneity of responses to mass culture. The crisis is an effect of a demand for a historicized understanding of reception and representation and has come into focus as those working on lesbian and gay sexualities, race and ethnicity, and postcoloniality have turned a critical eye on the dominant feminist paradigm for the analysis of visual culture. They have raised serious questions about the value of the psychoanalytically based "apparatus theory" feminist film scholars critically adapted, which they argue reproduces the ahistoricism and universalism of psychoanalysis. Reconceiving "the subject" as "multiple, rather than divided," in Teresa de Lauretis's words (de Lauretis 1987b, x), they have articulated a re-vision of spectatorship through the lenses of new approaches, often Foucauldian or Deleuzian rather than Lacanian, which would correct for psychoanalytic feminism's oversights.

This task is assigned to "queer theory" in particular when the latter is understood as an attention to the intersection of a range of differences that cannot be disarticulated from sexuality and which may function as resistance to normalization through modern "discipline" as Foucault has theorized it. "[Q]ueer gets a critical edge by defining itself against the normal rather than the heterosexual," Michael Warner writes in the introduction to a recent collection of essays about queer politics (Warner 1993, xxvi). Although he believes it enables "a more thorough resistance" as it deconstructs identities and the norms presumed to found them and identity-based homogeneous communities, Warner argues that "queer politics has not replaced older modes of lesbian and gay identity" (Warner 1993, xxviii), by which he means "minority-based" activisms grounded in the very conceptions queer theory would call into question. While he does not justify this claim by directly referring to Gayatri Spivak's notion of "strategic essentialism," often cited at this juncture in other critiques of deconstructive approaches to subjectivity, he recognizes the importance of making demands in the name of subjects who have been defined and specified (and therefore limited and "normed") in certain ways. However, Warner knows that strategic essentialism is necessarily complicit with the sorts of social science administrative knowledges which must serve both the state and those who would critique it on behalf of minority interests and political programs. He therefore emphasizes the importance of a queer protest against "the *idea* of normal behavior" (Warner 1993, xxvii) and the methodologies it founds. Ultimately, queers must question any identity, even a queer identity, since the very fact that it is fixed enough to be recognizable implies an idealized norm and an imperative to identify with it.

For Warner, as for Spivak, the ethical force of deconstructive theory is just this interrogation of norms and proper names, which results in bringing to crisis the practices they ground, since, as Spivak reminds us, "people are different from the object of emancipatory benevolence" (Spivak 1990, 136). Judith Butler makes a similar point when she urges us to be "critically queer":

> And if identity is a necessary error, then the assertion of
> "queer" will be necessary as a term of affiliation, but it will not
> fully describe those it purports to represent. As a result, it will
> be necessary to affirm the contingency of the term: to let it be
> vanquished by those who are excluded by the term but who
> justifiably expect representation by it, to let it take on meanings
> that cannot now be anticipated . . . (Butler 1993, 230).

The danger is that queer theory will supplant what it should only deconstructively supplement, as Warner suggests when he expresses some reservations about it by describing it as a "universalizing utopianism" with "an aggressive impulse of generalization" (Warner 1993, xxvi). Determined to do justice to differences, queer theory seems to sublate them into a higher non-identity, in which each particular difference is negated in turn as a small part of an implied whole bigger than all of them. When the queer becomes a new, more inclusive identity, rather than what queers any identity, its negativity is recuperated for a Hegelian project of the recovery of totality, and it reproduces the very identity politics it set out to counter. Paradoxically, queer theory queers itself as it articulates itself and a queer subject. What is queer about identity and theory disappears into queer identity and theory, whose idealized qualities suggest the phallus and its imaginary function of sustaining the dream of wholeness – even if as a wholly anti-phallic self or theory.

For these reasons, queer theory (and identity) has already come under fire in the academy for failing to live up to its promises. To date, the critiques have largely come from those in feminist, lesbian, and gay studies, the primary fields queer studies would seem to correct, and they echo Warner's own doubts about it. Like Warner, Stephen Seidman argues that queer theory over-generalizes, promoting "an undifferentiated oppositional mass" (Seidman 1993, 133), while Biddy Martin accuses it of being fascinated by a fluidity which is finally deadly in its desire to escape the limitations life imposes as "identity" (Martin 1994). De Lauretis, who according to Robin Wiegman actually coined the phrase "queer-theory" in 1990 (Wiegman 1994 17, n. 1), already repudiated "queer theory" only four years later as "a vacuous creature of the publishing industry" (Habit 297) because it is empty of any specificity. Are queer theorists so very vacuous? Does queer theory screen us from differences, or can it be a prescription for a far-sighted theory of differences on the screen or in the other arts and fields in which difference persists as a problem? Has it worked through the problems of feminism and other minority-based studies, or does it repeat them, even if in a disguised or displaced form? Should we develop a theory of the queer spectator and an apparatus for producing that subject, or should we queer any theory of the spectator and the apparatus, including identity itself as an apparatus? As I hope to demonstrate, the resistance to queer theory – including queer theory's resistance to "itself" as whatever it is in the process of becoming – is a symptom, rather than a cure, of the problem of difference and marks the latter's difficulty for all theoretical discourses, including film studies, in which difference is a repeating and structuring theme. It seems we are always on the point of a metaphysical gesture of *aletheia*, which (un)veils our differences in what proves to be a cover-up. We are never satisfied, no matter what is on screen or in screen theory (or feminist theory, lesbian and gay theory, or queer theory). We never see ourselves there in all the details of our specificity. The trouble with any theory is that it is never quite queer enough; it inevitably leaves something out, unspecified, which is evidently too queer for it.

Why does difference queer theory, even a queer theory which would reflect it in its totality? I would suggest it is because difference is first and foremost a matter of self-difference, rather than totality, which inevitably queers how we see and say things. This is something psychoanalysis and deconstruction in particular have emphasized, but it is also a central insight of other fields, each in its own way: feminism, lesbian and gay studies, Marxism, postcolonial studies, African-American studies, and other "minority based" discourse or culture studies (the list is potentially endless). Queer theory does not transcend these as the completion of more limited undertakings, nor do these approaches address the multiple parts of a larger whole or queer identity. The modern project of Enlightenment does not achieve closure in queer theory or queer identity because closure is impossible. The field of identity (and the language about it) is non-totalizable, not only because we will continue to discover some new difference yet to be named which must be taken into account, as recent transgender and intersexual activisms remind us (we might term this the difficulty of empiricism), but also because what has been left out enables the field to exist as such (which is the difficulty of language or naming itself, through which identities are constructed).

Difference, as a constitutive subtraction or lack, can never finally be disclosed. Any name, as a signifier, must function as an inadequate supplement for the reality it "ghosts," a "presence" which we experience as a revenant whose life is in the uncanny effects of representation that we cannot escape. Language does not re-present what is already present before it, which we could intuit without it. There is neither queer theory nor queer identity in "the real," as harmonious wholes lacking nothing which we must strive to approximate by dialectically sublating each theory or identity which precedes it. Nor is there "the woman" or "the lesbian" as identities more "specific" than the vaguely queer as the transcendental Absolute or "Spirit of Difference" itself. "The apparitional lesbian" Terry Castle has discussed is not simply a murder victim, done in by "people [who] can't see what's right in front of them," who consign her to "the world of vapors" (Castle 1993, 2, 19), which for Castle seems to be a Platonic realm of shades and shadows. "The lesbian," like any other identity, is an effect of representation, a negotiation between language users who (re)create themselves through their linguistic performances, their encoding and decoding or writing and reading of signs. And no matter what we bring to those negotiations, something will always be missing which is finally more ourselves than everything else we are: what we had to negate to represent a self in the first place.

Lacan terms this mysterious absence which founds our desire the *objet a*. The particular objects we use to represent it and supplement the lack at the center of our subjectivity impede the self-realization they also figure as a possibility. This lack is what is queer about theory and other subject-object relations, jamming the machinery of any self-regulating apparatus, whether bourgeois, male, or heterosexual, as successive theories of the cinema apparatus and its subject would have it. Difference is not in the good or bad object but in the dialectical relation between subjects. They impact retroactively on each other in an object relation structured as the superimposition of two lacks which cannot be harmonized, making for a radical non-reciprocity which "queers" things for the subjects involved and ensures their lack of satisfaction with each other. No one has what the other wants – not even queers or their theories. Queer theory?! The phrase is at once a question, a curse, and a mandate, naming a process which is weird, impossible, and an ethical necessity, dangerous in its overweening ambition and disturbingly fascinating as it brings to crisis identities, institutions, and practices along with the theories which are in a dialectical relation with them, each (re)creating the other(s).

Double Vision: The Cinema "Apparatus" and Feminist Theory

Film studies owes much to Althusser in its conceptualization of cinema as an ideological apparatus geared to the mass production of the subjects necessary to the reproduction of our social formation. For Christian Metz, Jean-Louis Baudry, Jean-Louis Comolli, and other "apparatus theorists," domination is immanent in the popular realist film text projected in typical "institutional" conditions (a darkened theater with a large screen and silent, immobile viewer). According to them, Hollywood cinema helps to reproduce capitalism through the constitution of a bourgeois subject, a spectator who is sutured into a position of imaginary coherence and power as an omniscient and omnipotent eye, which structures an "I" with an illusory autonomy, self-mastery, and freedom. They argue that cinema centers the subject as "the gaze," an imaginary point outside the frame and picture which is an analogue for the internal vanishing point of the haptic space the camera constructs. The subject mistakes himself for the source of the image, instead of its effect, and misrecognizes the other's "fantasy" as his own because the labor of its production is hidden. The lack of a complete visual mastery of space is concealed through realist montage, in which the subject sutures two frames or shots with absent fields and times: the space of the apparatus which guides the subject's "free" gaze, and the duration between the frames of a shot and the shots of a sequence. Profoundly confusing self and other through the agency of the film fantasy implanted in him, the spectator seems to see himself seeing himself, and he likes what he sees. There is nothing lacking in the picture, and no lack of satisfaction at the pictures. According to apparatus theory, cinema is the quintessential "good object," with which the subject necessarily has good relations not despite his narcissism, but because of it. Sociality *is* narcissism when desire is reduced to a need – albeit a manufactured one, with a commodity object to assuage it.

In this realm of the ideological genesis of needs, our needs are needed. There is nothing beyond the pleasure and reality principles as a homeostatic regulation of the narcissistic system, which endlessly reproduces the needs it needs and the subjects who are their bearers. Apparatus theory sacrifices the enigma of desire, which for Lacan is in excess of any need and beyond both pleasure and social "reality" as what holds the former in check for a while. Desire interrupts the functioning of the apparatus – of both the psyche and of cinema/culture. The subject of apparatus theory is a robot in the service of consumption, rather than production, as the alienated workers of *Modern Times* or *Metropolis* were. If sexuality threatens the cyborg future envisioned by Ford, Taylor, and others who wished to "modernize" labor to make it more efficient and less "entropic" or wasteful of energy, as Peter Wollen argues, sexuality becomes the very means of modernizing consumption, according to apparatus theorists. Jacking off and in to commodity culture, modern man has ceased to be "meat"; he is a virtual object, a synthetic composed of the commodity-prostheses which "supplement" his body image and the world about him, adding to and substituting for them.[1] Like androids from Pinocchio to Data of *Star Trek: The Next Generation*, the cyborg consumer merely resembles the human, which he mimics.

The initial feminist critique delimited these apparently monolithic effects of the cinema apparatus by revealing it to be what Constance Penley subsequently termed a "bachelor machine." As Laura Mulvey argued in her landmark essay on visual pleasure, the subject of the cinematic gaze was specifically masculine, rather than universal. Film was about the fear of castration or "lack", the sacrifices necessitated by subjection to the Symbolic against which man defends himself through his representations of gender difference. Mulvey emphasized that "primary identification" with the camera was bound up with a secondary (and symbolic) identification with characters as narcissistic ego-ideals. Hollywood film reproduced patriarchy by interpellating men as subjects and women as objects of the gaze, offering voyeuristic , sadistic, and fetishistic pleasures to its male heroes and spectators, and passive, exhibitionistic identities to women. In a follow-up essay on female spectatorship, Mulvey more directly addressed the question of women's pleasure in cinema, suggesting that if women enjoy a film, it is because they can participate transvestically in the logic of the "masculinization of the spectator position" (Mulvey 1988, 69), while also identifying with the heroine. Woman's supposed greater bisexuality would allow her to take up a masculine subject position by cross-identifying with the male hero and his freedom of action and control over the diegetic world; such a woman would find herself hysterically "torn between the deep blue sea of passive femininity and the devil of regressive masculinity" (Mulvey 1988, 70), as do some of the heroines of the genre marketed specifically for women: melodrama.

For Mulvey, subjects in a patriarchy were necessarily masculine – and implicitly white, middle class, and heterosexual. She never considered the pleasures and difficulties of identifications across class, race, and ethnicity, or of identifications across gender which might express a gay or lesbian desire, nor did she address the effects of showing First World films in Third World theatres). She also assumed that films as fantasy can be reduced to their human objects and actions and treated as unitary objects themselves, with only one meaning, although their signifying material incorporates a variety of objects, part objects, erotogenic zones and aims or activities which may not originate from a single desire or identification.[2] As Jean Laplanche and J.-B. Pontalis argue in their now often-cited work on fantasy, any scenario has multiple enunciations; in addition, the subject may be present in it in a desubjectivated form, in its syntax (in this Laplanche and Pontalis stress the performative, rather than merely representational dimension of reading and writing a fantasy or self). As Mulvey saw it, the only pleasure available to women as women was the passive, narcissistic (and exhibitionistic) identification with the good object as fetish.[3]

Mulvey's approach was more theoretically sophisticated than that of earlier feminist film theorists, such as Marjorie Rosen or Linda Artel and Susan Wengraf, who had looked for "positive images" instead of negative and unrealistic stereotypes. Like apparatus theorists, Mulvey rejected the reductive model of realism as a transparent reflection of a pre-given world and showed how filmic realism participated in the constitution of reality and subjects. According to her, identification was part of the problem for an ideological cinema, rather than the solution to it, as the call for positive and/or realistic images assumed. Mulvey took seriously the Althusserian notion that ideology structures behavior at a level which is not simply that of consciously held ideas, whereas advocates of "positive images" discussed the problems of and solutions to sexism in terms of liberal humanism's sovereign subjects, whose consciousnesses were to be "raised" to truth from falsehood and, if they were female, replaced by those of "better" role models.[4] "Images" criticism was consistent with ego-psychology as an imaginary fortification of a weak ego. Mulvey, however, was committed to psychoanalysis and its assumption that the subject does not coincide with the ego, although hers was a psychoanalysis informed by a feminist critique which used it against itself. Mulvey's argument that Hollywood cinema was a symptom of a perverse patriarchal psyche, unable to accept feminine difference, called into question the "developmental maturity" of male heterosexuality, which Freud all too often assumes.

Her conclusions were quite similar to those of the feminist philosopher and psychoanalyst, Luce Irigaray, who at about the same time maintained that the symbolic was a masculine imaginary in which feminine difference was reduced to opposition, "castration," so that man could misrecognize himself in women's "penis envy" as having what she lacked. Reversing the usual psychoanalytic judgments about gender and narcissism, Irigaray and Mulvey argued that men, not women, were the real narcissists, effacing difference in favor of the reproduction of the same. This resulted in an economy of relations which Irigaray described as "hom(m)osexual" (Irigaray 1985b, 171), anticipating by several years Eve Sedgwick's notion of the "homosocial,"[5] But Mulvey and Irigaray proposed very different "cures" for this masculinism. Irigaray called for the elaboration of a specifically feminine imaginary, in which women's (presumptively) different relation to language (what feminists now discuss as *écriture feminine*), desire, and the body would be expressed, rather than censored. Drawing on her work (and related efforts on feminine narrativity), both Mary Ann Doane and Annette Kuhn have suggested there might (or could) be an essentially feminine cinema aesthetic expressing and reproducing feminine identity.

However, many critics have questioned the value of such a notion because of its essentialism. While debates about the latter have been structured primarily as a choice between biologism or social constructionism, we might investigate instead the place of differences within "the" essentially feminine Imaginary as Irigaray conceives it. How does she represent "other" women or take into account the differences between women of different classes, races, ethnicities, and sexualities, given that she presumes to speak for and about all women? She is necessarily caught up in the representational problematic which Spivak outlines in "Can the Subaltern Speak?" Whenever we represent the other we speak in her name, on her behalf, about what we claim are her interests, needs, and desires, and thereby represent ourselves as qualified or sanctioned to speak for and instead of her. We represent her both as a delegate or proxy (which Spivak, drawing on Marx, terms "political representation" or *Vertretung*) and as a portrait artist who must depict the other's character (Spivak links this more common, textual definition of representation to Marx's *Darstellung*) (Spivak 1988, 275–9). Spivak is very critical of any "standpoint epistemology" that assumes that a person's identity guarantees a certain experience or knowledge of the world, reminding us that class consciousness and class position do not necessarily coincide (Spivak 1988, 277–8). Because the oppressed may not experience and know their oppression as oppression, they must be represented; indeed, to eschew this responsibility is to sanction ignorance as an alibi for refusing to engage with oppressions which we imagine are not part of our "experience" (Spivak 1990, 62–3). We must remember, however, that to represent the other is to confront (or indulge in) our own narcissism because "people are different from the object of emancipatory benevolence" (Spivak 1990, 136).

Irigaray can be critiqued, as advocates of "positive images" have been, for failing to consider the politics of offering certain representations of a whole, powerful, and genuine femininity that are to function as good role models or ego ideals.[6] What does she envision when she argues for "[v]alid representations of [women] themselves in actions, words, and images in all public places" (Irigaray 1993, 86)? Would women of color be represented by these images? Would working-class women – or lesbians, or Third World women – see themselves in them? Whose values will determine the "validity" of the traits of the feminine ego-ideal which the subject is to incorporate, and through whose gaze she is to see herself? Because Irigaray offers no sustained discussion of any differences between women other than those deriving from the mother–daughter relation, her "women" is unspecified and uninflected, a new universal (and therefore implicitly white and middle class).[7] Could such a feminine imaginary avoid the specular rivalry of the masculine imaginary, in which difference is disavowed, signifying castration as the failure to measure up to an ideal from which the male subject must screen himself? Would Irigaray's subjects have an unconscious or id and a super-ego – or would they be egos driven by need only, rather than desire, with no bad or castrating objects to leave them wanting and nothing to repress, disavow, or foreclose? Does Irigaray's theory allow for change, or is her feminine imaginary a static utopia, ordered by that "women's time" which Julia Kristeva has described as cyclical or monumental and eternal (Kristeva 1986)?

Mulvey's solution to the patriarchal cinematic imaginary does not give rise to some of these questions because she did not appeal to essentialism, however deconstructively complicated, as Irigaray's is according to a number of feminist critics.[8] Instead, Mulvey called for a counter-cinema the effects of which would be analytic and deconstituting, rather than orthopedic like those of ego-psychology or the feminine imaginary. As she envisioned them, the techniques of this counter-cinema were very similar to those on which apparatus theorists themselves pinned their hopes for subversion of hegemony: a self-reflexive modernism which – as in the work of Theodor Adorno – is associated with critical negativity, the destruction of passive pleasures, and disidentification from the subject effect(s) of bourgeois culture.[9] Mulvey proposed to shatter the mirror of the imaginary by offering the subject a "bad object," one that would destroy visual pleasure and therefore frustrate man's ideologically generated needs, in effect starving him to death. Her strategy was the inverse of that of Irigaray and other critics advocating positive images, which like apparatus theory proposed a subject who could be adapted to reality by the good object of needs – whether the true needs of genuine femininity or the false, ideologically manufactured needs of bourgeois subjectivity.

However, as its opposite, Mulvey's theory of counter-cinema was still apparatus theory's double, an imaginary reproduction of the imaginary it wished to "raise" to the level of the symbolic and acceptance of difference.[10] To be captivated by the good or the bad object relation, the other of narcissistic love (*Verliebtheit*) and hate, is to remain within the logic of the imaginary. Such a subject is caught up in the narcissistic drive for self-mastery through an alter-ego who could iconically reflect the whole and wholly lovable self, "fixing" it (in both senses of the word) by eliminating spaces and times of difference in which the Other might be master. Mulvey's bad object was the projection of the subject's disintegration as what would ineluctably promote (self) difference (and the anxiety accompanying it?), the other side of the imaginary narcissistic jubilation associated with the projection of the good object. For her, the bad object guarantees the bad subject, which it reflects and (re)produces. Like Irigaray, Mulvey doubled the apparatus theory's effect of doubling or cloning masculine subjects, which she wished to subvert. She too expelled difference by reducing it to an identity with its object-signifier. Collapsing together fantasy's dimensions of representation and performance, enunciation and address, she sutured the splitting of the subject which ensures that the I who speaks is never identical with the I who is spoken.

Out of Focus: Subjects, Objects, and the Decentered Gaze

Mulvey's turn to modernism was an effort to decenter both the apparatus of the subject and of the cinema that constituted him. Although Mulvey does not mention Kristeva, the contemporary critical notion of a link between modernism and feminism derives primarily from Kristeva's theory of the semiotic as pre-signifying sounds, colors, etc. associated with the maternal, which disrupt (patriarchal) symbolic signs, theses or meanings and identities.[11] Kristeva finds the semiotic at work in (generally male) modernist writing but also in some earlier art and literature, including Reniassance paintings by Bellini (Kristeva 1980, 237–70). According to her, the semiotic is "maternal" in that it is an expression from the time when the child is still differentiating itself from the mother as the object of the satisfaction of vital needs. It achieves that separation through its entry into the patriarchal symbolic, which will make the mother a "lost object" for the child by virtue of the lack the father's prohibitions institute, severing their fantasmatic phallic dyad. Lack is the condition and effect of substitution through symbolization in desire, enabling subject–object distinctions and relations. Ultimately, it is both the mother's and the child's lack of complete satisfaction in their relationship which drives them to other objects and activities.

According to Kristeva, lack must be introjected by the child in a primary identification with what is not so much an object as a relation, figured by the imaginary father as the mother's desire for the phallus the child is not (Kristeva 1983, 41). For both Kristeva and Lacan, the father as third term always already interrupts the dual relation of mother and child. Kristeva describes his function as an "archaic reduplication" of the structure of signification, the potential for desire in the possibility of metaphor, or similarity, difference, and substitution which the semiotic (pre)figures (Kristeva 1983, 25, 30). Lack is the unwitting gift of the father to the child. It is not just a signifier of the patriarch's phallic power but also a mark of respect for the otherness of the M/Other as desiring subject, especially if we consider that the father is not the only one who can function as a reason for the mother's absences, which can include any desirable ideal other than that which the child might represent for her as a phallic substitute. Lack is equally a sign of respect for the otherness of the child, who through it is given a "self" which could be distinct from the mother (which enables us to speak of "the child" before there is such a subject), a self caught up in both narcissism and desire as the ongoing subversion of the narcissistic ego and the object-choices which would reflect and secure it.

The psychoanalytic notion of lack accounts for what humanizes the cyborg subject of the ideological apparatus, the machine whose desires to "be real" (a real boy, a real human) disrupt narcissistic homeostatic regulation. Lack feeds that desire, which makes the cyborg's mimicry a masquerade, an alienating charade that seems to veil or screen him from some other self and gives him the uncomfortable sense of being "in the closet," not quite not ignorant of what he really is at the level of his unconscious desires. "Willing the cyborg into being appears to be the equivalent of wishing the problems of organic life away," Margaret Morse writes, "Yet unless the human is erased entirely, food and waste will enter the cyborg condition . . . What do humans who want to become electronic [cyborgs] eat?" (Morse 1994, 158). Her question implies that for humans there is something beyond the pleasure principle, narcissism, and homeostasis, something which wastes energy and drives us to consume. That something is desire. It ensures that no matter how many ego ideals we introject at the cinema, we will still be hungry for something else. Consumption can never be a "lubrication cycle"; because we do not know what we lack in order to be real, no object can finally smooth our functioning. Despite his manufacture by and for the symbolic, the cyborg is human in his desires, which fractures his self-identity as a perpetual motion machine for ideology.

Kaja Silverman demonstrates this in a persuasive reading of *Blade Runner*. She argues that in fact we are all cyborgs because we are structured by certain cultural fantasies, like Oedipus, which we have incorporated as the desire of the other. It does not really matter whether one's memories are real or fake, implanted by "experience," the hypnotist of "false memory syndrome," the cyborg engineer who "fathered" one's memory chips, or the ego of defensive "screen memories"; their effects are the same – lack and the desire which is its metonymy. As the term reveals, the "replicants" of *Blade Runner* embody the ideological problematic, the tendency of "parental" fantasies to "repeat" in the next generation as the child is caught up in what Lacan describes as the "circuit" of the symbolic machine, which functions at the level of the unconscious as the discourse of the desire of the Other. According to Laplanche, the child is seduced into a negotiation with these fantasies which accompany the care given by mothers and fathers and take the form of the enigmatic signfiers of demands, the import of which is not clear (Laplanche 1976, 44–5). The child therefore does not know just what the parent wants. Like the replicant, the child is addressed or interpellated by the parent and must participate in the adult's desire and the lack which founds it in order to respond to those mysterious demands or calls, even if only to refuse the name(s) by which s/he is addressed. If there is no response, there can be no intersubjective relation; the other does not exist as such for those who are autistic.

Lacan's is a radically anti-humanist theory of the subject, which is emphasized by his recurrence to the metaphor of the machine in his seminars. He describes both the system of the ego and the system of the unconscious as machines characterized by different mechanisms of functioning or managing energy, which Freud discusses as the secondary and primary processes. As a machine, the organism has a tendency to return to a state of equilibrium. However, Freud outlines two different human equilibriums. One is associated with life as a reduction of tension to a level previously established, which involves the binding of a certain amount of energy to signs and objects to hold it in reserve for the work necessary to maintain the system. This machine is governed by feedback mechanisms for homeostatic regulation, the pleasure and reality principles (the latter is simply delayed gratification and no real contravention of the pleasure principle). The other equilibrium is linked to death as the system's entropic dissolution into inorganic forms and the free discharge of unbound energy. While both machines involve repetition, the restitutive function of the narcissistic ego, which lends itself to notions of "adaptation" to reality through good object relations, is finally at odds with what Lacan terms Freud's "original contribution" (Lacan 1988b, 79), that repetition which is beyond the pleasure and reality principles and subverts both narcissism and adaptation to reality. "Freud chose to remind us that the unconscious as such cannot be reached and makes itself known in a fashion which is paradoxical, painful, and cannot be reduced to the pleasure principle," Lacan explains (Lacan 1988b, 65). The symbolic machine manifests itself as an interruption in the functioning of the ego apparatus, which nevertheless "maps out a certain curve, a certain persistence" (Lacan 1988b, 80): "The principle which brings the living being back to death is situated, is marked out behind the necessity it experiences to take the roads of life – and it can only take that way. It cannot find death along any old road" (Lacan 1988b, 80–1).

According to Lacan the only vital principle is the libido as the energy at stake in a fundamental disequilibrium which splits the drive (into life and death drives). There is no unique individual or self at the center of the drive from birth, no little ego which simply grows bigger and stronger until it can resist the invasive desire of the Other. Lacan's figure for the infant libido, the lamella or *hommelette*, is a shapeless blob, rather than an ego, and it has more to do with the Other than the self. As a life drive, the lamella represents the immortality the being subject to sexual reproduction lacks on its own (Lacan 1978, 205), which compels what Lacan refers to as "being for the Other": the drive is "given the task of seeking something that, each time, responds in the Other" – the gaze, the voice, the phallus, and the other *objets a* the subject of symbolic castration lacks (Lacan 1978, 196). There is an Other beyond the ego that seeks recognition as its master: "[T]he other become[s] less and less truly other to the extent that it takes on more and more exclusively the function of support" or imaginary alter ego in whom the subject's mastery seems to be alienated and against whom the subject's aggression is directed (Lacan 1988a, 51). Lacan insists that childhood play, including the *fort-da* game invented by Freud's grandson, reaffirms loss and does not just seek to master it through situating the child in an active relation to what was passively experienced. The drive therefore is fundamentally self-reflexive and passive, literally carving up a self through a primordial masochism which brings it into being through subjection to a master and the loss of the vital bits that are the *objets a:* "The activity of the drive is concentrated in this *making oneself (se faire),*" Lacan explains, offering as one example the oral drive, which is "getting sucked, it is the vampire" (Lacan 1978, 195).

The subject is caught up in an automatism, rather than the autonomous self-making of bourgeois individualism or ego-psychology, at both the imaginary and the symbolic levels. This automatism takes the form of mimicry as a negotiation between imaginary and symbolic, a compromise between the split imperatives of a life drive which is also a death drive. It compels the subject to identify with the master who must be preserved and annihilated as both self and other, and therefore to identify with the master's desire as what must also be repressed. The other is not so much a mirror as a screen: the other's masquerades conceal from the subject the lost object or cause of desire, which the subject cannot have or be. Ultimately, the other as truly the Other lacks what the subject wants, and lacks even the knowledge of that desire (the Other is not the "subject supposed to know" of transference love). The subject's only freedom is this lack of the Other, which is also his or her own lack. It opens the subject to the call of others whose interpellations s/he will accept or refuse in an "inmixing" of subjects that results from the trauma of symbolic castration.[12] It is a death drive in its attack on the ego, the object the subject was for others s/he loved – but it is also a life drive in its renaming of the subject as a different object, an ego lovable in a different way. Identity is at once a defense against and expression of the desire of the Other we can only know through the demands s/he makes; it is a witness to our encounter with alterity.

As Homi Bhabha points out, new demands – or new readings of demands – negate old certitudes and necessitate a rehistoricization, in effect a rewriting of self and other and their relationship (Bhabha 1988, 11, 19, 21). For psychoanalysis, otherness is not in the good or bad object but in an object relation between two subjects which is dialectical because each impacts retroactively on the other. Just as the realist picture could never finally consolidate the ego, as Lacan demonstrates in his reading of Holbein's *The Ambassadors* (Lacan 1978, 85–90), so the modernist film could never definitively destroy it. The Lacanian theory of the gaze is not imaginary, like that of apparatus theory. Lacan's subject is not centered in the eye/I that corresponds to the vanishing point of haptic space but is actually split between it and the gaze of the Other, which is the effect of the belief that there is something behind, veiled by what we can see, as Joan Copjec explains (Copjec 1989, 68). The gaze symbolizes what both subject and other must lack as they try to catch the other's desiring eye. What do they hope to see in the exhibitionism of masquerade? According to Lacan, the voyeur looks for "not, as one says, the phallus – but precisely its absence . . . What one looks at is what cannot be seen" (Lacan 1978, 182). The gaze is refracted through the masquerade, which is a screen for the lack it signifies.

The basis of the relation between the subject and the Other, the link between their desires, is the superimposition of their two lacks, which are fundamentally different, making for a radical non-reciprocity and lack of satisfaction in their encounter, and so sustaining them as subjects of desire. For such subjects, appearances are deceiving, as the saying goes, some-thing Freud demonstrates with the joke about the man who wonders why his friend tells him he is going to Cracow so he will think the actual destination is Lemberg, when it really is Cracow (Freud 1963c, 115). Trying to outwit the other by identifying his or her desire, determining what s/he is up to, we identify with a projection of our own desire. Analysis should reveal this to us: we do not grasp the alterity of the other but of our self through it, which is why Lacan believes a genuine analysis is a psychoanalysis and requires a recognition and assumption of our desires as they have been rehistoricized through our encounters with new and "other" demands. Anything else is an imaginary technique involving projection – like the analysis of "resistances" undertaken by ego-psychologists. As a therapy, such practices consist of an effort to dominate the other aggressively, "adapting" him or her to "reality" through the imposition of our idea of a good object, as in hypnosis. Such an object can never come into focus, which is why the subject of the gaze is decentered by the desire to see.

Queer Spectacles? The Resistance to Queer Theory

The object cannot be a device for securing the ego, since it is caught up in the subject's desires as well as the ego's defenses against them. Although the most influential feminist revisions of apparatus theory drew on psychoanalysis, they did not use it to smash the ego machinery of the apparatus. Instead they redefined the latter as masculine and proposed a counter-apparatus for the production of feminine egos – or at least egos which were not masculine. Ultimately, Mulvey's utopic vision of modernism is symptomatic of a desire for the difference of desire itself, which was repressed by apparatus theory and her response to it. Because she and other feminist film theorists reproduced the apparatus in their work, queer theorists and others have viewed it critically, noting that Mulvey and her successors seemed to account for only one kind of subject, who was not only male but also First World, white, middle class, and heterosexual. Queer theorists have been interested in some of the differences feminist film studies left out of the picture(s), which they wish to make visible. In the pursuit of this politics of visible differences, they have been looking through – and for – queer spectacles.

Raising questions about differences the apparatus disavowed, queer theory undoubtedly has queered its smooth functioning. All too often, however, queer theory, like feminist theory, imagines an apparatus of its own which would ineluctably reproduce good objects – queer spectacles – for good subjects, queers who would resist hegemonic identities. Can it be surprising if the queer bug in the works of the apparatus of the imaginary turns out to have a few bugs in its own works, which jam the machinery of the reproduction of resisting, queer egos? In the final analysis, what any ego resists is the subject's own self-difference, the desires which queer identity, even the queer identities queer theory might like to secure. The risk of any politics of visibility, as both Lee Edelman and Peggy Phelan have emphasized, is voyeuristic surveillance and the fetishism of being reduced to the same or its opposite – which can happen within, as well as to, queer communities. Confronting one kind of narcissism, the queer theorist may well reproduce another. The effort to get latent queer identities out of the apparatus can become a project of getting the apparatus out of "manifestly queer" identities by disavowing what marks identity, that "difference within" which signifies a lack of self-identity and drives desire, from which the ego seeks to defend itself.

This is the paradox of what Eve Sedgwick discusses as the structuring or "dynamic impasse" between a "universalizing view" of sexuality, the belief that "desire is an unpredictably powerful solvent of stable identities," and a "minoritizing view" of sexuality, which assumes there are distinct populations of hetero- and homosexual people (Sedgwick 1990, 85). Does desire queer identity and its reproduction, or is there a queer identity and a desire proper to it, a "queer psychology" which would reproduce it? Barbara Johnson highlights this dilemma in a discussion of lesbian films and novels, which she recognizes could be works by or about manifestly lesbian subjects, or simply works which lesbians manifestly enjoy. In either case, however, one must confront the problem of recognizing what a manifestation of lesbianism is:

> If I tried to "speak as a lesbian," wouldn't I be processing my understanding of myself through media-induced images of what a lesbian is or through my idealizations of what a lesbian *should* be? Wouldn't I be treating as *known* the very predicate I was trying to discover? I needed a way of catching myself in the act of reading as a lesbian without having intended to (Johnson 1993, 160).

The queerness of identity appears in the other, which is identity's imaginary dimension of specular alienation. Wiegman explores what is implicit in Johnson's questions, the alienation of the lesbian self through the commodity, the glossy image on offer in films, popular fiction, magazines, and advertisements which increasingly seek to address lesbian and gay consumers. This notion of alienation at once assumes and denies the possibility of authentic, unalienated lesbianism, since lesbian identity – like any other identity – can only take the form of a misrecognition. It is a paradox all identity-based discourses come to address sooner or later and has already been discussed at length in African-American studies by critics and authors such as bell hooks, Kobena Mercer, Toni Morrison, and Susan Willis, who have explored the possibilities of authenticity and "hybridity," black representations, and (white) commodity culture. Are black consumers addressed as white "replicants" (Willis's term) who must assimilate white values and mime white identities? Or can they creatively consume commodities to (re)produce resistant black identities, as Mercer argues in his well-known essay on black hairstyle politics? Of course, questions similar to these also prompted the initial work of Mulvey and other media feminists, who confronted the fact that women's visibility was through and as commodity fetishes, which were also sexual fetishes.

Ultimately, every version of "minority-based" criticism (re)stages a debate about identity and visibility in a compulsive return to the trauma of alienation through the image and visual signifiers. Wiegman repeats it when she notes that the consolidation of lesbian identity as a category of consumption is not "liberation" but a form of discipline (Wiegman 1994, 10). Butler, too, reiterates it in her even more sweeping critique, which questions not only commodified images but any signifiers of identity. Drawing on Foucault, she argues that "identity categories tend to be instruments of regulatory regimes, whether as the normalizing categories of oppressive structures or as the rallying points for a liberatory contestation of that very oppression" (Butler 1991, 13–14). Discourses construct identity, rather than representing or distorting something that already exists: "[T]he I only comes into being through being called, named, interpellated . . . [R]ecognition is not conferred on a subject, but forms that subject" (Butler 1993, 225–6). Why then do subjects feel that misrepresentation and misrecognition can occur? Butler offers an answer by modifying the theory of discourse as a pure productivity or performativity, affirming instead that the subject generated is split, rather than "pure," divided between "itself" and a remainder whose alienation or exclusion is constitutively necessary, an "outside" which therefore is included in the subject's formation. In this, she is in agreement with Lacan, of whom she is often critical.

Butler evokes this splitting in her comments about coming out as a lesbian:

> For it is always finally unclear what is meant by invoking the
> lesbian-signifier, since its signification is always to some degree
> out of one's control, but also because its *specificity* can only be
> demarcated by exclusions that return to disrupt its claims to
> coherence. What, if anything, can lesbians be said to share?
> And who will decide this question, and in the name of whom?
> If I claim to be a lesbian, I "come out" only to produce a new
> and different "closet" (Butler 1991, 15).

Her exploration of this issue alludes to the problematic of representation discussed by Spivak as the intersection of *Vertretung* and *Darstellung*, the political proxy and the portrait, which emphasizes the non-coincidence of ego and Other, the "I" who speaks and the "I" who is spoken, the eye which sees and the gaze.

Edelman also stresses the splitting of the subject, challenging the institutionalization of identity and pleasure by emphasizing the remainder, the excess between desire and a representation that can never reflect it (Edelman 1989, 345). That negativity which queers identity cannot be recuperated for it in a queer identity. There is no final "synthesis" (as in Hegel) which could reduce difference into the self-same, eliminating it. Paradoxically, queer theory and identity represent a resistance to queering theory and identity, a refusal of what is beyond the calculations of any totalized, closed, and self-regulating system or apparatus, whether theory, identity, or community. The queer theorist must read for those differences (and self-differences) which even queer theory and identity would exclude, which disrupt the reproduction of the machine; s/he must disclose the human desires animating it. There is no end to such (re)reading or analysis. If queer theory and its critiques are mutually constitutive, they are no more reciprocal complementary than consciousness and the unconscious. Theirs is a queer relation in which each brings the other to crisis or disequilbrium. Something insists beyond any given reading, an absence or lack to which the queer theorist compulsively returns, but always in disguised or displaced form, since it has no other, more authentic representation. The name for what queers theory therefore is not "the queer" – "woman," "lesbian," "Chicana," etc. will always specify that. Queer theory describes a relation with alterity, in which calculation comes undone and the name or identity fails. What is queer therefore is neither the multiplication nor the sum of differences, but the division and difference from any particular difference one could name, identify, unveil, or "out." The other in whom I would see myself inevitably alienates me from my perfected or completed self-identity.

Unfortunately, this destabilizes the lesbian self Johnson looks for and Wiegman critiques in the media, as any would-be lesbian finds herself *mise en abyme* by an endless substitution of self and alter-ego as representations of "the lesbian" which can never finally locate the original or essential lesbian the other lesbians must resemble. The imaginary object, the lesbian one loves (or hates) as one's self, cannot secure identity, whether this imaginary is conceptualized as a heterosexual apparatus in which "the original" is straight, or as a homosexual apparatus. The performative dimension of discourse ensures that any apparatus produces the desire it represses, even if only as a repressed desire. Furthermore, the "epistemology of the closet," as Sedgwick terms it, at once recognizes and denies such a desire. Its constant policing of masculine (and, modifying her argument, feminine) identities through a suspicious reading for signs of homosexuality involves an active ignorance about the latter, the constitution of the presumptive universal as an un(re)marked difference. The two faces of fetishism are visible in this disavowal of queer difference, which is at once everywhere and nowhere. Anyone might be queer – or straight; appearances are deceiving, including one's own. The epistemology of the lesbian "closet" which Butler mentions would result in the very same dilemma.

When all the players are masquerading, identity becomes a game of strategy, a "skill of reading," as Amy Robinson phrases it in her discussion of passing (Robinson 1994, 716). But such guessing games about identity are inevitably imaginary, since one can only know the other's desire by projection or "reading into" it, as ego-psychology does. Robinson acknowledges this, arguing that such reading skills actually constitute as queer what is apparently straight: "Naming as real what cannot be ontologically substantiated, in-group recognition serves to safeguard members of the group from which one passes from the interpretive authority of the group to which one passes" (Robinson 1994, 731). This is the strategy of the fetishist, who is able to discern in the women he finds attractive that special something which might be invisible to everyone else, such as the "shine on the nose" in the case with which Freud opens his essay on the topic (Freud 1963b, 214). Like the fetishist, Robinson's ingroup privileges the gaze as the vehicle of an imaginary (mis)recognition in which the difference between self and other is disavowed to sustain identity and community. She provides a very clear example of such a scene of identification of – and with – the gaze of the gay other, which is described by one of the subjects of a book of case studies of "sex variants" published in 1955:

> The eyes of the homo usually stare right through you. He
> looks a second or two longer than the average, and as you gaze
> into his eyes, if you are a homo, there is a lightninglike
> magnetic response, and a thrill passes through the very heart of
> you. *The confirmed homo needs only to use his eyes.* (Robinson
> 1994, 720; Robinson's emphasis.)

The queer is "confirmed" as such through the imaginary use of "the eyes of the homo," which are at once his own and the other's, able to penetrate through both their masquerades, cutting right to the heart.

Can such violence go unpunished? The narcissistic imaginary which would heal the splitting of the subject between enunciation and utterance, eye and gaze, ego and Other, is characterized by aggressive, as well as jubilatory, "thrills." For that reason many theorists have wished to emphasize the symbolic, rather than imaginary, dimension of lesbian and gay identity. Warner notes the long history of associating homosexuality with narcissism as "an interest in self rather than in the other," while heterosexuality is affirmed as other-oriented (Warner 1993, 190). Diana Fuss also focuses on this alleged queer narcissism, pointing out that gay sex is all too often represented in straight culture as "cannibal murder," an oral insatiability associated with identification, rather than object choice, whose exemplars would be the Hollywood villains of *Silence of the Lambs* and the real-life killer Jeffrey Dahmer (Fuss 1993, 182), Fuss emphasizes the violence Freud associates with identification as the earliest form of relation to the object, which she describes as a non-relation, since through it the other is assimilated to the self, his or her otherness apparently negated. Hannibal Lecter's identifications only perversely literalize the process as "the oral-cannibalistic incorporation of the other person," in his case, with "favva beans and a nice Chianti" (Fuss 1993, 188).

While Warner accepts the argument that queer relationships involve narcissistic object choice and identification with the other, he nevertheless maintains that alterity and lack is recognized in them because the queer seeks in another "some ideal excellence missing from his own ego" (Warner 1993, 192). In queer relationships, he asserts, "the Imaginary transcends its limitations" (Warner 1993, 199). He reaffirms Simone de Beauvoir's evaluation of lesbian relationships as "the miracle of the mirror": "[I]n exact reciprocity each is at once subject and object, sovereign and slave; duality becomes mutuality" (Warner 1993, 199). In the mirror of "the eyes of the homo," lack seems to disappear. However, any mirror can only screen or conceal it for a time. The Other's mastery alienates the subject from the ideal which s/he would incorporate. Desire returns as the question to the mirror, whose answer will one day displease "his majesty the ego," as the fairy tale about the evil queen and Snow White reveals. Lacan therefore is sharply critical of any valorization of intersubjective reciprocity, sympathy, empathy, understanding, or love, which are based on an imaginary confusion of self and other whose other "face" is hate and aggressivity:

> We have been intoxicated for some time in analysis by themes
> that have indisputably come from so-called existentialist
> discourse, where the other is the *thou*, the one who can
> respond, but in a symmetrical mode, one of complete
> correspondence, the alter ego, the brother. One forms a
> fundamentally reciprocal idea of intersubjectivity. (Lacan 1993,
> 273)

Whenever self-sameness or self-difference is projected in the other, otherness is denied. The other is reified as an object for – or against – an equally reified subject, who through the other denies his or her own self-difference. Instead of an "inmixing" of subjects in the response to the other's call, which changes both participants in a dialogue, there is a substitution of subject and object, rendered absolutely disjunct yet equivalent through the fetishistic negation of difference in the double.

The Apparitional Lesbian

Seeking to undermine the association of homosexuality with regressive narcissism, de Lauretis emphasizes object choice, rather than identification, in her work on fantasy and lesbian subjectivity, criticizing essays by Fuss, Valerie Traub, and Jackie Stacey for conflating identification and object-choice just as the Hollywood films they discuss do.[13] Linking the identificatory confusion of self and other with the pre-Oedipal imaginary of the child, de Lauretis argues that Irigaray's appropriation of it for an image of genuine feminine eroticism is not lesbian (de Lauretis 1991, 233). Her analysis implies that the structure of the imaginary is regressive, a point Constance Penley also makes in her discussion of women fans of *Star Trek* who reinvent the relationship between Kirk and Spock as erotic (Penley 1992, 480). Like Penley, de Lauretis wants to situate women, particularly lesbians, in the symbolic realm of adult, post-Oedipal sexuality. According to her, the latter is an affair of object-choice, rather than identification (de Lauretis 1991, 236). She assumes that "the practice of love" in object-choice respects the other's difference from the self as desire, whereas identification negates alterity; love is symbolic and constitutes differences, while the imaginary confuses them. The ultimate stake for de Lauretis in this privileging of loving object-choice is the very possibility of lesbianism, since without it, she argues, lesbianism dissolves into the identification with another woman as ego-ideal and rival, which is heterosexual. As she sees it, identification is implicitly and essentially heterosexual because the unmarked woman is presumed to be so, as she discusses at length in an earlier essay (de Lauretis 1987a).

For Irigaray, the unmarked woman, withdrawn from circulation on the masculinist and heterosexual market of commodity exchange, is lesbian, although hers is a lesbianism which de Lauretis refuses to recognize as such because it blatantly confuses object-choice and identification. De Lauretis prefers Wittig's essential figure of lesbian eros, the *J/e-tu* doubled protagonist of *The Lesbian Body*. Wittig's doubled subject is for de Lauretis an example of something supposedly different, the lesbian "coupled, rather than split, subject," two women who "inhabit the subject position together" and thereby constitute themselves as lesbian. She adapts this idea from Sue-Ellen Case's description of the butch-femme relationship which, in the latter's memorable phrase, replaces "the Lacanian slash with a lesbian bar" (Case 1988–9, 57). Nevertheless, de Lauretis does not believe the lesbian disproves the psychoanalytic theory of castration; she draws on that concept to avoid Wittig's essentialism, deriving the lesbian from her social construction in heterosexuality as a woman. Lesbianism is an affair of *female* object choice, that is, by and of women, who are themselves the effect of a constitutive heterosexuality. A woman is interpellated as a lesbian by another woman who interpellates her as a lesbian through their mutual desire for each other, expressed in a shared fantasy. Each sees herself as lesbian only through the eyes of the other, with whom she must identify as subject of a desire whose object she is. The two women must inhabit together not only the subject position (as desiring women) but also the object position (as desired women). Without the object to reflect her identity as desiring subject, the lesbian is just a woman, presumptively heterosexual. Yet the object also must reflect the lesbian's identity as woman. Because she must interpellate the other as a woman with whom she identifies as such, she at once creates and negates the lesbian desire she would bring into being, necessarily confusing object-choice and identification – exactly what de Lauretis finds so problematic in Irigaray. Ultimately, de Lauretis's lesbian subject is caught up in a specular feminine imaginary like Irigaray's.

In fact, lesbianism as de Lauretis theorizes it accomplishes what Irigaray argues the feminine imaginary does: the restoration of a libidinally invested body image which can be narcissistically loved (de Lauretis 1994a, 300). Irigaray's feminine imaginary incorporates many symbolic functions, such as desire and language, as an alternative to a symbolic which is really a masculine imaginary. She repeats the mixing of the imaginary and symbolic which characterizes patriarchy – but she does so for women, rather than men, in an effort to repair the psychic trauma of women's castration by repudiating it. Unlike Irigaray, de Lauretis asserts the importance of castration, recognizing its constitutive function for the feminine subject, whom it splits from the first love object, the mother, which gives the girl a separate "self" and restructures her relation to her imaginary morphology and the ego that is its projection. However, because de Lauretis in effect abolishes the role of the phallus in castration, she evacuates the concept of lack from subjectivity and reproduces the very essentialism which she wishes to avoid. She replaces what Lacan characterizes as *"manque-à-être"* or "lack in being," which is the effect of the drive's submission to the signifiers of the Other, with a "lack *of* being" (de Lauretis 1994a, 300; my emphasis) that can be overcome through lesbian fetishism, in which being and meaning coincide, with nothing lacking: "[P]erverse desire is sustained on fantasy scenarios that restage the loss and recovery of a fantasmatic female body" (de Lauretis 1994b, 265). Relocating castration in the mirror stage, de Lauretis resolves it through an imaginary cure, a new self-image. Whereas psychoanalysis explains castration as that which *gives* the girl a feminine body by denying her the phallus as the signifier of the mother's desire, de Lauretis argues that castration *denies* the girl a feminine body:

> Failing the mother's narcissistic validation of the daughter's body-image, castration means the lack or loss of the female body; that is to say, the castration complex rewrites in the symbolic a narcissistic wound, a lack of being (Lacan's *manque-à-être*), already established in the imaginary matrix of the body-ego; it rewrites it in terms of anatomical ("natural")

> sexual difference, refiguring as lack of a penis what was first
> and foremost lack of a lovable body. (de Lauretis 1994b, 242)

In de Lauretis's model, sexual difference is not socially constructed but natural (her scare quotes notwithstanding), always already there in the presence or absence of the penis which is an essential expression or cause of it. The girl has a lovable girl's body from the start, which the mother perversely refuses to love, depriving her of it.

Reducing the phallus to the penis as an imaginary organ with a *Gestalt* fixed by nature, rather than by the symbolic, de Lauretis resolves through elimination the problem of lack as the impossibility of having or being the phallus for the other. Because we all know a penis when we see one, there can be no mistake about it. It can never be an object of exchange between women, who clearly do not have it (that is what makes them women in the first place) and do not *want* it, in both senses of the word, since it is not a part of the whole and wholly lovable feminine self which is there from the start, if only the mother would recognize it. De Lauretis conflates nature with culture, male or femaleness with having or lacking the penis, which for her is identical to having or being the phallus for the other. Ironically, the penis as she theorizes it is missing the very symbolic characteristics which would make it a phallic object of exchange in desire. Such an object can always be replaced by other symbolic "gifts" with a different imaginary shape, as Lacan reminds us: "Where one is caught short, where one cannot, as a result of the lack, give what is to be given, one can always give something else" (Lacan 1978, 104). Because the phallus is a signifier subject to exchange and substitution, both men and women can masquerade as having or being the phallus for any other subject; these are psychic, rather than biological positions, and in any case, no one really has or is the phallus; love is an affair of phallic deception and pretense. The phallus designates the lack which makes every self something less or other than what the mother wants and loves; everyone loses a lovable self through castration. By separating the phallus from castration (at least for some women), de Lauretis situates lesbians outside the problematic of lack and phallic exchange which is the very meaning of castration, disavowing it; her theory therefore repeats the fetishism she argues characterizes lesbian psychology. She finds a precedent for this fetishistic theory of fetishism in the work of Leo Bersani and Ulysse Dutoit, who also reinvent the phallus as a fetish which cannot be a phallic symbol. Echoing them, de Lauretis argues that unlike the lesbian fetish, the phallic symbol "stands for an actually perceived penis" (de Lauretis 1994b, 225), inverting the Lacanian psychoanalytic explanation of the penis as a fetish which stands for the phallus. She requires this fetish to signify the difference and even the mastery (the ideal or lovable self) which structures desire, but by severing it from the phallus as the signifier of lack, she makes difference and mastery unthreatening, leaving the couple completely satisfied with and as the other in whom they see themselves whole.

Separating off and repudiating lack, de Lauretis sutures the split subject of psychoanalytic theory to produce the lesbian couple as a narcissistic machine very like Irigaray's feminine imaginary. In what is finally a Hegelian model of subjectivity, feminine object-choice sublates feminine identifications and heterosexual desires, negating and synthesizing them into a higher unity, a new and transcendent identity which absorbs each object's otherness through love as reciprocal recognition. Emphasizing the other as the good object, de Lauretis substitutes the togetherness of the lesbian bar for the Lacanian slash, which fetishistically bars the violence of the cut severing the subject from the object as a part of itself, creating difference. An imaginary apparatus for the production of lesbian egos, the bar facilitates the assimilation of differences along with the Chianti, the differences of the desiring object relation that disrupt it and divide the coupled subject in a break-up of loving identity, turning it into masquerade. Those differences symbolize the lack which creates discord in the most harmonious object relation, even transforming the fetish into a phobic object in which the subject would not recognize herself. However, the disavowed and repressed signifiers of a potentially castrating difference continue to haunt the lesbian couple, returning as symptoms or delusions which testify to lack and the desire which is its metonymy. The lesbian/feminine ego ideal defends itself from this desire through fetishism because its self-mastery is menaced. Ultimately, the cause of desire is a lack for which there can be no imaginary compensation because it moves the subject beyond a calculus of profit and loss, disrupting the apparatus of any ego, including that of the lesbian.

The return of such disavowed and repressed differences is manifest in the film de Lauretis considers at length, Sheila McLaughlin's *She Must Be Seeing Things* (1987), and in the conference discussion which followed the paper she delivered on it (they have been published together in *How Do I Look?*). De Lauretis's essay concentrates on lesbian fantasy without addressing the film's inscription of racial difference because, she argues, the film itself does not allow one to deal with it "beyond locating it as a problem" (de Lauretis 1991, 264). The discussants repeatedly return to questions of race until de Lauretis defensively asserts that everyone is avoiding the issues she did raise in her paper, "the difficulties and problems in representing lesbian sexuality ... difficulties and problems that clearly exist for white lesbians as well as lesbians of color. So that it seems as if the specificity of lesbian sexuality must remain unspoken or unspeakable" (de Lauretis 1991, 272). In fact, what de Lauretis finds unspeakable is difference within "lesbian sexuality," in this case, the difference of race, the specificity of which she believes she has already spoken about as "lesbian specificity." Confronting racial difference, the coupled subject splits into its raced components, those "white lesbians" and "lesbians of color" in the film and audience to whom de Lauretis refers who do not equally reflect her identity and some of whom refuse her interpellation. The phallicism of lesbian fetishism reveals itself in the aggression and anxiety which are the other face of what de Lauretis has depicted as beneficent and benevolent, a defense mechanism the function of which, as such, she has denied.

The lack the film's protagonists, Jo (a white femme) and Agatha (a black, Brazilian butch), would disavow or repress returns in their shared fantasies or "visions" of white women, white men, and their "dildos." Each woman is, in her own way, "seeing things." Agatha hallucinates Jo's infidelities with white men when she spies on Jo or snoops into her belongings, but she also envisions social justice in Latin America, a dream which she hopes to realize through her practice of law. Jo's visions are brief daydreams of sex with white men and a long, and very complex fantasy represented by the film version she directs of Thomas de Quincey's *The Spanish Military Nun*, the story of Catalina, a seventeenth-century Spanish woman who escapes from a convent, cross-dresses, and saves a woman with whom she may be in love from two men who have a murderous quarrel over her. We see occasional scenes from this film, including its final rescue sequence, which also serves as the resolution of *She Must Be Seeing Things* itself, and which de Lauretis characterizes as the lesbian "primal scene" of origin (since the fight between the men breaks out while one of them is having sex with the woman Catalina saves). There are no people of color visible in any of these fantasies (that is, there are no bodily or other cultural signifiers of racial difference, as there are in Agatha's case). This is symptomatic of the disavowal and repression of Agatha's own racial difference, which is inextricable from her sexual difference and which comes to signify castration for both of them as they negotiate their relationship and identities in their practice of love. Lesbian fetishism takes the form of racialized sexual fetishism in the film and de Lauretis's reading of it; racial difference is finally what both negates and creates lesbianism itself as de Lauretis has theorized it.

According to de Lauretis, Jo's film is a fantasy she shares with Agatha, although it is "enunciated" by Jo as the film's director (and at least in part by de Quincey, since it is based on his novel, and by the actors and technicians who collaborate with Jo in the making of the film). Explaining what makes it a joint production, de Lauretis first tells us the film is put together by Jo as "a *figure of her desire* for Agatha " (de Lauretis 1991, 228). At that point, when de Lauretis says, "Catalina represents Agatha" (de Lauretis 1991, 228), we understand her to mean "for Jo," since Agatha has not created this sign of herself for herself. Yet de Lauretis goes on to emphasize Agatha's spectatorial identification with "Jo's fantasy," following Laplanche and Pontalis on the spectator position as one of the ways of being in a fantasy which marks it as one's own, even though it appears to be enunciated by some other. De Lauretis therefore concludes that "the Catalina primal fantasy is shared by both Agatha and Jo" (de Lauretis 1991, 231). However, when she elaborates on this, she implies she is countering our assumption the fantasy really has been Agatha's, rather than Jo's. "[I]t only *apparently* refers to Agatha alone, thematically and in its setting (the Spanish locale, Catholicism, Catalina's cross-dressing)," she writes; "Jo is as much the subject of the Catalina fantasy, a subject present and participating, if in a 'desubjectivized form'" (de Lauretis 1991, 231–2), a phrasing which recalls the occluded clause, "as Agatha is." But de Lauretis has constructed the preceding argument as if to persuade us the fantasy is as much Agatha's as it is Jo's, since Agatha is only "addressed" by it, whereas Jo "enunciates" it, making it up "with absorbed, passionate involvement" (de Lauretis 1991, 231). This confusion of address and enunciation ("you" and "I") characterizes the imaginary but is also the vehicle for an implantation and incorporation of signifiers from the symbolic (the fantasy itself). It is an instance of the "inmixing" of subjects Lacan theorizes and suggests the transformative power of identification through interpellation, in which the other changes the self, something most discussions of identification ignore when they explain it only as an annihilation of the other by the narcissistic self.

Perhaps the most compelling evidence that Jo and Agatha share the fantasy is a structural one engineered by the film itself as a fantasy about their fantasies, which it arranges and frames: as de Lauretis points out, "[T]hroughout the film, all the scenes with Catalina are crosscut with shots of Agatha" (de Lauretis 1991, 228). "Jo's fantasy" is in effect a "reply" to Agatha's, whose fears and desires centering on Jo are "worked through" by *Catalina* and resolved in its last sequence, the lesbian primal scene, answering the question of Jo's desire which Agatha's paranoid jealousy clearly raises: "What does she really want from me?" However, Agatha's fantasies are themselves a reply to Jo's, not only those her film suggests, but also the substance of her daydreams, which Agatha quite accurately guesses, gleaning it from both legible clues and insignificant details. These range from Jo's diary entries concentrating on her sexual history (there is even a photo of one lover's penis) to a certain look in Jo's eyes when they are in bed together (in one such scene early in the film, when Agatha asks Jo what she was thinking about, Jo responds with a half-truth, saying her mind was on Catalina, although she has been fantasizing about Richard too). After they watch the ending of *Catalina*, Agatha tells her it is very good. She and Jo are framed together in a mirror in the screening room and each smiles at the other, as if in happy agreement that their problems are over along with the film; then they move out of the mirror to the "real world" outside, where they run into extreme long-shot in the night, accompanied by a "jazzy" soundtrack, in what is a classic movie finish. Jo's film has apparently "cured" Agatha of her paranoid jealousy and supplanted Jo's own earlier fantasies about heterosexuality.

It seems the phallus – or at least the father's penis – as the signifier of castration has been abolished, as each recognizes the other as her desire. This penis has been an issue in the film as the heterosexual desire which interrupts not only the idealization but the very realization of the lesbian coupled-subject and suggests the meaning of the woman's difference is castration, as de Lauretis herself notes (de Lauretis 1991, 239), albeit a castration in the anatomical sense it generally has for Freud. However, it is not simply a question of whether Jo wants a penis, as her daydreams and diary entries appear to suggest; it is also a question of whether Agatha desires one, if not "for" Jo, then for herself, and why that penis must be white. The wish for a penis for Jo might be indicated by Agatha's "butch" identity, which is often read as a lesbian "masculinity complex" by psychoanalysts and others, and which in this case also might be supported by fantasies of black hypervirility and a US history of "true womanhood" as white femininity, which makes it difficult for black women to be perceived as "femme" and casts them in the role of "stud," as B. Ruby Rich, Jackie Goldsby, Alycee Lane and others have remarked. The film explores the issue of Agatha's masculinity when Jo asks if she ever wanted a cock shortly after performing a (semi-comic) striptease for her. Agatha first admits that she sometimes has, then insists she has never wanted to be a man, adds with a half-smile that she is a misogynist because the Church taught her to hate women, and finally concludes by claiming she did not desire her father but identified with him and the practice of law (he too is a lawyer), a series of comments whose vacillations and ironic tones clearly signal disavowal.

Does she or doesn't she? Not surprisingly, Jo playfully asks to see "it," a request which Agatha refuses. Although both have treated the whole thing as something of a joke, just a few scenes later, Agatha makes a trip to a sex shop where she looks over several dildos, lingering only over the white ones, in particular the dildo whose dimensions suggest it is a fantasy phallus, a fetish at once sexual and racial.[14] The music, the setting, and her behavior all mark this as a much more serious (even "gothic") matter than it seemed in the conversation with Jo, a sign that Agatha finds herself a rival with white men, and is anxious lest she be "caught short," as Lacan puts it (Lacan 1978, 104). Even if the black woman has the phallus (and if black people "really are" hypermasculine, they might), it would not be a white phallus, which is evidently the one Jo wants. Agatha only determines not to buy the dildo after watching a white man purchase a blonde, blow-up "judy" doll. A fetish and a caricature of the white woman, as the dildo is of the white man, it is literally deflated before her eyes, reduced to a mere instrument of male pleasure; its phallic pretensions, and through them, the man's, are revealed as such. Both fetishes lose their charm: the incident has an anamorphic effect like that of the skull in Holbein's *The Ambassadors*. Agatha sees that something is awry in this picture and removes herself from its scene, leaving the shop without purchasing anything. Nevertheless, just a few days later she prepares tongue for Jo and herself while joking about the dish of bull's balls her grandmother used to make another reminder of her ethnic "difference," but a difference which is insistently fetishized and linked to the question of virility by the film.

If Agatha's paranoid jealousy seems relatively "rational," given Jo's daydreams about heterosexual encounters, its delusional dimension suggests that irrational desires may be at stake, desires Agatha, rather than Jo, has denied, which psychoanalysis explains can return in the real as hallucinations. Classical psychoanalytic theory locates the cause of paranoia and jealousy in a homosexuality which seems to threaten castration and from which the subject defends himself through a variety of mechanisms, including projection, negation, and reversal into the opposite.[15] As a result of these, desire takes the form of a sentence such as the following: "I (a man) do not love him; she does." In Agatha's case, however, it is heterosexuality which must be denied and projected on to Jo, a denial which is constitutive of lesbianism in de Lauretis's theory and has been discussed as such by other queer theorists, including Lynda Hart and Peggy Phelan (1995, 227). The sentence which expresses the denial is very queer indeed from a normative perspective: "Agatha does not love the father/man; Jo does – Agatha identifies with him" (of course, if Agatha has made a masculine identification, then she is still denying homosexuality). But it is perfectly in accord with psychoanalysis, since, as Freud notes, "[F]rom the point of view of psychoanalysis the exclusive sexual interest felt by men for women is also a problem that needs elucidating and is not a self-evident fact" (Freud 1962, 123). The fact that the man in Agatha's (as well as Jo's) fantasies is always white could be a symptom of the part played by race in Agatha's psychic defenses: "Agatha does not love the father; Jo does, and he is not Agatha's father in any case because he is white." The desire to abolish the father who signifies castration returns as an anxiety about whiteness (and a whiteness with a possible metonymic link to the paternal phallus), which is present in all of Jo's fantasies, but lacking in Agatha herself.

If Agatha has a white identity in Jo's fantasies, then Jo is indeed "seeing things," disavowing or repressing a key component of Agatha's symbolic identity, which Agatha must also misrecognize. Through the lens of Jo's film (her gaze), Agatha must see herself in white people of early modern Spain, displacing her postcolonial present by the colonizer's past (Brazil is historically linked with Portugal, and through it to Spain, which itself has colonial ties to other South American countries bordering on Brazil). The Oedipal rescue fantasy of saving the white mother substitute from the white father, which Jo has "for" Agatha, gives the latter a white man or woman to identify with and a white woman to desire in the primal scene that de Lauretis argues structures her lesbianism and restores her ideal femininity. Jo interpellates Agatha as white, a whiteness unmarked by the history of imperialist and racist oppression, which is displaced on to the Church's oppression of women and lesbians. There is little difference between the women in the primal scene of the film: both are apparently white, Catholic, and Spanish. Through Catalina's eyes Jo would see herself as the desirable white femme, her femininity renewed. Yet that lack of difference between the women in the fantasy threatens a lack of desire – as de Lauretis points out, we do not know what will happen to the women after they leave the convent (de Lauretis 1991, 277); perhaps they only identify with each other.

In Agatha's paranoid fantasies, a question about desiring object-choice is raised, in which oppression returns as persecution, the fantasies and hallucinations of Jo's infidelity with white men. Why does Jo pretend she wants a black woman, Agatha, so Agatha will think she wants a white man, the "father" of the primal scene, when she really wants a white woman – or perhaps only wants to be a white woman – Catalina or the "mother"? All these are possibilities raised by the fantasy of the film within the film and Jo's feminine masquerade, which addresses Agatha as what she is not, a white man or woman, making the latter's identity a masquerade, rather than the real thing. It is Agatha's impossible white feminine identification with Jo which enables the latter's impossible white feminine object-choice but undermines the satisfied narcissism of the lesbian coupled subject through the non-reciprocity of their lacks. Castration ruptures lesbian *Verliebtheit*, in which each would see herself as lovable through the other she loves; however, it opens the

subject to desire, which is ultimately neither homosexual nor heterosexual, but queer, since its object is lost. What frustrates love (and
causes us to fall in love again) is something outside, rather than inside the
subject, that "Otherness within" without which there would be no subject
at all.

De Lauretis repeatedly grounds her theory in the work of Laplanche
and Pontalis, who argue that fantasy cannot fix an object or a subject
because it only represents the scene of desire, in which the subject has no
fixed place and may be present simply as a spectator or even in a
desubjectivized form, "in the very syntax of the sequence" (Laplanche and
Pontalis 1986, 26). Nevertheless, she reaffirms the "subject effect" of
fantasy and quotes Silverman to emphasize that point: "[A]lthough at the
deepest recesses of its psyche the subject has neither identity nor nameable
desire, the fantasmatic and the *moi* [ego] work to articulate a mythic but
determining vision of each" (de Lauretis 1994b, 144, n. 35).[16] It is not the
phallus which homogenizes but the imaginary content which seeks to
fill up and screen the lack phallic castration brings into being (including
the misrecognition of the penis as the phallus which our patriarchal
and heterocentric culture encourages). Silverman's words remind us all
identities are compromise formations, the symptoms which result from
negotiations between the imaginary ego and the desire of the Other, the
life drive and the death drive. Yet de Lauretis theorizes a lesbian fantasy
which would function as an apparatus for lesbian egos, something desire
renders impossible. The discussion following de Lauretis's essay on
MacLaughlin's film and the film itself reveal how the unexpected return of
disavowed or repressed desire queers the fantasy of an apparatus, opening
the subject to the self-difference that is a reply to the demands of the
Other.

It is that queer self-difference that Johnson emphasizes when she says
she will have to catch herself in the act of reading as a lesbian without
having intended it. Lesbian desire is at once something familiar and unknown, the effect of a call from the Other whose fantasy changes both self
and other if the subject receives it and responds, assuming the desire of the
Other as her own. Each subject in the object relation (mis)recognizes
herself in her alter ego as she finds herself looking at and through queer
spectacles. How will they inscribe alterity in their relationship? Will race
– or some other difference – occupy the place vacated by gender, as Rich
suggests it can (Rich 1993, 321)? Or will other differences inflect gender so
that there is a sexual difference even between women as a cause of desire
and the defenses against it, as I have argued? "The long looks between the
two women are looks across class, education, profession, and size,"
Johnson writes of the female protagonists of the manifestly straight film,

The Accused. "They fill each other's screen as objects of fascination, ambivalence, and transformation" (Johnson 1993, 163). The queer desire latent in this fantasy of "the eyes of the homo" makes manifest Johnson's own queer desire, as the women catch her eye with what she sees is just a masquerade of heterosexuality. Captivated by the gaze of the Other, she is photographed by it, and identifies with the picture of herself it seems to offer. The apparition of lesbianism appears. Beyond it there are other things to see, the ghostly presences of a desire that queers all identities, even queer identities, leaving the skeletons of old selves in our closets. Queer theory is a mandate to see such things; queer reading and writing demands that we attend to them, requiring, in Hart and Phelan's words, "an allegiance to the radicality of unknowing who we are becoming" (Hart and Phelan 1995, 277).

Notes

1   As such he may bring to crisis sexual difference itself, putting in question the pronoun which is appropriate for him. Jonathan Goldberg argues that the very hypermasculinity the cyborg bodies of Arnold Schwarzenegger's body in *Pumping Iron, Terminator 1*, and *Terminator 2* feminizes him: "Making every inch of the body hard, having erections everywhere, entails a massive denial of the adequacy of the penis," (Goldberg 1995, 235–6). While Goldberg emphasizes the imaginary, phallic qualities of such cyborg bodies, Donna Haraway maintains that the cyborg refuses "seductions to organic wholeness through a final appropriation of all the powers of the parts into a higher unity" and is therefore beyond Oedipus and sexual difference, "a creature in a post-gender world" (Haraway 1994, 425). Haraway links imaginary totalities only to Oedipus, which is just one element in the psychoanalytic narrative of gender she critiques and less important for the structuring of sexual difference than the phallus and symbolic castration, which engage the notion of totality more directly than the Oedipus complex does. Here and elsewhere I explore how symbolic differences of sex, race, and class are aligned with the phallus and symbolic castration so as to consolidate or question imaginary bodies and identities – without which there can be neither a self nor desire. I do not believe subjects of hierarchized social distinctions are beyond the phallus or desire which would drive the affinity politics and other exchanges of the groups Haraway discusses. She offers no alternative to "desire" as an explanation of why such groups come together, why hierarchies continue to exist, and

how the gender hierarchy came to an end. Her cyborg is rather too like the fully conscious, rational, and intending thinking machine poststructuralist theory has critiqued as the Cartesian cogito, the very apparatus this essay questions, which is most often identified as masculine. For that reason, I will use the gendered pronoun "he" for the cyborg subject of the apparatus, although I will argue that social differences besides gender can be articulated with the phallus so that sometimes women can seem to "have" the phallus.

2   This is a common assumption of film theory of the 1970s and 1980s, including feminist work. For example, in her ground-breaking essay on masquerade, Mary Ann Doane conflates the masquerade of the film heroine with that of the spectator, who is able to have a critical distance from femininity because the character's exaggeration of it suggests she is playing a role with which she is not deeply identified: "The effectivity of the masquerade lies precisely in its ability to manufacture a distance from the image, to generate a problematic within which the image is manipulable, producible, and readable by the woman" (Doane 1981, 54). The woman in question here is the film heroine, such as Dietrich, with whose masquerade the spectator is assumed to identify as masquerade, rather than as genuine femininity. Doane does not consider whether the woman in the theater might find a heroine's presentation of femininity to be a masquerade because her own is at odds with it, a question an exploration of the issue of identification across class, race, nation, and sexuality might have addressed, something I consider at length in *Female Impersonation* (forthcoming from Routledge).

3   Mulvey did not elaborate a possible masochistic pleasure for women who identified with the bad object, the villainess who is punished when she cannot be rehabilitated, although the absence of masochism in her schema is striking. Undoubtedly this was because as a feminist she did not wish to align women with masochism, which is generally understood as victimage. For a discussion of the absence of masochism in Mulvey, see D. N. Rodowick, "The Difficulty of Difference." In *Hard Core*, Linda Williams argues that masochism is not a site of victimage, since the masochist has a great deal of control over the sado-maosochistic scenario. Her reading, shared by others, has implications for the other passive forms of the partial drives, such as exhibitionism, which may be equally active and powerful, something Kaja Silverman explores in her discussion of fashion and sumptuary law in "Fragments of a Fashionable Discourse."

4   "Better" was usually defined in terms of an "equal rights" notion of equal access to "universal" – First World, bourgeois, and, some would argue, ultimately masculine – subjectivity and its prerogatives.

5 Eve Sedgwick develops the idea of the "homosocial" in *Between Men* to describe the English-speaking West's homophobic and heterosexual patriarchy. For an argument that Irigaray's usage is itself homophobic, and therefore very unlike Sedgwick's deployment of what might seem a similar concept, see Craig Owens, "Outlaws."

6 Because Irigaray's imaginaries – both feminine and masculine – have characteristics more often associated with the symbolic, it is unclear whether other differences linked to those two orders would still be operational, such as the difference between the ideal ego, as the core of the ego developed during the mirror stage and therefore "properly" imaginary, and the ego ideal(s) as the source(s) of ego traits formed through subsequent and symbolic identifications (nor is it clear whether there would be a feminine super-ego with any relationship to the ego-ideal).

7 I discuss whether she is implicitly heterosexual later in the essay, when I consider the debates about object-choice and identification in de Lauretis's work on lesbian fetishism.

8 See Doane, "Woman's Stake"; see also Diana Fuss, *Essentially Speaking*, 55–72, and Naomi Schor, "This Essentialism Which Is Not One."

9 In fact, the feminine aesthetic linked to Irigaray – and sometimes to Hélène Cixous and Julia Kristeva – also has much in common with this avant-garde cinema practice, as Kuhn's essay suggests.

10 At a minimum, this difference would take the form of man's own castration or anxiety about it; Mulvey defers a discussion of what sexual difference "really" might be, which is the focus of Irigaray's work.

11 For critical reevaluations of modernism's feminist potential, see the work of Rita Felski, Jane Gaines, and Janet Wolff, among others. Two important books by Kristeva which focus on the semiotic are *Revolution in Poetic Language* and the essays collected in *Desire in Language*.

12 Lacan addresses interpellation in his analyses of psychosis. See his consideration of Melanie Klein's treatment of "little Dick," *The Seminar of Jacques Lacan*, Book I, 68–88; see also Book III, 281–323. Shoshana Felman discusses this material, 1987, 98–159. The "inmixing" of subjects is implicit throughout Lacan's discussions of interpellation. See also *The Seminar of Jacques Lacan*, Book II, 160, and Book III, 193–195, and Felman, 60–66.

13 De Lauretis mentions Fuss only in a note to the longer version of the essay which appears in her book, *Practice of Love*, 190, note 20. The Fuss essay in question is "Fashion and the Homospectatoral Look."

14   For more on dildos and fetishism, see Heather Findley and Parveen
     Adams.
15   See, for example, Freud's essay, "Certain Neurotic Mechanisms in
     Jealousy, Paranoia, and Homosexuality" (1963b).
16   Despite her recognition that "address is quite another thing from
     audience" (De Lauretis 1991, 228).

References

Adams, Parveen. "The Three (Dis)Graces." *New Formations* 19 (1993):
    130–8.
Artel, Linda and Susan Wengraf. "Positive Images: Screening Women's
    Films." *Issues in Feminist Film Criticism*. Ed. Patricia Erens.
    Bloomington: Indiana University Press, 1990. 9–12.
Baudry, Jean-Louis. "The Apparatus: Metapsychological Approaches to
    the Cinema." 1975. Trans. Jean Andrews and Bertrand Augst. *Narra-
    tive, Apparatus, Ideology: A Film Theory Reader*. Ed. Philip Rosen.
    New York: Columbia University Press, 1986. 299–318.
——. "Ideological Effects of the Basic Cinematic Apparatus." 1970. Trans.
    Alan Williams. *Narrative, Apparatus, Ideology: A Film Theory Reader*.
    Ed. Philip Rosen. New York: Columbia University Press, 1986. 286–98.
Bersani, Leo. *Homos*. Cambridge: Harvard University Press, 1995.
Bersani, Leo and Ulysse Dutoit. *The Forms of Violence: Narrative in
    Assyrian Art and Modern Culture*. New York: Schocken Books, 1985.
Bhabha, Homi. "The Commitment to Theory." *New Formations* 7 (1988):
    5–23.
Butler, Judith. *Bodies That Matter: On the Discursive Limits of "Sex"*.
    New York and London: Routledge, 1993.
——. *Gender Trouble: Feminism and the Subversion of Identity*. New
    York and London: Routledge, 1990.
——. "Imitation and Gender Insubordination." *Inside/Out: Lesbian
    Theories, Gay Theories*. Ed. Diana Fuss. New York and London:
    Routledge, 1991. 13–31.
Case, Sue-Ellen. "Towards a Butch-Femme Aesthetic." *Discourse* 11, 1
    (Fall–Winter 1988–9): 55–73.
Castle, Terry. *The Apparitional Lesbian: Female Homosexuality and
    Modern Culture*. New York: Columbia University Press, 1993.
Commoli, Jean-Louis. "Technique and Ideology: Camera, Perspective,
    Depth of Field" (Parts 3 and 4). 1971–2. Trans. Diana Matias et al.
    Narrative, Apparatus, Ideology: A Film Theory Reader. Ed. Philip
    Rosen. New York: Columbia University Press, 1986. 421–43.

Copjec, Joan. "The Orthopsychic Subject: Film Theory and the Reception of Lacan." *October* 49 (1989): 53–72.

De Lauretis, Teresa. "The Female Body and Heterosexual Presumption." *Semiotica* 67, 3–4 (1987a): 259–79.

———. *Technologies of Gender: Essays on Theory, Film and Fiction.* Bloomington: Indiana University Press, 1987b.

———. "Film and the Visible (Includes 'Discussion')." *How Do I Look?* Ed. Bad Object-Choices. Seattle: Bay Press, 1991. 223–76.

———. "Habit Changes." *differences* 6, 2–3 (Summer–Fall 1994a): 296–313.

———. *Practice of Love: Lesbian Sexuality and Perverse Desire.* Bloomington: Indiana University Press, 1994b.

Doane, Mary Ann. "Woman's Stake: Filming the Female Body." *October* 17 (1981): 23–36.

Edelman, Lee. "Homographesis." *Yale Journal of Criticism* 3, 1 (1989): 189–207.

Edelman, Lee. "Queer Theory." *Gay and Lesbian Quarterly* 2, 4 (Dec. 1995): 343–8.

Felman, Shoshana. *Jacques Lacan and the Adventure of Insight: Psychoanalysis in Contemporary Culture.* Cambridge, MA: Harvard University Press, 1978.

Felski, Rita. *Beyond Feminist Aesthetics: Feminist Literature and Social Change.* Cambridge, MA: Harvard University Press, 1989.

Findley, Heather. "Freud's Fetishism and the Lesbian Dildo Debates." *Feminist Studies* 18, 3 (Fall 1992): 563–79.

Freud, Sigmund. "Certain Neurotic Mechanisms in Jealousy, Paranoia, and Homosexuality." 1992. Trans. Joan Riviere. *Sexuality and the Psychology of Love.* Ed. Philip Rieff. New York: Collier Books, 1963a. 133–59.

———. "Fetishism." 1927. Trans. Joan Riviere. *Sexuality and the Psychology of Love.* Ed. Philip Rieff. New York: Collier Books, 1963b. 214–19.

———. *Jokes and Their Relation to the Unconscious.* 1905. Trans. James Strachey. New York and London: W.W. Norton & Co., 1963c.

———. *Three Essays on the Theory of Sexuality.* 1905. Trans. James Strachey. New York: Basic Books, 1962.

Fuss, Diana. *Essentially Speaking: Feminism, Nature, and Difference.* New York and London: Routledge, 1989.

———. "Fashion and the Homospectatorial Look." *Critical Inquiry* 18 (Summer 1992): 713–37.

———. "Monsters of Perversion: Jeffrey Dahmer and *The Silence of the Lambs.*" *Media Spectacles.* Ed. Marjorie Garber, Jann Matlock, and Rebecca L. Walkowitz. New York and London: Routledge, 1993. 181–205.

Gaines, Jane. "Women and Representation: Can We Enjoy Alternative Pleasure?" *Issues in Feminist Film Criticism*. Ed. Patricia Erens. Bloomington: Indiana University Press, 1990. 75–92.

Goldberg, Jonathan. "Recalling Totalities: The Mirrored Stages of Arnold Schwarzenegger." *The Cyborg Handbook*. Ed. Chris Hables Gray. New York and London: Routledge, 1995. 233–54.

Goldsby, Jackie. "What It Means to Be Colored Me." *Out/Look* 9 (Summer 1990): 8–17.

Grosz, Elizabeth. "Experimental Desire: Rethinking Queer Subjectivity." *Supposing the Subject*. Ed. Joan Copjec. London and New York: Verso, 1994. 133–57.

Haraway, Donna, "A Cyborg Manifesto: Science, Technology, and Socialist-Feminism in the Late Twentieth Century." *Theorizing Feminism: Parallel Trends in the Humanities and Social Sciences*. Eds. Anne C. Herrmann and Abigail J. Stewart. Boulder, CO: Westview Press, 1994. 424–57.

Hart, Lynda and Peggy Phelan. "Queerer Than thou: Being and Deb Margolin." *Theater Journal* 47 (May 1995): 269–82.

hooks, bell (Gloria Watkins). "The Oppositional Gaze: Black Female Spectators." *Black American Cinema*. Ed. Manthia Diawara. New York and London: Routledge, 1993. 288–302.

Irigaray, Luce. *Je, tu, nous: Toward a Culture of Difference*. 1990. Trans. Alison Martin. New York and London: Routledge, 1993.

——. *Speculum of the Other Woman*. 1974. Trans. Gillian Gill. Ithaca: Cornell University Press, 1985a.

——. *This Sex Which Is Not One*. 1977. Trans. Catherine Porter. Ithaca: Cornell University Press, 1985b.

Johnson, Barbara. "Lesbian Spectacles: Reading *Sula, Passing, Thelma and Louise*, and *The Accused*." *Media Spectacles*. Ed. Marjorie Garber et al. New York and London: Routledge, 1993. 160–6.

Kristeva, Julia. *Desire in Language*. Ed. Leon S. Roudiez. Trans. Thomas Gora et al. New York: Columbia University Press, 1980.

——. *Revolution in Poetic Language*. 1974. Trans. Margaret Waller. New York: Columbia University Press, 1984.

——. *Tales of Love*. 1983. Trans. Leon S. Roudiez. New York: Columbia University Press, 1987.

——. "Women's Time." 1979. Trans. Alice Jardine and Harry Blake. *The Kristeva Reader*. Ed. Toril Moi. New York: Columbia University Press, 1986. 187–213.

Kuhn, Annette. "Textual Politics." *Women's Pictures: Feminism and the Cinema*. London, Boston, Melbourne, and Henley: Routledge & Kegan Paul, 1982. 156–77.

Lacan, Jacques. *The Four Fundamental Concepts of Psycho-Analysis.* 1973. Trans. Alan Sheridan. New York and London: W.W. Norton & Co., 1978.

——. *The Seminar of Jacques Lacan: Book I. Freud's Papers on Technique, 1953–1954.* Ed. Jacques-Alain Miller. 1975. Trans. John Forrester. New York and London: W.W. Norton & Co., 1988a.

——. *The Seminar of Jacques Lacan: Book II. The Ego in Freud's Theory and in the Technique of Psychoanalysis, 1954–1955.* Ed. Jacques-Alain Miller. 1978. Trans. Sylvana Tomaselli. New York and London: W.W. Norton & Co., 1988b.

——. *The Seminar of Jacques Lacan: Book III. The Psychoses, 1955–1956.* Ed. Jacques-Alain Miller. 1981. Trans. Russell Grigg. New York and London: W.W. Norton & Co., 1993.

Lane, Alycee. "What's Race Got to Do With It?" *Black Lace* (Summer 1991).

Laplanche, Jean and Jean-Bertrand Pontalis. "Fantasy and the Origins of Sexuality. (Includes 'Retrospect, 1986')." 1964. *Formations of Fantasy.* Ed. Victor Burgin et al. London and New York: Methuen, 1986. 5–34.

Laplanche, Jean. *Life and Death in Psychoanalysis.* 1970. Trans. Jeffrey Mehlman. Baltimore and London: Johns Hopkins University Press, 1976.

Martin, Biddy. "Extraordinary Homosexuals." *differences* 6, 2–3 (Summer–Fall 1994): 100–25.

Mercer, Kobena. "Black Hair/Style Politics." *New Formations* 3 (1987):33–54.

Metz, Christian. *The Imaginary Signifier: Psychoanalysis and the Cinema.* 1977. Trans. Celia Britton et al. Bloomington: Indiana University Press, 1982.

Morrison, Toni, *The Bluest Eye.* New York: Washington Square Press, 1977.

Morse, Margaret. "What Do Cyborgs Eat? Oral Logic in an Information Society." *Culture on the Brink: Ideologies of Technology.* Ed. Gretchen Bender and Timothy Druckrey. Seattle: Bay Press, 1994. 157–89.

Mulvey, Laura. "Afterthoughts on 'Visual Pleasure and Narrative Cinema' Inspired by *Duel in the Sun.*" *Feminism and Film Theory.* Ed. Constance Penley. New York: Routledge, 1988. 69–79.

——. "Visual Pleasure and Narrative Cinema." 1975. *Feminism and Film Theory.* Ed. Constance Penley. New York: Routledge, 1988. 57–68.

Owens, Craig. "Outlaws: Gay Men in Feminism." *Men in Feminism.* Ed. Alice Jardine and Paul Smith. New York and London: Methuen, 1987. 219–32.

Penley, Constance. "Feminism, Film Theory and the Bachelor Machines." *m/f* 10 (1985): 35–59.

——. "Feminism, Psychoanalysis, and the Study of Popular Culture." *Cultural Studies*. Ed. Lawrence Grossberg et al. New York and London: Routledge, 1992. 479–94.

Phelan, Peggy. *Unmarked: The Politics of Performance*. London and New York: Routledge, 1993.

Rich, B. Ruby. "When Difference Is (More Than) Skin Deep. *Queer Looks: Perspectives on Lesbian and Gay Film and Video*. Eds. Martha Gever, John Greyson, and Pratibha Parmar. New York and London: Routledge, 1993. 318–39.

Robinson, Amy. "It Takes One to Know One: Passing and Communities of Common Interest." *Critical Inquiry* 20, 4 (Summer 1994): 715–35.

Rodowick, David N. "The Difficulty of Difference." *Wide Angle* 5, 1 (1982): 4–15.

Rosen, Marjorie. *Popcorn Venus: Women, Movies, and the American Dream*. New York: Avon Books, 1973.

Schor, Naomi. "This Essentialism Which Is Not One: Coming to Grips with Irigaray." *differences* 1, 1 (Summer 1989): 38–58.

Sedgwick, Eve Kosofsky. *Between Men: English Literature and Male Homosocial Desire*. New York: Columbia University Press, 1985.

——. *Epistemology of the Closet*. Berkeley: University of California Press, 1990.

Seidman, Steven. "Identity and Politics in a 'Postmodern' Gay Culture: Some Historical and Conceptual Notes." *Fear of a Queer Planet: Queer Politics and Social Theory*. Ed. Michael Warner. Minneapolis: University of Minnesota Press, 1993. 105–42.

Silverman, Kaja, "Back to the Future." *Camera Obscura* 27 (Sept. 1991): 108–33.

——. "Fragments of a Fashionable Discourse." *Studies in Entertainment: Critical Approaches to Mass Culture*. Ed. Tania Modleski. Bloomington: Indiana University Press, 1986. 139–52.

Spivak, Gayatri. "Can the Subaltern Speak?" *Marxism and the Interpretation of Culture*. Eds. Cary Nelson and Lawrence Grossberg. Urbana: University of Illinois Press, 1988. 271–313.

——. *The Post-Colonial Critic: Interviews, Strategies, Dialogues*. Ed. Sarah Harasym. New York and London: Routledge, 1990.

Stacey, Jackie. "Desperately Seeking Difference." *Screen* 28, 1 (Winter 1987): 48–61.

Traub, Valerie. "The Ambiguities of 'Lesbian' Viewing Pleasure: The (Dis)Articulations of *Black Widow*." *Body Guards: The Cultural Poli-*

tics of Gender Ambiguity. Ed. Julia Epstein and Kris Straub. New York and London: Routledge, 1991. 305–28.

Warner, Michael. "Homo-Narcissism; Or, Heterosexuality." *Engendering Men: The Question of Male Feminist Criticism.* Ed. Joseph Boone and Michael Cadden. New York and London: Routledge, 1990. 190–206.

——. "Introduction." *Fear of a Queer Planet: Queer Politics and Social Theory.* Ed. Michael Warner. Minneapolis: University of Minnesota Press, 1993. vii–xxxi.

Wiegman, Robin, "Introduction." *The Lesbian Postmodern.* Ed. Laura Doan. New York: Columbia University Press, 1994. 1–20.

Williams, Linda. *Hard Core: Power, Pleasure, and the Frenzy of the Visible.* Berkeley: University of California Press, 1989.

Willis, Susan. "I Want the Black One: Is There a Place for Afro-American Culture in Commodity Culture?" *A Primer for Daily Life.* London and New York: Routledge, 1991. 108–32.

Wolff, Janet. *Feminine Sentences: Essays on Women and Culture.* Berkeley: University of California Press, 1990.

Wollen, Peter. "Modern Times: Cinema / Americanism / the Robot." *Raiding the Icebox: Reflections on Twentieth-century Culture.* Bloomington: Indiana University Press, 1993. 35–72.

Chapter 7

André Gide and the Niece's Seduction

Naomi Segal

In this essay I want to try to set two semi-fictitious figures in front of each other. One is Gide, immobilized like any object of criticism or desire, with all the subtlety or flexibility in the figure he makes ambiguously accredited to the perceiver. The other is myself, undertaking a feminist analysis from a position which needs explanation and perhaps justification. I shall try to do justice to both the complexities of Gide's position in gender and sexuality and also the ambivalences of the critique I have directed at him. On what authority and with what aim can an anti-homophobic hetero-sexual-identified female critic work on Gide? What is feminism to do with gay men?

André Gide, who died in his eighties in 1951, is perhaps unique among a rich generation of French gay writers.[1] For one thing, unlike both Proust and Wilde, he believed it right and proper to speak of homosexuality in the first person,[2] though the ways in which he did so may seem very incomplete to readers of the 1990s. For another, his apologia for pederasty, based as it is in a Platonic tradition, seems to look both far back and uncannily forward in its strange combination of good citizenship, natural hedonism and pure masculinity. Gide is the 'straight man' of twenties gay creativity: he placed himself in more or less overt contrast to his contemporaries Wilde,[3] Proust and Cocteau in his rejection of the inversion theory and the varieties of [male] femininity which for him were true perversion (and hence loathsome). At the same time, he lived with and lived off the [female] feminine in a number of ways: the 'mystical orient' of his life was

his cousin Madeleine Rondeaux,[4] to whom he committed himself in early
adolescence when he learned of her mother's adultery, and whom he
married thirteen years later following the death of his own mother and just
a few months after he had euphorically discovered pederastic pleasure as
an emancipating identity. There seems little doubt that he had no sexual
contact with Madeleine; but twenty-eight years after they married, he
had a child with Elisabeth, the feminist daughter of his friend Mme Théo
van Rysselberghe – to his disappointment, it was a girl – and he lived
more often in the large apartment in Paris adjoining that of Mme Théo and
occupied from time to time by Elisabeth and their child and his onetime
lover, Marc Allégret, than in the family estate in Normandy where
Madeleine lived near her own extended family and waited for his visits.

And what of his desire? Gide's parents were bourgeois Huguenots, his
mother from a well-to-do business family in Normandy, his father a
southern-born academic.[5] His father died when he was eleven, and the
story of his upbringing is told by both himself and a string of biographers
as that of an isolated boy surrounded by strictly religious women, his
mother in particular, with her large square body, sideways unsmiling eyes
and embarrassing dress-sense, representing simultaneously all that is negative in a prescriptive and proscriptive religious education and all that
terrorizes western culture as a dominating feminine.[6] Madeleine appears to
have been her desirable substitute, the mirror in which he looked for his
own reflected face, the fixed point from which he continued to make his
limited escapes, the pole by which he measured creative emancipation.
With her went the same religion, more tenderly packaged but still
feminized as the soul which opposes the body. The wife in the house, the
spirit (in a more mystical than stringent guise now, or so he tried to make
it) possessing the body from within – what does the body do to escape
these? It dwells in closed rooms, at first, and learns of pleasure in the form
of sin, battling with the tireless 'temptation' of masturbation in a way we
can only gawp at nowadays. Later it absorbs itself in friendships of an
intellectually freer but still chaste kind – in his late teens and early twenties, when Madeleine was continuing to refuse his proposals, Gide describes himself as 'completely virgin and depraved'[7] – and it finally defines
itself in the discovery of real warmth and multiple pleasure in the wordless
embrace of a brown-skinned boy in the sand outside Biskra. He is horrified by penetrative sex, seeing in it only violence and predation in the
briefly evoked scene of his friend, Daniel, descending under a black coat
vampire-like over the frail body of an Arab boy. Gide comments:

> He laid him on his back, on the edge of the bed, at right angles;
> and soon I could see nothing but, on either side of the grunting

Daniel, two slim legs hanging down. . . . As for me, who can
only understand pleasure when it is face to face, reciprocal and
without violence, and who often, like Whitman, get satisfaction
from the most fleeting [*furtif*] contact, I was horrified both by
what Daniel was doing and by seeing Mohammed accept it so
obligingly.[8]

As an adult, he writes a solemn and frustrating journal explicitly aimed at
the public, for whom he begins to publish it from 1939, and a string of
fascinatingly direct and indirect fictions; he travels, cruises and roosts; he
plays mayor and juror in Normandy and amateur ambassador, sycophant
and critic in Africa and the USSR; and he preaches a strange kind of
sensual pleasure, that of *attente* (expectancy, waiting) which, along with
its psychological corollary of *disponibilité* (availability) is poised midway
between release and abstention.

Put all this together, and we find a man who seems to desire two things:
a feminine mirror he may both fix and abjure, and a masculinity he seeks
in the child who is by preference brown or bad or both.[9] He lives in
voluminous clothes, in which he 'settles himself' when he reclines to
read,[10] and embarrasses his friends in railway stations or cinemas by his
roving eye, his gawkiness, his habit of shedding underwear or losing
suitcases.[11] His second family call him 'the Bipede' [*sic*, pronounced
'Bypeed']. He argues, with Plato, that desire is something to do with
stopping short, pleasure is in *waiting*, and that the man–boy bond is
not indulgence or exploitation but pedagogic and educative, and yet in
his fictions the older man is always the more simple, even stupid, of the
two, and it is the knowing child who invites while the man holds back in
ignorance.[12] Just once in his writing an adult comes near to seducing a
child, with a hand slipped into the shirt-front then creeping further
down . . . – and the boy leaps away, tearing his collar, runs down to the
end of the garden, dips his handkerchief into the rainwater tank and rubs
his face, cheeks, neck and body to get rid of the contaminant touch – but
here the grown-up is a woman, the same adulterous aunt whose negative
figure guided him to the love of the pure girl-cousin.[13]

This pell-mell of details should suggest what a complex thing we
undertake when we look to any life, available only in texts made public by
the subject and others, in order to analyse the other's desire. But if to
apprehend is always to oppose (and knowing of course that nothing is less
innocent than a binary), let me begin by trying to arrange the elements of
Gide's life into a number of oppositions for us to think him by.

The first opposition is male/female. Female, his main educators and
some of his 'best friends'; female, his wife and his daughter; male, his
schoolfriends, his fellow writers and copious correspondents, and his

lovers – the last two groups seldom overlapped. Then class: Gide's rare
contacts with people other than wealthy middle-class intellectuals (Sartre
with fair justification despised his writing for being only about 'rich kids')
were tenants on his wife's estate and the boys he picked up. Colour
coincides with class here, for the latter were very often also non-French,
'mediterranean': Roman, Tunisian or Algerian street boys, or other children met on his travels. With the opposition masculine/feminine the picture becomes of course more complicated. It is tempting, and perhaps
convenient at least as a preliminary, to set up a chronological argument
here. In this scheme, up till 1918, when he fell in love with family friend,
Marc Allégret, thirty-five years his junior, who for the first time offered
Madeleine a rival for Gide's serious affections, gender seems to have
functioned along the lines of a conventional oedipal/Christian split: the
female/feminine as a mirror-soul in which perfection can be glimpsed and
aimed at, haunted of course by the horror of a sexuality which is its dimly
thinkable obverse; and the male/masculine as the body-self which exists
against it to rebel or be controlled, the universal 'us' of Goethe's 'das
Ewig-Weibliche zieht uns hinan [the eternal feminine draws us onward]'.[14]
After 1918 and the crisis which resulted from Madeleine's recognition of
Gide's new love, he begins work on Les Faux-monnayeurs (The Counter-
feiters, 1926), the first fiction in which there is, he claims, no version of her
as moral pole, and returns to Corydon (1911, 1920, 1924), in which the
feminine is what a good pederasty pushes aside, both in male inverts and
in the female consort who, as in the Greek idyll, is left free by her masters
to enjoy a chaste domesticity; here femininity no longer has, it seems, that
mirror-function in which Narcissus gazes and knows not if he desires
himself as boy or girl.

Then there are other oppositions. Jonathan Dollimore in his Gide/
Wilde dichotomy argues that it is Wilde who overturns the depth theory,
using paradox and play to advocate an aesthetic of surfaces, Gide who
holds to theories of depth-meaning and high seriousness.[15] Indeed, this is
true of both the periodically Christian Gide and the writer of Corydon,
whose apologia justifies a sometimes absurd argument by way of a
'deeper' masculinity of social and natural rightness. But it is not true of the
desiring Gide whose fantasy cleaves to the skin, to the pleasures of touch
or embrace,[16] and to a relation of pleasure with his own body which
remains primary in his encounters with others.[17] It is no chance that he
quotes in Corydon the dazzling aphorism of Chamfort that love in society
is 'the exchange of two fantasies and the contact of two epiderms'.[18] Gide's
sexual aesthetic is that of the sculptor for whom surface is not so much
the tease of a penetrative gaze – stone drapery suggesting an impossible
unveiling – but actually the only level there is, not thickness but a journey
of the two-dimensional line around a solid space. Let us oppose the Wilde

and Gide principles, then, not so much as theories of surface and depth but as two positions on the relation between skin and its covering. Just as it is impossible to conceive of Wilde unclothed, even in his imagined nudity, so Gide seems always to be reaching a clothed arm towards skin – and stopping there.[19] Sartre once wrote of the way in which [masculine] 'possession' occurs less by ingestion or penetration than by making a mark on a surface: the line of a skier, the mapped colony, the caress of a breast.[20] This, it seems, not penetration, is Gide's fantasy of possession: neither to 'take' nor to be 'be taken', but to be *allowed to touch*.

The body for Gide, then, is male and understood in specific transgression of the Christian *noli me tangere*. To touch one's own flesh – his first fiction, *Les Cahiers d'André Walter* (*The Notebooks of André Walter*, 1891), bounces with the effort to resist this simple temptation, which the eight-year-old Gide first discovered to be a sin, he says, when he was suspended from school for masturbating and eating chocolates at the same time. And from this, another opposition: the flesh as own and other. Is it, when the pious adolescent resists or chastises the desire to masturbate (we have a similar drama in the life of the young Anna Freud),[21] the body as self or as other that is being desired? Gide speaks, here and later, of transgressive desire personified as the demon, specified as 'l'Autre',[22] and we can, I think, assume that in touching or resisting touching his penis he is dividing his self into two along the castratory lines of a familiar Freudian prohibition. For him, at the same time, masturbation implies a more specific and perhaps unusual question. Temptation resisted is temptation repeated. It may often be that what is fantasized and refused is a one-act drama, the arc of a rise which ends in detumescent orgasm. But Gide was multi-orgasmic, as he joyfully affirms in his autobiography.[23] Perhaps, then, we are to understand the pleasure/unpleasure of masturbation as sin to be the fear of unstoppable repetition, a series of rises and falls, the impossibility of release from desire once it is started, or the very undirectedness of that series, which, having no other, may have no end. He writes of the terror of spending himself to the point of idiocy or insanity – that is the only closure he can conceive for his surrogate, André Walter, who dies mad. Fluidity, the flow of release, may in itself be the fear,[24] as we recognize from the imaginary of our folktale heritage, with its stories of sorcerers' apprentices, boys or girls who cannot halt the discharge of the magic porridge pot until the sudden intervention of the parental Other turns the spell off again.

Along with the desire of the skin, then, is the desire/fear of repetitious flow. In Gide's texts, in the place of couples, we often have a different kind of plurality, for the 'innocent' man rarely follows the beckoning boy to consummation; rather, a chain of male others, or of way-stations in some unmarked search, is stoppable only in *Le Voyage d'Urien* (*The Voyage of Urien*, 1893), *Les Nourritures terrestres* (*Fruits of the Earth*, 1897) or *L'Immoraliste* (*The Immoralist*, 1902) by the advent of a female figure who puts an end to the movement of language or desire. In *Les Faux-monnayeurs* – and even pointing out the end of the text – there is always a younger boy not quite within reach. As in the pederastic tradition, the succession of lovers will continue as long as only beardless youths can be desired, for each child is disqualified for love when he becomes a man;[25] but more children will be born as the lover himself grows old. To turn around Lacan's pessimistic dismissal of heterosexual intercourse, in pederasty, it seems, there is no couple.

If, then, this sexuality looks to an other while still always also being turned towards the self, how can we understand those kinds of sameness and difference that are being sought at the instant of desire? All the evidence I have offered so far of Gide's modes of desire shows that, in seeking an other he wanted a body that would both endorse and espouse his own, skin to skin, and yet also be that other by which he could position his subjectivity: man to boy, white to black, middle-class traveller to Arab servant, educator to wild child. These figures may perhaps not be so very different, as processes, from either his desire of the unsexualized female other, or of the pleasure and risk involved in solitary masturbation, whether directly narcissistic or joined to fantasy.

In all these oppositions, I have not yet broached the most obvious one: homosexuality/heterosexuality. Central without being at all clearcut, it is difficult to situate the opposition in Gide's life. He proposes to resolve it by a sharp genderizing split between the deep, pious and lasting love, which was unsexual and female-directed, and sexual desire, impermanent, promiscuous and skin-deep, which was directed only towards boys. But as his love for Marc Allégret and his fathering of a child illustrate, the dichotomy does not hold, or not for long. And this problem raises another issue, in which we can no longer understand desire as wholly connected to sexuality. Gide is a man who appears to have needed – and as a powerful person to have been able to have – homosexuality and heterosexuality in equal measure, located in a number of centres and theoretically kept apart (so that one did not properly know of the other) and exemplarily suspended both in the writing and speaking life.

For this, after all, takes place now in language, since its events are past and have left only a trace to know them by. What I want to suggest is that there are issues here over and above the universal grave-robbing of the reader's relation to text. What are the motives and what if any are the rights of my plunder of this dead matter?

One answer, the less conscious, is a motive of sexual voyeurism, and I will come to that later. The other is conscious, and engages fundamentally with theoretical questions of the relation between a feminist reading, undertaken as a critique of masculinity in culture, and the textual object of a gay male writer.

However overtly confessed, feminist criticism of male-authored writing is an oppositional activity, acquiring by its own logic a triumphalism wholly different from the euphoria that belongs to what Elaine Showalter once called 'gynocritics' – the rediscovery, identification and explication of female-authored texts. That the political difference is something to do with canonicity is proved by the rather more complicated task that faced the 'gynocritic' of George Eliot or Virginia Woolf; in the latter readings, something of feminism's second-decade discovery of its own divisiveness began early. In the feminist reading of men's writing we find the joys of a now inverted chase – we the hunters, they the prey, and psychoanalysis the undisprovable method for highlighting the murkier areas of their 'unthought'. Their fear, envy and bitterness against women, unpleasant enough to read, has been endlessly pleasurable to expose.

It is important to recognize, I think, that this counter-attack, justified still by millenia of prejudice and oppression, remains pleasurable even when the feminist critic understands that she is among the relatively privileged of her sex, is perhaps being paid (by men and others) to carry it out in conditions of fair comfort, and that not only is there no such simple thing as 'us' and 'them', but there never was. I still want to muscle in on/ grub inside/ tease the secrets out of male writing: it is a Zuyder Zee which is far from cleared. But the conditions are irrevocably changed. Feminists can no longer claim an innocent triumphalism. We know too much about our own complicities and the complexities of any position on any spectrum of power.

In Gide, I want to argue, I am facing a very complicated knot of differences. He was wealthy, leisured, white and culturally assured from childhood. When he travelled, published or seduced, it was as a powerful man. Nowhere in his writings does one discover a voice unsure of its right to be heard; he is, in other words, always masculine. His masculinity operates in relations with a variety of others – women, black people, children, working-class people, readers, animals, posterity – whom he holds in a position of distance coloured sometimes by respect, sometimes by desire, sometimes by a rarely admitted contempt (his unashamed antisemitism is an exception to the latter modesty). This mastery is a fascinating mixture of pedagogy and coquetry; he is the ideal target for a feminist critic, who seeks an address not meant for her and disinters exactly how it is not meant for her. But in other ways he is vulnerable in the way that women are vulnerable. As a hysteric, as a Protestant, as someone whose body, voice and appearance drew embarrassed attention in public places – but much more than this, as a homosexual.

There is no doubt that Gide put his reputation on the line by certain more or less overtly confessional texts – far more directly than Wilde, Cocteau or Proust, however much these others may have been voluntarily or involuntarily outed. And any heterosexual critic retains a privileged position in relation to that, woman or not, which demands due recognition and respect. But what interests me most about Gide are the ways in which his power-position (his *masculinity*) functions within the writing of his homosexuality. The unusual material he affords is that of a gay man who deals overtly with femininity as his other, whether it resides in women, men or himself and whether he commands/contains it in action or in fiction. If all first terms of a binary necessarily parasitize the second, if masculinity is that thing which lives off and out of femininity (again, understanding the latter as immanent anywhere) and if it is the job of feminism to continue asking after the place of the feminine – then how does this gay man live off and out of the feminine in the texts he has left us to read him by?

With his usual charm, Leo Bersani has recently confessed that many gay men do not much like women, in a 'more or less secret sympathy with heterosexual male misogyny'.[26] Of course this is true and it is true in an inevitably more complicated way than the (already labyrinthine) way in which heterosexual men dislike women. The man who valorizes the phallus in himself and his love-object, has the woman as potential rival and, with a feminist heterosexual woman, will also have her as critic, dedicated to the devalorization of what he prizes.[27] The word 'femininity' occurs no more than once in *Homos* (on p. 111), but it is implied and exploited everywhere. For where some gay men get off on the 'suicidal ecstasy of taking their sex like a woman' (p. 19), they are living a fantasized femininity which has no more exact relation to the female body than to their own – less, indeed, since those conventional aspects of womanhood which are less sexually suicidal, like the wish for endorsement at the price of pastoralization, are roundly condemned. Femininity for Bersani, then, is a privileged signifier as long as it occurs in men, that is, in gay men, and only in certain gay men, at certain moments. It has to do with positionality conceived very literally rather than politically. The woman's position, taken by a man, confers a familiarly masculine pride.

Gide does something different but no less absolute. He too robs women of their fire in the name of a deviant masculinity. But to say this is to highlight only one side of the interest he offers feminism. The feminine exists in his texts differently both from the traditional between-men operation of heterosexual, homosocial writing, and from the other kind of exclusion/exploitation that we find, say, in Bersani or Genet. He relies on women's feminine as a measure of something else which is not women's and not feminine but he does it in the name of a different kind of sexuality (that of the surface) and a different kind of relationality (familial but not oedipal).

Feminism has grown up rather conventionally since it sprang full-grown and aged about twenty in 1970. Quarrels with father and (differently, of course) with mother have given way to other explorations of generational relations. We theorized (late) maternity and now we are theorizing the menopause. Of course we also talked siblings and other differences, but essentially (*pace* Deleuze and Guattari), oedipus held pretty solid, and the relation between generations was still comprehensible on a model of the domestic incest motive. None of this has gone away; it still remains to be dissected.[28] But with the advent of lesbian, gay and queer studies, the differences have become different. Who inherits now?

I would like to suggest that lesbian/gay/queer studies offers the feminist critique a possible model of relationality which is neither vertical nor genealogical, and a conception of the communicativeness of desire – love, pedagogy, or pollution – that has little to do with inheritance. Such models do not exactly abandon the profit motive of the reproductive family, but necessarily turn it aslant. They are unlikely to do without triangularity, but perhaps they are abandoning the shortest distance between the three points.[29] Generations without generation: this is what the homosexual model can offer a feminist analysis of power.

Gide exceeds (or perhaps more precisely evades) the oedipal pattern by taking a sideways step away from the parent/child plot to that of uncle/nephew.[30] There is a well-trod history for this: it is no coincidence that bastardy so often hid its shame under a supposed uncle–nephew relation, nor that Gide took the family romance theme of bastardy from Romanticism, updating Julien Sorel's quest for a new *nom du père* into the much sexier Lafcadio and his entourage of educating uncles.[31] The masculine chain that I mentioned earlier is different from the genealogical one: not so much by circular or triangular links but by the mini-war of the chess-board, it crosses generations in a knight's move. Being seduced by your much older cousin (effectively an uncle, and with the permission of your mother, who sees in him a loving educator with no taint of exogamy) is safe sex. Plato would have approved. The avuncular embrace grounds a social-economic system of nepotism in something pedagogic, not incestuous. While Romanticism started off at least in explaining incest as the only true innocence – in *Paul et Virginie* (1788) and *Atala* (1801) Bernardin de Saint-Pierre and Chateaubriand designed colonial Edens where everyone had access to 'those ineffable unions, when sister was bride to brother, love and fraternal friendship mingled in the same heart and the purity of the one increased the delights of the other'[32] – Gide brings back chastity to desire by a different family relation. But only on one side of the gender variable. The seducing aunt is a horror and a danger – for the same reason that colonists of sexuality always take more care to control women's transgressions: because we are vessels. The image of dirt in the scene from *La Porte étroite* quoted earlier here connects in perhaps an unexpected way with the horror of Daniel's vampiric 'possession' of Mohammed. Both pass into a forbidden space something pollutant called femininity.

The French term for a 'queen' is *tante* (aunt). Gide's repulsion from the seductive aunt in both senses is a fear of the feminine in desire which makes it something other than chaste, socially justified and skin-deep. Penetration, as we are all too aware, is not safe. To be so it requires either an extra skin of rubber or a monogamy so certain that it is almost familial – and here we smile knowingly at the poverty of the trust any of us might still naïvely attribute to the family relation. In a world so permeable that we no longer define crime/work/sex etc. as that which happens outside the four walls of domesticity,[33] where is the safe space? Love and cleanliness? Manliness? Is that what Gide is telling us?

Telling us? In *Les Nourritures terrestres*, the narrator addresses a named narratee, Nathanaël, in a familiar blend of tease, instruction, arousal and evasion, framed at start and finish by the exhortation to 'throw this book away, leave me, go out and live/let me live instead'.[34] If not the desired boy, then whom? Refusing the aunt's seduction, Gide clearly did not intend to seduce any nieces.[35]

And here I think we can place the sexual motive of the feminist reading. There is a seductive tease in not being addressed by a writer's desire, especially if that desire is the only point of the text where need escapes from prideful decorum – I shall return to this later. Where Gide lets himself momentarily look a fool – as who does not when addressing the beloved, all the more if that beloved is unknown – we can catch him satirically, and knowing ourselves outside the circuit of that appeal, be as ruthless as we like without the usual risk of offence to the vanity of men. But, vulnerable for his moment, is he then still the enemy? I have not yet decided this. Gide's unselfconscious lust, lust of the skin for his pastoral Amyntas, both affirms and breaks him as a man. Does he ever lose face? He looks like 'a criminal or a madman',[36] but is neither outlawed nor abashed. He never drops his guard because he never quite needs to. If, as I suggested earlier, the thing he is not letting himself lose is still his masculinity; then perhaps this can only be understood in terms of his final inability to desire.

This undesire may be made clearer if we look at a scene from near the

beginning of *La Porte étroite* (1909). Alissa's adulterous mother has just
left home and her uncle, a pastor, is preaching:

> Alissa was sitting a few rows in front of me. I could see her
> face in profile; I gazed at her, so forgetful of myself that it
> seemed, as I listened in desperate intensity to those words, that
> I was hearing them through her. – My uncle was sitting next to
> my mother, weeping.
>
> The pastor had begun by reading the whole verse: *Enter ye
> in*
> *at the strait gate: for wide is the gate and broad is the way that
> leadeth to destruction, and many there be which go in thereat.
> Because strait is the gate, and narrow is the way, which leadeth
> unto life, and few there be that find it.* Then, dividing up his
> subject, he began by speaking about the broad way. My mind
> took off and as if in a dream, I saw the door to my aunt's
> room; I saw my aunt reclining there, laughing; I saw the
> brightly-clad officer laughing with her ... and the very idea of
> laughter and joy became wounding,[37] outrageous, seemed like
> the hateful excessiveness of sin.
>
> *And many there be which go in thereat*, continued pastor
> Vautier; then he described and I saw a crowd of people all
> decked out, laughing and processing in festive mood, forming a
> cortège in which I knew I could not, would not find a place
> because every step I might have taken with them would have
> parted me further from Alissa. – And the pastor came back to
> the beginning of the text, and I saw that narrow gate by which
> we must endeavour to enter. As I plunged deeper into my
> dream, I imagined it like a sort of rolling-mill in which I
> inserted myself with great effort and an extraordinary pain, in
> which however there was a foretaste of the bliss of heaven. And
> that gate [*porte*] became the very door of Alissa's room; in
> order to go in, I made myself smaller, emptied myself of all the
> egoism left in me ... *Because strait is the gate which leadeth
> unto life*, the pastor went on. And beyond all mortification, all
> sorrow, I imagined and sensed another kind of joy, pure,
> mystical and seraphic: already my soul was athirst for it. I
> imagined this joy like the song of a violin, at once piercing and
> tender, like a sharp flame in which Alissa's heart and my own
> were exhausted [*s'épuisaient*]. Both of us were striding forward,
> dressed in the white garments of the Apocalypse, hand in hand
> and gazing at the same goal ... What do I care if these childish
> dreams make you smile! I am retelling them without alteration.

Whatever may seem confused in them comes from the words
and the imperfect images that try to render an emotion which
was very precise.

'*Few there be that find it*', pastor Vautier concluded. He
explained how to find the narrow gate . . . '*Few there be*' – I
will be one of them . . .

I had reached such a pitch of moral tension by the end of the
sermon that, as soon as the service was over, I fled without
trying to see my cousin – out of pride, wanting to put my
resolutions (for I had already made some) to the test, and
believing that I would deserve her better if I went away from
her at once.[38]

As in the rest of this text, so in this passage, Jérôme – both as hero and
narrator, and he insists that the gap between the two is very small – is
doing his thinking and fantasizing via the imagined body of his cousin.
Staring at her face, he seems to hear and feel through her. A few pages
earlier, he discovered her mother's adultery and swore to censor and
protect himself from women's desire through the imagination of Alissa's
discovery, her horror and her need of protection. Now he enters a state of
mingled intensity and forgetfulness, this time more or less literally
channeled through her.

Readers of *La Porte étroite* will know how it appears to chart Alissa's
choice of the narrow path through a series of refusals and anorexias until
she dies alone in a grim little hospice room aware suddenly that she is
bereft not only of her rejected suitor but also of the seraphic surrogate,
God. A careful rereading will find all these motives originating in Jérôme,
from the opening scenes in which he divides their two mothers into the
scarlet and the black to his choice of travel and distance, his co-opting of
her reading and writing, his use of her as mirror and Echo even beyond the
grave. In the scene of the sermon, we see most clearly that the fantasies of
refusal, together with their justification, are his, and that their masculinity
operates purposefully through a series of images of the feminine.

The doors/gates are of course the doors to the two women's bodies. His
aunt's is wide open and everyone streams in to perdition. Alissa's is
narrow: you enter only by making yourself very small, detumescing the
ego, and the pain and bliss (yours, not hers) are equally intense. The
imagery of religious mortification is familiarly the pretext for a masochistic excitement, but there is more than simple masochism here.

Gide's texts are, I have suggested, informed by a sexualized ethic of
undesire. After all the imagery of penetration in and through Alissa,
Jérôme's first impulse is to go as far as possible away from her, in order to
'deserve her better'. This can be understood, of course, as his fundamental

wish to distance her, not to test his exploitation of her image against the resistance of a real other, but it is also a way of amplifying the pleasure by not knowing it. For what he is refusing to know here are the modes of desire which underlie his refusal of heterosexuality. There are, I think, five levels of the central image in the passage, and we need to take them one at a time.

Entry into the bad woman is easy and shocking. Entry into the good woman is an act for which one must become more narrow in the effort and almost two-dimensional in the execution. The imagery of pain surely suggests both the tension of *not* penetrating and also the sympathetic sensation of a fantasized rape which all the angelism cannot quite hold at bay. Remember the double identification with both Daniel and Mohammed, the former doing all the grunting, the latter remaining graceful and complaisant within an image of violent pain? Jérôme's fantasy here makes him both man and boy, and Alissa has become the place, the occasion, of that fear/desire of penetration.[39]

Three levels, then: the bad woman, the good woman and the anal penetration which follows from the image of feminine virtue and constraint. In the last of these images, all the anxiety of forbidden wishes multiplies, so that the 'I' is both the body and in the body, feeling and giving pain/pleasure; and so that (and this ambiguity remains problematic all through the *récit*) it is not clear whether the space is just wide enough for two or one. Then, on the fourth level, we sense that the whole *dramatis personae*, rooms and bodies, has disappeared. Angelism takes over. Like nativity play angels or Tamino and Pamina, the identical white dresses of the girl and boy stride through the 'exhausting' flame. This incongruous participle is not casual: it is used repeatedly in Gide for the depletion that follows masturbation. We surely sense in this imagery of the 'heavenly path', in which Alissa reappears as one of the seraphs who has made its way through her body, a scenario in which only self-pleasuring is left.

Finally, on the fifth level we find the typically Gidean way in which all of this disappears, the body itself disappears, and all that is left is the effort not to penetrate or be penetrated by desire. The only figure that remains, as Jérôme escapes with his angelism intact, is the abandoned shell of Alissa, whose conceivable thoughts or sensations have been crowded out by the path his thoughts have etched through her corporeality out into disincarnation.

In all these ways, the feminine provides the site and occasion of masculine desire/undesire. Opening and closing the gates into the female bodies, the Gidean narrator regulates a flow conditioned by constraint and refusal. Masculinity, in this scheme, is what is left when, purified by the tempering flame, all that other stuff has been consumed.

Gide was a notorious flirt. The term most commonly used by his friends is *'coquetterie'*. Pierre Herbart more precisely judges that all his actions were motivated by a fundamental wish neither to be disaappointed nor to disappoint. The flirtation is not always, or even mainly sexual: the 'furtive satisfaction' of his desire seems to have demanded less ceremony. He wanted, like many a star, to be loved severally but exclusively by all those whom his solipsism could magnetise.[40] But how authors operate with their acquaintances may not affect the fact that their books are instruments of seduction. The question is, when I read, how do I attend to that siren call voiced for or against me? Barthes wrote in 1973: 'the text is a fetish-object, *and this fetish desires me*'.[41] Peter Brooks, fourteen years later, exhorts us to 'refuse a text's demand in order to listen to its desire'.[42] The delight of one man and the suspicion of the other are both claims that the text, popping up out of its author's body's motive, smells me out with or without the aid of pheromones.

A feminist critic treads unwarily into the world of textual desire which, like sex, is rarely meant to go direct from gender to gender. Most published books are of course an intercourse between men. I would argue, however, *contra* Sedgwick,[43] that the man-man play of texts is only homosocial up to a point – it masks a *corps-à-corps* that climbs over Oedipus to murder the mother before, during and after the main course. They are not only passing the port. The reader who enjoys what was not written for her is a voyeur. When I deliberately overhear the tongue of Genet at work on his masculines and feminines, I am intervening on a kiss forbidden to a woman. Gide has better manners but he is also asking me to keep my lips closed when he speaks.

What is seduction anyway? What Strachey called by this term (Freud's original *'Verführung'* means very much the same thing) we may nowadays be more inclined to call rape or abuse. But each of those words is perhaps equally inappropriate for what may be a slow or sudden event involving a complex process of mixed coercion and consent. Whatever the detail, the term implies on the one side an element of resistance deemed appropriate and on the other an overcoming of that resistance considered equally appropriate – though in both cases the arbiter of appropriateness is the seducer alone. The latter blandishes, persuades, tickles or caresses; the seducee lets her-or himself be blandished, persuaded, etc. and eventually enters a state in which there is no going back and also no going forward. The process can only be carried out across a power differential, with resistance initially narrowing the space and capitulation fixing it either open or closed. One keeps their cool, the other succumbs. You may let yourself be seduced, but can you let yourself seduce? We find ourselves back here with the image of Gide's pederastic pedagogue, who seduces but pleads that he has been led to do so, that the brown-skinned child or laughing boy-scout was the one with the wiles and he, top-heavy with education, more taught-against than teaching.[44]

In the pederastic model of Gide's writing, the only place available, it seems, for the feminist critic is that of the niece whom it radically excludes. But we are unlikely to sit comfortably there. Everything in his turned about homosexuality has suggested how masculine authority remains intact in the role of author/uncle/pedagogue. Something in our non-negotiated contract makes me just as assertive. Intervening in a story in which I am not wanted, I am positioned as the niece but enter as the aunt. And this perhaps is the last theoretical point to emerge from this *corps-à-corps* between absentees. Consciously, I will not allow my critique to be between generations – neither he nor I is willing to play the child.

But unconsciously? I still have something in my hand. What role in this scenario belongs to the book as 'desiring object'? Like an artfully placed item in a window-display, it is in order to create and control my desire that it appears to solicit me. It invites me to break in, shoplift or incur debt – and all the while I will know that it wasn't for me after all (does it even fit?) because it comes as a message without any sender and whose receiver can only be arbitrary. If this is so, then is my seduction as unintended critic of Gide, which I practise without him, a rather exact copy of his seduction of himself in all those exhausting nights of resistance of his own flesh? He in his room, with chastity, heterosexuality and the Bible as his only defence, and I in mine, determined to catch him at it without exposing myself?

Notes

This essay is based on the preparatory work for my book *André Gide: Pederasty and Pedagogy,* to be published by Oxford University Press. Throughout this chapter, translations are my own and reference is given to the original-language text. Unless otherwise stated, all italics are the author's and all ellipses mine.

1   See Christopher Robinson, *Scandal in the Ink: Male and Female Homosexuality in Twentieth-century French Literature* (London and New York: Cassell, 1995).

2   See André Gide, *Journal 1889–1939* (Paris: Gallimard, 1951), p. 692: Gide reports on 14 May 1921 that Proust told him '"You can say everything . . . as long as you never say *I*." Which would not suit me'. In *In Memoriam: Oscar Wilde* (Paris: Mercure de France, 1910, 1989

p. 46, Gide reports Wilde's parting shot: ' "In art, don't you see, there is no *first* person." '

3   See Jonathan Dollimore, *Sexual Dissidence* (Oxford: Clarendon Press, 1991), Parts 1–3.

4   The cited phrase actually comes from Jean Delay, *La Jeunesse d'André Gide*, vol. I (Paris: Gallimard, 1956), p. 301; he purports to be quoting a sentence from Gide's autobiography *Si le grain ne meurt* (*If It Die*) in *Journal 1939–1949; Souvenirs* (Paris: Gallimard, 1954), where however it appears on p. 434 as 'nouvel orient' [new orient].

5   Gide was enough of a man of his time, conventionally influenced by Taine and Barrès, to take pleasure in the idea of being the crux of various imagined contraries across space and time: 'Nothing could be more different than these two families; nothing more different than these two provinces of France which conjugated their contradictory influences in me. I have often thought that I was forced into creative art because only it could harmonise such opposing influences which would otherwise have gone on battling or at least arguing inside me' (*Si le grain*, p. 358). But, as Jean Delay shows in Part I, chapter 9, the choreography of opposites derives more from desire than fact. Beside this fantasy, let me offer two alternative, more blatantly gendered ways of reading the family: Lautréamont's 'as handsome as the chance meeting on a dissecting table of a sewing machine and an umbrella' (from the *Chants de Maldoror*, in *Œuvres complètes*, vol. 1, ed. L. Genonceaux et al. (Paris: Corti, 1969, p. 327) and Woody Allen's 'I come from a mixed marriage: my father was a man and my mother was a woman' (from *Take the Money and Run*, 1969).

6   A whole book could be written about Gide's mother, whom critics and biographers universally describe in the terms of an aberrant 'virility' – that fatal combination in any Jocasta of ugly appearance and the disciplinary rod of iron – but whom Gide himself, having digested his resentments, evokes rather as a desperately girlish timidity harsher to herself than others. Cloaked in that hulking frame, is this not precisely the mother as *anima mulieris virili corpore inclusa*?

7   In his *Journal*, p. 33, March 1893.

8   *Si le grain*, pp. 595–6. The contrast Gide is drawing here is not entirely clear, since Daniel is obviously penetrating Mohammed from the front; the phrase 'face to face' (*face à face*) is, I think, meant to be understood literally: what he is expressing is a horror of the exclusive use of the lower body.

9   See *Si le grain*, p. 567: 'how beautiful he was! half naked under his rags, black and slim as a demon, his mouth open, his gaze wild'; or pp. 593–4: 'how then can I name my joy at clasping in my naked arms

that perfect little wild, ardent, lustful, shadowy [*ténébreux*] body? . . .', ellipses Gide's.

10   See Mme Théo van Rysselberghe, in her invaluable *Les Cahiers de la petite dame*, 4 vols (Paris: Gallimard, 1973–5), for instance vol. 1, p. 194: 'I can see him now, stretched out on the large yellow sofa in the drawing-room, cosily embedded among the cushions; no one could be more supple, more nobly nonchalant; but he is incapable of casualness, of being carelessly casual; he cannot let himself sink into comfort, he settles himself in it carefully, with precaution, finding the best position for [*pour le plus grand bien de*] his limbs and his clothes, always taking his pleasure with deliberation [*en voluptueux réfléchi*]'; or on p. 217, seeing Gide for the first time after an operation: 'I'd forgotten that slightly twitchy, nervous habit he has of moving his shoulder around in his clothes, as if trying to find the best position for it.'

11   See again the *Cahiers de la petite dame* or, for a briefer and even less starry-eyed view of Gide in his body, the beautifully observed Roger Martin du Gard, *Notes sur André Gide 1913–1951* (Paris: Gallimard, 1951).

12   This trope is familiar both in the fantasies and the self-justifications of child-seducers – though, as the social/legal services know, these can vary in their modes and levels of exploitation as much as other desirers – and in the literature of such as J. M. Barrie or Lewis Carroll. Like the latter, Gide's fiction needs both a Wendy/Sylvie (the fair, chaste, timid elder sister) and a Peter/Bruno (brown, semi-taught and temperately wild).

13   An early scene in *La Porte étroite* (*Strait is the Gate*), in André Gide, *Romans; Récits et soties; Œuvres lyriques*, ed. M. Nadeau, Y. Davet and J.-J. Thierry (Paris: Gallimard, 1958), p. 500.

14   Johann Wolfgang von Goethe, the final words of *Faust II*.

15   Dollimore, pp. 74–6.

16   See *Si le grain*, p. 565: 'what attracts me is the trace of sun on brown skins'. On the subject of skin, it is interesting to note that Gide tended, in adulthood at least, to suffer above all from skin disorders; in later middle age, from recurrent pruritus, and all his life from warts and cysts. In the *Cahiers de la petite dame* and Martin du Gard, as well as in Pierre Herbart, *A la recherche d'André Gide* (Paris: Gallimard, 1952), there is talk of having these warts and cysts removed. Gide must have been much vainer than Oliver Cromwell, because they do not seem to show up in any of his published photographs.

17   This erotics of the skin is noted in two recent analyses by Kevin

Kopelson (in *Love's Litany*, Stanford: Stanford University Press, 1994) and Leo Bersani (in *Homos*, Cambridge, Mass. and London: Harvard University Press, 1995). Both symptomatize the narcissism of the sunbathing episode in *L'Immoraliste*, but Bersani somewhat inexplicably connects the pleasure of the skin with a kind of pantheistic merging between self and world. On the contrary, skin-pleasure retains the sense of self in contact with other to the most extreme degree, whether or not it is fleeting or indiscriminate. Theorizing the body, Elizabeth Grosz offers 'a model which insists on (at least) two surfaces which cannot be collapsed into one and which do not always harmoniously blend with and support each other; a model where the join, the interaction of the two surfaces, is always a question of power' (in *Volatile Bodies*, Bloomington and Indianapolis: Indiana University Press, 1994, p. 189).

18 Chamfort, *Maximes et pensées* (Neuchâtel: Paul Attinger, [1796], 1946), p. 89. Diderot offers the penetrative correlative in his more vibrant 'the pleasurable rubbing of two intestines': Denis Diderot, *Supplément au voyage de Bougainville*, in *Œuvres*, ed. A. Billy (Paris: Gallimard, 1951), p. 998.

19 See Kopelson, who remarks on 'this tendency to keep the pederastic subject clothed . . . Gide wants to strip with, if not for, attractive boys but is too mindful of his power over them to do so' (pp. 54–5).

20 Jean-Paul Sartre, *L'Etre et le néant* [*Being and Nothingness*] (Paris: Gallimard, 1943), pp. 672–3.

21 Anna Freud had surprisingly similar reasons to turn her piety towards a dominant parent of the opposite sex into an 'addiction' to masturbation. In 'A child is being beaten' (1919) Freud shows that her accompanying fantasy was always focused on a bad boy being beaten for her by her father – the pleasurable chastisement of the naughty masculine self allowing various kinds of relief. Gide's characterization of himself as 'a little boy having fun and his double, a protestant pastor who bores him' expresses a very similar structure. In later life, as we know, Anna Freud created a permissible space of authority for herself by becoming a full-time pedagogue. Her most important psychoanalytical writing, however – surely a powerful brew of parental piety, resentment and the longing for a kind of castration – is the article 'On losing and being lost' (written 1948, published 1967); see Elisabeth Young-Bruehl, *Anna Freud* (London: Macmillan, 1988), chapter 7.

22 This term has Lacanian resonances now, but in everyday French (normally without a capital letter) it would simply mean '*him*'. See Delay, vol. I, Part III, ch. 3.

23   *Si le grain*, p. 594.
24   And of course the desire; see Delay, pp. 200–4, 231, 250, 536–9.
25   See Michel Foucault, in the sections on pederasty in the latter two volumes of *L'Histoire de la sexualité* (Paris: Gallimard, 1984) *The History of Sexuality* (Harmondsworth, Penguin, 1987 and 1988).
26   *Homos*, p. 64.
27   There is a corollary to this, of course. A heterosexual woman experiences both identification and rivalry in the desire of a gay man for other men – see Lynne Segal's paean to James Baldwin in *Straight Sex* (London: Virago, 1994).
28   Lesbian theory, especially in its more direct relation to feminist theory, remains haunted by an aetiological model of mother/daughter incest – see the essays in this volume by Biddy Martin and Trevor Hope.
29   Matrilineal societies, of course, trace inheritance through the mother's brother. These societies, while not matriarchal, locate relations of rights and property in the mother's line. They do not eschew the triangular relationship which takes possession from male to male via a female, but amend it in two important ways: as first focal point of the triangle, the mother is less expendable than she is in the oedipal triangle; and by the use of the maternal uncle the whole structure is taken outside the nuclear-familial space, moving one step out into the social sphere and relations of exogamous exchange.
30   Such is the speed of research in this field, I am superseded in this observation – though not with regard to Gide – by Eve Kosofsky Sedgwick's declaration: 'Forget the Name of the Father. Think about your uncles and your aunts', in 'Tales of the Avunculate', *Tendencies* (London: Routledge, 1994), p. 59.
31   I refer here to the heroes of Stendhal's *Le Rouge et le noir* (1830) and Gide's own *Les Caves du Vatican* (*The Vatican Cellars*, 1914).
32   François-René, vicomte de Chateaubriand, *Atala, René, Les Aventures du dernier Abencérage*, ed. F. Letessier (Paris: Garnier, 1962), p. 131.
33   In 'Sexual harassment and sexual abuse: when girls become women', in Clare Brant and Yun Lee Too (eds), *Rethinking Sexual Harassment* (London and Boulder, Colorado: Pluto Press, 1994), pp. 148–64, Suzanne Raitt draws important parallels between the false dichotomies public/private, woman/girl and harassment/abuse.
34   This paraphrases a set of playful/painful parting gestures in *Romans*, pp. 153 and 248.
35   This is not to ignore the potential and *disponibilité* of a series of young women in Gide: Alissa, Gertrude, Sarah, Laura, Geneviève,

even Alissa's mother in retrospection. His fiction is not without its audacious girls, but, like Shakespeare's sister, they are quickly netted by pregnancy or its threat, almost inescapably becoming mothers as soon as they are out of the nest, and adulterous ones at that. (As in Freud, there is not much for young Jocasta to look forward to as she hops from phallic masturbation to the desire of the son.) They then produce the bastard who may enjoy in their place, and their lovers will become his uncles.

36 This is the comment he reports Madeleine as having made, with 'more sadness than reproach' when, during their journey in Algeria, he spent a railway journey catching at the bare arms of the schoolboys in the adjoining carriage; in *Et nunc manet in te*, in *Journal 1939–1949; Souvenirs*, p. 436.

37 Apropos of this image of laughter, Max Marchand, in his unpleasant book *Du Marquis de Sade à André Gide* (Fouque, Oran, 1956) finds it repeatedly used by Gide to describe desirable boys.

38 *Romans*, pp. 505–6, all ellipses Gide's.

39 Who or what is the channel here is a complex question. Both the male and the female body are 'passed through', multiplying the traditional genderised penetrator/penetratee division. There is evidence from classical and modern sources (for instance in the climax of *Emanuelle*) for the importance of a fantasy of a triple structure of intercourse in which the central male body takes both roles simultaneously. For a negative version of this fantasy, see Sartre's Roquentin, in a frenzied stream-of-consciousness set by off the rape/murder of a little girl: 'a sweet bloody desire for rape is taking me from behind', in *La Nausée* (Paris: Gallimard, 1938), p. 144.

40 Herbart, pp. 14*ff*. But Herbart also describes the suddenness with which he would drop one person when 'the little fever of seduction' (p. 65) passed on to the next one. Enid Starkie – in *André Gide* (Cambridge: Bowes & Bowes, 1953), p. 8 – likens the turned-off tap of Gide's charm to the smile of the Cheshire cat.

41 Roland Barthes, *Le Plaisir du texte* (Paris: Seuil, 1973), p. 45.

42 Peter Brooks, 'The idea of a psychoanalytic literary criticism', in Shlomith Rimmon-Kenan (ed.), *Discourse in Psychoanalysis and Literature* (London & New York: Methuen, 1987), p. 12.

43 In *Between Men* (New York: Columbia, 1985)

44 For two versions of the interchangeability of this pedagogical differential in gay male couples, see Kopelson, *Louis Litany*, pp. 61–2 and Lee Edelman, *Homographesis* (New York and London: Routledge, 1994), pp. 132–4, on the Pygmalion imagery of Frank and Gobie.

Chapter 8

Savage Nights

Mandy Merck

In 1987, an unusual essay appeared in what was perhaps an even more
unusual edition of an academic journal. Under the editorship of Douglas
Crimp, *October* 43 devoted 271 pages to the 'critical, theoretical, activist
alternative to the personal, elegaic expressions that appeared to dominate
the art-world response to AIDS'.[1] The contributors to this issue included
two video producers, an attorney, a community activist, a medical
editor, a former Executive Director of the New York City Minority
Task Force on AIDS, and a performance artist campaigning for the
rights of prostitutes. Its contents ranged from a critical glossary of
the epidemic's 'keywords' ('In discussions of AIDS, because of distinctions *not* made – between syndrome and disease, between infectious
and contagious – there is often a casual slippage from *communicable* to
contagious'[2]) to a manifesto for New York City policy in regard to the
medical, housing and educational needs of women and children devastated
by HIV infection.[3]

Introducing this issue, its editor notes several cultural projects which
stimulated its production. The first to be listed is Simon Watney's study of
'Pornography, AIDS and the Media', *Policing Desire*, published in the
same year. Watney's book is a pioneering investigation of the popular
representations of male homosexuality in the first decade of the epidemic,
among them that cluster of morbid figurations which render the two terms
of the expression 'gay plague' effective equivalents:

> as if the syndrome were a direct function of a particular sexual
> act – sodomy – and, by extension, of homosexual desire in all
> its forms.[4]

AIDS offers a new sign for the symbolic machinery of
repression, making the rectum a grave.[5]

Describing the norms which pathologize homosexuality, he maintains
that the practice

as it is currently construed, contravenes both limited codes
concerning the depiction of specific acts such as sodomy
between men, as well as much larger, regulative dichotomies
which are derived from the anatomical distinction male/female,
the attributes of which inform the entire taxonomic field of
Western logic. Above all, homosexuality problematises the
casual identification of primary power with the figure of the
biological male as masterful penetrator. It equally problematises
the parallel identification of powerlessness and passivity with
the figure of the biological female as submissive and
penetrated.[6]

Given the influence of Watney's study (in the United States – it has been
almost wholly ignored in his native Britain) and the stress it lays on (male)
homosexuality as a contravention of gender dichotomies, it is not surprising to find a lengthy meditation on its premises in the same edition of
October. But Leo Bersani's questioning reply to *Policing Desire*, 'Is The
Rectum a Grave?', sounds a darker note. Together with other lesbian
and gay polemics for the radical subversiveness of sadomasochism, the
democratic *camaraderie* of the bathhouse, and the parodic performativity
of the lesbian butch-femme couple, Watney's attempt to separate the
significations of anal sex from those of sickness and death is subjected to
severe critique. '[W]e have been telling a few lies,' Bersani announces, 'lies
whose strategic value I fully understand, but which the AIDS crisis has
rendered obsolescent.'[7]

Chief among these lies is any attempt to distinguish the fantasies of
homosexuality from the dichotomous imaginary Watney ascribes to
heterosexuality. In Bersani's view, the leather queen desires, rather than
discomfits, masculinity, just as the butch-femme couple submits to, rather
than subverts, sexual difference. And to those who would contest the
condemnation of sodomy as a lethal violation of that difference's fateful
protocols, he replies with a celebration of its murderous power – to slay
the imperial ego, 'the masculine ideal . . . of proud subjectivity', in the very
act of gay sex. 'Male homosexuality,' his essay concludes,' advertises the
risk of the sexual itself as the risk of self-dismissal, of *losing sight* of the
self, and in so doing it proposes and dangerously represents *jouissance* as
a mode of ascesis.'[8]

The argument here derives in part from a more extended meditation on sexuality, *The Freudian Body*, which Bersani published the previous year. There, in a reconsideration of Freud's writings on sex and metapsychology indebted to Jean Laplanche's *Life and Death in Psychoanalysis*, Bersani reads 'beyond' *Beyond the Pleasure Principle* to a general definition of sexuality as pleasurable unpleasure. To this end, he adopts Laplanche's elaboration of Freud's argument for 'the marginal genesis of sexuality and the genesis of sexuality in a moment of turning round upon the self'.[9] According to this account, 'sexuality' emerges as a drive through the detachment of an instinctual function (such as infantile sucking) from its natural object (nurturance) and the reflexive redirection of that function at an object reflected within the subject (the breast as fantasised source of pleasure). *Life and Death in Psychoanalysis* links this reflexivity to Freud's description of how the subject's primary aggressiveness spirals into a sexualixed sadism via a masochism which ultimately displaces its apparent primacy. (As Freud maintains in 'Instincts and Their Vicissitudes', it is only in the turning back of the subject's aggression upon himself that the resulting pain can be transformed through fantasy into sexual excitation.) Combining these observations, Laplanche concludes that (1) all nascent sexuality involves the conversion of a non-sexual activity into sexual excitation via fantasy; and that (2) such excitation involves a necessary breach of the subject's defenses, causing its 'first psychical pain and is thus intimately related, in its origin, to the emergence of the masochistic sex drive'.[10]

The logic is difficult to evade: all sexuality must be founded on masochism, Bersani argues, finding support in the contradictions of Freud's successive discussions of sex and death in his metapsychological speculations. Rejecting the various hierarchies of libidinal and death instincts which Freud erected and inverted across these writings, he discerns 'a collapse of Freud's dualisms and a reconsideration of sex *as* death, or, more exactly, the hypothesis of an identity between a sexualized consciousness and a destabilized, potentially shattered consciousness'.[11] *The Freudian Body* assigns this masochism to human sexuality in general, forced from birth to find pleasure in sensations which overwhelm its infantile capacities for psychic organisation. Indeed, it proposes masochism as an inherited survival mechanism for a species whose lengthy sexual maturation would otherwise ill-adapt it to reproduction.

One year – and the acknowledgement of a new, sexually transmitted epidemic – separate this hypothesis from Bersani's *October* article. The latter recapitulates his general observations on 'sex as self-abolition', this time alluding to Georges Bataille's contention that eroticism signifies 'a violation of the very being of its practitioners', 'a violation bordering on death, bordering on murder'.[12] (This resort to *Erotism*, it should be noted, appears somewhat selective. Where Bataille describes stripping naked as a quest for bodily 'communication' in the face of our 'discontinuous existence',[13] Bersani cautions that he nevertheless 'seems to be describing an experience in which the very terms of communication are abolished'.[14]) Whether this violent sexuality constitutes a threat to the solipsism of the contemporary subject (as Bataille seems to be arguing) or its intensification ('the irremediable privacy of a masochistic *jouissance*' as Bersani puts it in *The Freudian Body*[15]), both commentators perceive a political dimension to its transgressions: 'Eroticism,' Bataille insists, 'always entails a breaking down of established patterns, the patterns . . . of the regulated social order.'[16]

If this is the macro version of a potentially politicizable account of eroticism, Foucault provides Bersani with the micro version, in the second volume of his *History of Sexuality. The Use of Pleasure*, on sexual protocols in ancient Greece, underwrites what might be the motto for the *October* article, and its final phrase: '*jouissance* as a mode of ascesis'. The provenance for this usage of 'ascesis' ('training' or 'exercise' in the Greek) is Socratic, specifically, the physical and mental preparation enjoined for the ethical exercise of power.[17] But, in his later interviews, Foucault employed the term to describe a method by which the contemporary subject might exceed his own limits – go beyond himself. To this purpose he stressed the self-transformative potential of using one's sexuality to invent new forms of 'pleasure . . . relationships, co-existences, attachments, loves, intensities'.[18] The most notorious of these, particularly since James Miller's biography,[19] is homosexual sadomasochism, a practice which Foucault regarded, not as a reversion to an aggression and submission latent in the culture or the unconscious, but as a means to different indices and temporalities of pleasure than those which 'climax' with ejaculation. Such innovations he praised for assuaging men's shame at sexual passivity, a shame which *The Use of Pleasure* considers at some length.

There Foucault argues that, despite the ancient Greek idealization of love between men and boys, an adult male's sexual submission to another could disqualify him from public esteem and political position. For this argument he is indebted to K. J. Dover's pioneering study of the moral and legal regulation of homosexuality in antiquity. These regulations included an Athenian edict which debarred a citizen who sold sexual favours to another male from a range of civic rights (on the grounds that 'one who had been a vendor of his own body for others to treat as they pleased would have no hesitation in selling the interests of the community as a whole'[20]) as well as moral strictures on the correct conduct of erotic relations between men. As Dover demonstrates, in a society which proscribed non-marital contact with citizen women, the Athenians sanctioned, indeed celebrated, sexual relations between an active adult male lover (*erastes*) and a younger male beloved (*eromenos*), but only if each observed the requirements of roles carefully calibrated to maintain the masculinity of both partners. Thus, the importunate *erastes* was encouraged to be loving, generous and gallant, while the object of his affections was enjoined to be modest, reticent and – even if he eventually conceded sexual favours – wholly without sensual pleasure.

In these circumstances, the approved method of intercourse involved a decorous upright embrace in which the active partner was allowed to place his penis between the thighs of the passive youth (a practice known to this day as 'Greek sex'). Protocols such as these not only precluded the youth's acceptance of payment for sex, but any 'readiness – even appetitite – for homosexual submission, adoption of a bent or lowered position, reception of another man's penis in the anus or mouth'.[21] Citing a ribald pastoral by Theocritus, as well as a vase which pictures a defeated Persian bending over for a Greek with his erect penis in hand, Dover observes that in classical Greek culture 'homosexual anal penetration is treated neither as an expression of love nor as a response to the stimulus of beauty, but as an aggressive act demonstrating the superiority of the active to the passive partner'. 'To choose to be treated as an object at the disposal of another citizen,' he concludes, 'was to resign one's own standing as a citizen.'[22]

In the third chapter of *The Use of Pleasure*, Foucault describes this ancient attitude as a 'principle of isomorphism between sexual relations and social relations'[23] in which both spheres are analogously divided between oppositions of activity and passivity, command and compliance, victory and defeat. This structural connection of sexual and social relations is the central theme of 'Is the Rectum a Grave?', enabling Bersani to turn from *The Freudian Body*'s account of human sexuality in general to the disparaged sexualities of two subordinated populations, gays and women. Taking its cue from Watney's comparison of Victorian representations of female prostitutes as 'contaminated vessels' of syphilitic contagion with AIDS-related characterizations of gay men, the *October* article relates the promiscuity attributed to both groups to their popularly imagined lust for annihilation:

The realities of syphilis in the nineteenth century and of AIDS today 'legitimate' a fantasy of female sexuality as intrinsically diseased; and promiscuity in this fantasy, far from merely increasing the risk of infection, is the *sign of infection*. Women and gay men spread their legs with an unquenchable appetite for destruction.[24]

A footnote to this rather extravagant description underscores the homology it proposes between the vagina and the rectum as 'privileged loci' of HIV infection as well as widely fantasized counterparts. Not noted is the homology of sexual position which secures the comparison. It recurs on the next page in Bersani's evocation of the 'seductive and intolerable image of a grown man, legs high in the air, unable to refuse the suicidal ecstasy of being a woman'.[25]

Seductive, intolerable, and, most of all, uncomfortable. While not uncommon for anal sex, the supine position so vividly evoked in this account is, I suspect, a contrivance, enforcing the identification of the penetrated gay man with the woman embracing her male lover, embracing – in effect – the fatality of sex. Unlike the more conventional *coitus a tergo* which Bersani makes so much of in his later *Homos*, precisely for the way 'the configuration of the front of one man's body against the back of the other most closely respects, so to speak, the way the anus (*as distinct from the vagina*) presents itself for penetration',[26] or the intercrural intercourse permitted the Athenian *erastes* and his *eromenos*, the image here of the man on his back ecstatically raising his legs to facilitate penetration combines a literally inferior position with intense volition. If the Greeks never expressed it quite so graphically,[27] this rendition of abandoned anality certainly can be taken to represent the lustful self-subordination which Foucault tells us they condemned as a culpable yielding to the appetites.

I dwell on this, as Bersani does, and for the same reasons. The combination of prostration and desire (of desired prostration) imputed to this particular practice of intercourse opens the way for the principle of sexual and social isomorphism identified by Foucault. Politically (the argument goes), gay men and straight women are *fucked*[28] – because they want to be. In their lustful receptivity to the phallus, they submit to the penetrator's superiority as a topographical and social fact, as well as to a narcissistic wound of potentially fatal proportions. Enter Andrea Dworkin and Catharine MacKinnon, admittedly 'unlikely bedfellows' for a gay sadomasochist like Foucault, but as convinced as any ancient Greek of what Bersani describes as 'the distribution of power both signified and constituted by men's insistence on being on top'.[29] Indeed, Bersani reads MacKinnon's description of the 'male suprematist definition of female sexuality as lust for self-annihilation' as a rhetorically enhanced version of Foucault's account of gender in antiquity, the social-sexual isomorphism on which her condemnation of pornography's fusion of 'the eroticization of dominance and submission with the social construction of male and female'[30] is also based. Not only does Bersani endorse her consequent claim that legal pornography is legalized violence against women, he congratulates both MacKinnon and Dworkin for condemning the practice as well as the representation of intercourse: '[They] have at least had the courage to be explicit about the profound *moral revulsion* with sex'.[31]

In this salute to their unflinching recognition of the awful truth about sex, feminism's greatest mistresses of hyperbole finally meet their match. For the joke, of course, is on Dworkin and MacKinnon, since Bersani will fan the flames of their philippic, endorse their critique of intercourse, in order to praise precisely what they regard as intolerable about it: 'Their indictment of sex – their refusal to prettify it, to romanticize it, to maintain that fucking has anything to do with community or love – has had the immensely desirable effect of publicizing, of lucidly laying out for us, the inestimable value of sex as – at least in certain of its ineradicable aspects – anticommunal, antiegalitarian, antinurturing, antiloving.'[32] Where sexual reformers lament the solipsism of sex without relation, a selfishness sorely emblematized for Dworkin and MacKinnon in men's masturbation to images of female submission, Bersani – via a glancing citation of Foucault's argument for the immanence of power in social relations – condemns the relational itself as the occasion of those narcissistic invest-ments which lead to the desire for mastery. Moreover, he goes on to mock the two women (and, albeit with slightly less derision, contemporary apologists for homosexuality like Weeks and Watney) for their 'pastoralizing, redemptive' attempts to clean up sex, to purge it of its power.

This argument anticipates its fuller development in Bersani's 1990 *Cul-ture of Redemption*, with its Nietzschean dismissal of the corrective power of thought, specifically those critical projects which could be said to elevate exegesis to a form of textual sublimation. Here Joyce's *Ulysses* comes in for a particularly pointed reproach, as a text which 'substitutes for the interpretative ordeals posed by such writers as Lawrence, Mallarmé, and Bataille a kind of affectless busyness, the comfortable if heavy work of finding all the connections in the light of which the novel can be made intelligible but not interpreted':

> The intertextual criticism invited by *Ulysses* is the
> domestication of literature, a technique for making familiar the
> potentially traumatic seductions of reading.[33]

This opposition of 'domestication' to trauma, both textual and sexual, structures Bersani's criticism. Thus the *October* article rebukes Watney's call for the recognition of sexual diversity as 'unnecessarily and even dangerously tame ... disingenuous about the relation between homosexual behavior and the revulsion it inspires'.[34] Moreover, Bersani suggests that machismo itself may simply represent the denial of 'the seductiveness of an image of sexual powerlessness', the same 'domesticating, even sanitizing' impetus which animates its feminist opponents.[35]

Counterposed to 'the domestic', 'the redemptive', 'the pastoral', 'the tame', we find – in a subsequent meditation on 'Sex and Death' much influenced by Bersani – 'the wild': 'the wild space of the promiscuous encounter', 'the wildness of a once vaguely defined illicit sexuality became in a sense even wilder'.[36] Jonathan Dollimore's recent discusion of these oppositions returns to the *October* article to quote its accusation against the 'normalizing vision of gay desire': 'unnecessarily and even dangerously tame'. His 'wilding'[37] of Bersani's already fierce denigration of any attempt to 'tame' the trauma of seduction brings the logic of both their arguments into relief. Not for the first time is 'our savage sexuality', as Bersani repeatedly describes it in *The Freudian Body*,[38] made to play nature to a culture variously associated with domesticity and dishonesty, religion and repression. In particular, sex is counterposed to 'homework' (as Bersani describes the endless exegetical exercises which Joyce sets the reader of *Ulysses*) and to housework, whether it be the anal character's 'compulsively renewed emptying of ashtrays'[39] or that of those feminists and queers obsessed with 'sanitizing aggression'.

With these distinctions before us, it is tempting to invoke Biddy Martin's recent observations on 'femininity's traditional association with attachment, enmeshment and home'[40] and read this opposition of wild and tame as one of gender, in which the libido is reconfirmed in its masculine character and femininity effectively set against sex itself. This is, in part, my complaint, but it must be qualified with the observation that, in his comparisons of heterosexual women and homosexual men, Bersani seems at times to be describing two different 'femininities'.[41] A cursory reading of his rendition of rectal sex reveals a heroic rhetoric of 'demolition', 'danger' and 'sacrifice' (all terms from his essay's final page) which is nowhere attributed to vaginal penetration. Might it be Bersani's view that male 'femininity' is butcher than its female equivalent, precisely because the subject's masculinity is at stake? The idea that subordination to another male can 'make a man of you', however alien to the Athenians, would be all too familiar to the Greeks on America's campuses, as well as to numerous other men subjected to sexual hazing by their male superiors in ritual inductions ranging from boot camp to stag night. While neither of these is legally available to Anglo-American gays at present, some homosexual equivalent (Bersani mentions a 'tough and brutal' evening of rejection at a bathhouse) might save them from what he portrays as a fate far worse than any shattering of the self – being taken home by a swaggering leatherman who turns out to talk like a 'pansy', reads Jane Austen, 'gets you into bed, and – well – you know the rest'.[42] Again, going home *tames* gay sex, transforming the phallic cruiser into the pansy, whose sexuality is as domesticated as (shades of *The Culture of Redemption*) his reading. His fate – and his sort of femininity – await gay men who accept recruitment into the relational. Only in the wrong place, in the 'wild', can femininity attain to the condition of its opposite, allowing the gay subject both his *horror feminae* and his disengendering adoration of the phallus.

Jonathan Dollimore's discussion of the 'wild space of the promiscuous encounter' is part of a larger project on what he describes as 'the perverse dynamic in western culture which binds together desire, death and loss (mutability), and especially the belief that desire is in a sense impossible.'[43] Although his general remarks on that dynamic adduce literary examples from Plato to Montaigne, those on the homosexual death-drive concentrate on gay men's writings since the 1970s, particularly contemporary works which take AIDS as their context, if not their subject. This focus on the epidemic is understandable, since Dollimore follows Watney in observing that the responses to it have construed homosexuality as 'death-drive, death-desiring and death-dealing'.[44] But, like Bersani, whose work is discussed at some length, Dollimore is profoundly ambivalent about this claim, arguing that 'it's one thing to disarticulate the lethal connections between death and homosexuality made by, say, the moral right, quite another to censor or disavow insightful gay writing about the death/desire paradox.'[45] Against the former's crude association of gay sex with morbidity, he counterposes the latter's exploration of a fundamental contradiction in subjectivity: 'the self riven by, constituted by, loss'.[46] Yet the very generality which Dollimore attributes to this paradox is immediately circumscribed by both its homosexualization and masculinization in his account. The fatality which culture assigns to homosexuality is matched by the male homosexual's own fatalism, an 'AIDS-related fatalism' evidenced in the recent fiction of Oscar Moore and the journalism of Rupert Haselden, 'both of whom . . . share an acute sense that desire is driven by a lack inherently incapable of satisfaction'.[47] In Moore's 1991 novel, *A Matter of Life and Sex*,[48] this conviction is represented in the unsatisfiable yearnings of the central character, a promiscuous youth whose intimations of mortality come true in the epidemic. Haselden's *Guardian* article of the same year argued that London's cruise bars were again busy because 'biologically maladaptive' gay men, unable to reproduce, continued to abandon themselves to a perpetual round of self-destructive pleasure, 'living for today because we have no tomorrow'.[49]

This is not, as Dollimore carefully points out, the only possible understanding of gay male sexuality and its relation to fatality. A footnote from Douglas Crimp[50] argues that it is precisely the plurality of homosexual practices which has enabled the invention of safer pleasures, while a flashback to the seventies fiction of John Rechy and Michael Rumaker reminds us that the promiscuous gay 'outlaws' of the decade, however much they were figured as the street-fighting revolutionaries of the period, still stood for 'satisfied bodies instead of dead ones'.[51] Nevertheless, both Rechy and Rumaker's acknowledgement of their own suicidal impulses, as a result of frustrated or condemned desire, are taken by Dollimore to support 'the death-sex connection' in what is an undeniably teleological argument. Just as the insatiability of the seventies cruiser is read to anticipate the unsatisfiability of desire registered in the AIDS writings of the nineties, so his suicidal longings come to fruition with actual death in the epidemic.

All of which makes me wonder if it is the case, as Bersani claims in his *October* article, that AIDS has merely 'literalized' the fantasmatic connection between sex and self-destruction, or whether it has played a more constitutive role in the new gay literature of the death drive. Although Dollimore can point to this theme in the pre-AIDS writings of Wilde, Baldwin and Holleran, his contention that the 'sexually dissident have always tended to know more about . . . the strange dynamic which, in western culture, binds death into desire'[52] consigns those activists with whom he disagrees to a sexual conformity even less radical than the redemptive project savaged by Bersani. Among those who would dissent from Dollimore's dissidence is Jeff Nunokawa, whose attempt to historicize the 'lethal characterization'[53] of homosexuality in both gay and straight culture is bizarrely appropriated in 'Sex and Death' to the opposite purpose. Where Nunokawa grounds his discussion of *Dorian Gray* and his Karposi's-scarred successors in a nineteenth-century hellenism preoccupied with beauty's brevity, Dollimore discards the genealogy from the gayness to claim his essay as yet more evidence that homosexuals have themselves regarded their sexuality 'fatalistically, morbidly, and as somehow doomed of its very nature'.[54]

If true sexual dissidents, in Dollimore's account, avidly await their rendezvous with death, the gay who associates homosexuality with healing and nurturance – to cite his sole example, the narrator of Michael Rumaker's 1977 novel *A Day and Night at the Baths* – is a big sissy, keen on moisturizer and personal hygiene, hilariously polite in pick-ups, his lunch packed all-too-literally with health food. '[C]autious, domesticated, and very much on the side of ordinary life' Rumaker's hero (whom Dollimore renders as a sort of gay lib Candide) wanders naively through an increasingly dangerous milieu, whose 'wildness' becomes 'even wilder' as bathhouse sex gets 'more transgressive'[55] in the sadomasochistic seventies and the epidemic looms ahead. When we learn that this exponent of 'mutually consenting and courteous erotic play' identifies with women while being fucked, the feminization of his anodyne vision of an American utopia 'where gay sex is free, benign and healing, and sufficiently sanitized to be reincorporated in civic society'[56] is contemptuously driven *home*.

So, 'Sex and Death' . . . and wildness, transgression and masculinity. My purpose in questioning these equivalences is not to deny the poignancy of Dollimore's account of lovers whose illness renders 'desire itself as a kind of grieving',[57] nor to refuse any notion of a sexual drive to an ecstatic self-shattering, nor to ignore the practice of homosexual sadomasochism. It is, however, to resist the conflation of these three instances, and their implicit gendering, in the 'epidemic of signification'[58] which he and Bersani survey. To do so, I suggest that we heed the call of the wild and pursue the political consequences of its erotic narratives. My model for this inquiry is Cora Kaplan's pioneering essay on feminism and eroticism, 'Wild Nights' (of which more below). My first object of investigation is a French novel whose author was described by *France-Soir* as 'convinced like Bataille that eroticism and death are inextricably linked' and whose Paris setting, promiscuous hero and references to AIDS lead Dollimore to compare it to Moore's *A Matter of Life and Sex*.

Cyril Collard's *Savage Nights* is better known in the 1992 film version in which its author starred. Seventy-two hours after his death from an AIDS-related illness on 5 March 1993, it was awarded four Cesars, the French equivalent of the Oscar. Collard's own appearance in a film about an HIV-positive film-maker, a film which he himself wrote and directed, and his death at the very moment of its recognition, accomplished a publicity coup to, so to speak, die for. The enthusiastic responses to a film which belatedly provoked public discussion of an epidemic long (and lethally) ignored in France are themselves instructive. But to understand its title, to pursue the savagery in Collard's portrait of a sadomasochistic cameraman with a taste for 'stiff cocks, degrading gestures, strong smells'[59] and Arab youths, it is necessary to turn to the original novel, first published in 1989 under the title *Les nuits fauves*.

Like the film, the novel follows the 30-year-old bisexual narrator's tortured relationship with Laura, a seventeen-year-old aspirant actress, across two years. But unlike the film, it deals at equal length with his friendship with Omar – a director with whom he is making a film about young Algerians in the Nanterre slums and their encounter with a white French doctor 'completely at the mercy of his desire for Arab bodies'[60] – as well as his sexual relationships with four young men: Kader, an eighteen-year-old whom he follows to Algeria; Sammy, who claims Spanish-Arab parentage, yet becomes a fascist; Olivier, a Burgundian of Arab extraction; and Jamal, a seventeen-year-old Islamic rapper. As one might expect, the hero of the novel is an aficionado of Arab culture, who travels to Morocco and Algeria, shoots a film about African musicians living in Paris and another about a gay white Frenchman who offers his services to the Fedayeen. Genet, as the narrator modestly observes, comes to mind. So do the French colourists who championed Islamic and African art and painted in the wild style that secured their nomination as 'Fauves'.

Here Collard exploits the multiple references of the French *fauve(s)*: 'fawn-coloured'; 'musky'; 'deer'; 'game'; as well as the Neo-Impressionist school of Matisse, Derain and Vlaminck, whose apparent recklessness with colour and brushwork earned them the sobriquet 'wild beasts'. Laura is the first of the narrator's lovers to be described in these terms. The daughter of an Algerian mother, she has skin which glows with 'a tawny colour, a savage colour',[61] and certainly the crazed intensity of her relation with the hero, and the risks they run in abjuring condoms, make their agonistic couplings as wild as any in the book:

> She came with a scream, clawing at my back. I fucked her
> again, then came with a throaty yell, feeling I was coming as I'd
> never come before . . . I was floating, knowing that I had shot
> her full of sperm that was infected with a deadly virus, but
> feeling that it was all right, that nothing would happen, because
> we were starting what could truly be called 'a love story'.[62]

But it is with the narrator's homosexuality that Fauvism is directly invoked, connecting the savagery of his masochistic encounters beneath the Seine bridges to the strange hues of their shadowy setting, and both with the tawny skin of his Arab amours.

> When I leave, with the skeleton of a night with the savages
> behind me, the bony shell of the miracle, my back is streaked
> with red welts, my chest bruised by combat-boot soles, my tits
> burning, my pants soaked, dried spittle on my face and streaks
> of cold piss tickling my thighs.

The savages take on the colours of the Fauve painters of the
past. Sombre, evanescent pastels in the jackets brushing pillars;
the washed-out greys of faces; blue fragments of jeans
enveloping arses, cocks and balls . . .
    The black and white memory of the tangled bodies bear
Fauve traces: Sammy and his fellows' golden colour, which the
darkness can't extinguish.[63]

Collard's description evokes only a little of the Fauve style – the purity
of colour, flattened perspective and arbitrary accents – but it is redolent
of its ethos, the cultivated primitivism with which Matisse painted,
among many subjects, his Moroccan series of 1912. Such primitivism,
with its associations of impetuosity, irrationality and intensity, is what
Collard's narrator seeks, a 'savagery' predictably represented by race,
but also by class, youth and an inclination to violence. This violence is
meted out to him in scenes of gay sadomasochism, in which his body,
unlike that of Bersani's subject, is not penetrated but beaten and dirtied.
Nonetheless, the narrator's ecstatic response to this pain and humiliation,
combined with the novel's knowing invocation of Bataille (to whose play
Le Mort the narrator is 'inexplicably' invited on page 112), seems intended
to signal the self-annihilating *jouissance* identified by both Bersani and
Dollimore with sexual radicalism. And yet, in the predictably perverse
dialectics of sadomasochism, these scenes prove not to be ones of submission, no funerals for proud masculine subjectivity, but celebrations of
mastery.

Some bodies hesistated, circled, spoke; for me, it had to be all
or nothing. I announced my tastes; if the answer was no, I
roughly shoved the man away; if yes, I'd follow him and
scream out my pleasure on the steps of an iron staircase on the
other side of the bridge.
    Standing soiled and bruised at the river's edge after orgasm, I
felt graceful and light. Transparent.[64]

Later, I went walking across the constantly erased footprints
left by the passengers of sex. A half-moon shrouded by clouds
shines on the roof of the barges. Dust and gravel mixed. For a
few hundred yards, full of an immediate desire, I am free of
restraints and powers. I feel I am lord and master.[65]

The narrator's tricks may beat him savagely, but they do it *to order*.
Like his Arab boys with their fawn-coloured skin and the attendant

cervine connotations of man's favourite quarry, the Parisian rough trade is ultimately dominated by its submissive superior in class and race, who rises again from their ministrations to stand 'graceful and light'. Far from illustrating any isomorphism between male sexual passivity and a commensurate social subordination, *Savage Nights* insistently – one might say narcissistically, given its autobiographical tenor – reveals its bourgeois bottom to be a top, older, wealthier and whiter than his sexual objects.[66] Indeed, the emphatic *non*-abjection of the hero may explain its cross-over success in France.

If this upends the social-sexual topography claimed by Bersani to subordinate gay men, via the heterosexual association of their sexual receptivity with a self-annihilating propensity to pleasure originally identified with female concupiscence, what of women themselves? Here it important to remember the political responses to the ancient isomorphic principle relayed by Foucault and summarized by Bersani as 'the distribution of power both signified and constituted by men's insistence on being on top'. Many feminists have recognized the *Weltanschauung* which informs this denigration of the supine position ('Dworkin takes a pornographic image as a kind of world view: the law on top, men in the middle, women at the bottom') and refused it: 'I don't see an image of a woman being penetrated in the missionary position as symbolic of a woman as a *victim*.'[67] And in a further questioning of MacKinnon's identification of sexual penetration with personal violation, they have noted how exquisitely *masculine* this terror is: 'What is the worst imaginable disaster to the masculine self? To be fucked.'[68] Reflecting ironically on the apocalyptic rhetoric so characteristic of this argument, Drucilla Cornell has asked 'But why is it the end of the world "to be fucked"?' The answer, in her reading of *Feminism Unmodified*, is that MacKinnon unwittingly subscribes to the phallic imaginary she purports to oppose and its equation of masculinity with selfhood, a selfhood defined as assertion rather than reception:

> Indeed, she cannot affirm carnality as long as she recasts the
> subject as seeking freedom, not intimacy, in sex. If it is accepted
> that to be masculine, to be a self, is not to 'be fucked', then if
> women are 'fucked', we cannot be individuals.[69]

Cornell reads this phallic identification in MacKinnon's diction as well as her logic, citing this exquisitely self-revealing salvo from *Feminism Unmodified*: 'I am getting hard on this and am about to get harder on it.'[70] And, in a related observation, Wendy Brown remarks on 'the insistent and pounding quality' of MacKinnon's prose, its 'stylistic mirroring' of the pornographic text's repetitive thrustings and rhythmic crescendos, 'suspending us in a complex pornographic experience in which MacKinnon is both purveyor and object of desire and her analysis is proferred as substitute for the sex she abuses us for wanting'.[71]

In comparison, Bersani's investments in the very phallic identification – 'the masculine ideal . . . of proud subjectivity' – whose demise he celebrates are both more overt and more oblique than MacKinnon's. The logic of the *October* article precludes the acknowledgement of the gay male top, as well as women's active eroticism, whether hetero- or homosexually directed. (The female superior position in straight sex is dismissed as a mere game compared to the powerful probing of the penis beneath, while lesbianism is wholly ignored.) Nonetheless, the gay man's desire for masculinity is distinguished from the collaborative longings of other oppressed subjects (those of blacks for whites, Jews for Gentiles, are instanced) by the possibility homosexuality offers for both appropriation *of* and identification *with* the erotic object. Bersani's 1995 *Homos* elaborates this point in a confession of gay men's misogyny and its 'narcissistically gratifying reward of confirming our membership in (and not simply our erotic appetite for) the privileged male society'.[72] The related reversibility of the supine position in sex, if not in society – the possibility of a gay man experiencing what Bersani terms 'sex as self-hyperbole', 'psychic tumescence'[73] – suggests another reading of 'Is the Rectum a Grave?', not as the funeral of the phallus, but rather as its resurrection. The penis, like the prostrate male to which it is attached, will rise again. Nothing in the anal receptivity of the penetrated male precludes its possession in actuality, let alone his identification with its potency. For what is all this talk of its 'shattering' and 'annihilating' powers but phallic narcissism by other means?[74] (And isn't this why both Bersani and MacKinnon, for all their ostensible interest in women's sexuality, so rarely address those women who fuck without the penis, the lesbians?)

This occlusion of the lesbian is not the sole liability of a sexual politics which reassigns femininity to passivity and (however positively) erotic receptivity to self-destruction, although it is an undoubtedly related effect. There are further drawbacks to Bersani's homology of the grave, the rectum and the vagina. As that historic exponent of anality, Guy Hocquenghem, so memorably observed, 'The anus is not a substitute for the vagina: women have one as well as men.'[75] Any equation of the rectum with the vagina effectively denies the very existence of the *woman's* anus, and the possibility of its own erotic deployment. Whatever 'the widespread confusion in heterosexual *and* homosexual men between fantasies of anal and vaginal sex'[76] on which Bersani remarks, that sex endowed with both organs of pleasure may prefer to keep all its options open.

Not that this has ever been a simple matter for feminism. If we turn from Collard's *Savage Nights* to Kaplan's 'Wild Nights', we are reminded that the liberal humanism which begot feminism out of *The Rights of Man* also propagated a modernised derogation of female sexuality. First published in 1983, the era of the 'sex wars' in which Dworkin and MacKinnon were such celebrated combatants, 'Wild Nights' looks back to feminism's foundational anxieties about women's sexual pleasure as the surrender of social power. Beneath three provocative epigraphs – from Dickinson's eponymous poem, Dworkin's *Pornography* and Wollstonecraft's 1792 *Vindication of the Rights of Women* – the last, 'the founding text of Anglo-American feminism',[77] is reread to remind us that it too identified female desire with a moral laxity meriting civil subordination. In unhappy anticipation of her successors two centuries later, Mary Wollstonecraft dedicated the *Vindication* to persuading women 'to become more masculine and respectable'.[78] Her argument – that femininity, in its vanity, coquettishness and cultivated ignorance, is tailored to the requirements of heterosexual attraction – established an uncanny precedent for Dworkin and MacKinnon's description of the eroticized engendering of female subordination.[79]

Writing at a time when a new perception of pleasure as danger meant that 'eros rampant [was] more likely to conjure up a snuff movie than multiple orgasm',[80] when pornography, rape and child abuse became central, if highly contested, issues in feminist politics, Kaplan opens her remarks by singling out sexuality as 'the wild card whose suit and value shifts provocatively with history. As dream or nightmare, or both at once, it reigns in our lives as an anarchic force, refusing to be chastened and tamed by sense or conscience to a sentence in a revolutionary manifesto.'[81] But if so exuberantly romantic a formulation threatens to put sex back into Bersani and Dollimore's wilderness – amoral, irrational, anarchic – Kaplan's own sense of how this spectacularly shifting signifier changes with history refuses it that naturalisation. Indeed, what makes her essay so exemplary is its historicization of both feminisms and femininities, and their complex relation to each other,[82] as well as to other conditions of existence. Sex is a wild card, she tells us, because its value is contextual rather than inherent. Reflecting, at her essay's conclusion, on the ironic similarities between Wollstonecraft the liberal feminist and her radical feminist successor Adrienne Rich, who respectively condemn and celebrate lesbianism for virtually identical reasons, she resists their appeals against a corrupting (Wollstonecraft) and compulsory (Rich) heterosexuality to insist upon the contingency of our sexual practices and the values we assign them:

> The identification of the sources of social good or evil in the
> sexual drive of either sex, or in any socially specific practice, is
> a way of foreclosing our still imperfect understanding of the

histories of sexuality. The moralization of desire that inevitably
follows from such an analysis colludes with those dominant
practices which construct human sexuality through categories
of class, race and gender in order to divide and rule.[83]

Surely it would be perverse to accuse a critic like Bersani, so resolutely
opposed to all that is 'redemptive', 'pastoral', 'salvational', of the moralization of desire? Better to take up Kaplan's opposition of a transcendent
sexual ethics to specific sexual histories and describe his homology of sex
and social standing as 'ahistorical'. This ahistoricism reappears conspicu-
ously in his more recent attack on the *bien pensant* presumptions of queer
theory, *Homos*. There, enlarging upon the *October* article's passing scorn
for those who would redeem 'fascistic S&M' as a parody of fascism,
Bersani argues that sadomasochism does nothing to undermine actual
social power. In what could be a comment on Collard's bourgeois masochist, he maintains that 'The concession to a secret and potentially ener-
vating need to shed the master's exhausting responsibilities and to enjoy
briefly the irresponsibility of total powerlessness allows for a comfortable
return to a position of mastery and oppression the morning after, when all
that "other side" has been, at least for a time, whipped out of the executive's system.'[84] But, having conceded the non-equivalence of sexual practice and social power, Bersani moves from sadomasochism's failure to
challenge actual authority to propose its *complicity with* that authority, as
the necessary principle of the master–slave relation. Foucault's attempts to
distinguish S/M from any structure of power are given short shrift. In
Bersani's view, S/M's eroticization of dominance without the practical
supports of racism or economic exploitation merely reveals its worship of
unalloyed authority, a devotion which need not be confined to the sexual
arena.

Curiously, Bersani offers these speculations on the non-ideological
appeal of dominance and the possible 'intractability of extreme forms
of oppression'[85] in the name of history. History is what S/M is said to
deny in its attempt to separate sexual fantasy from social consequence:
'[T]he polarized structure of master and slave, of dominance and
submission, is the same in Nazism and S/M.'[86] Why should the masochist,
he asks, having discovered the irresistible pleasure of 'bondage, discipline
and pain', confine his submission to sex? To assume that he will not
bring his erotic inclinations to his politics is to 'remove fantasy from
history'.[87]

This raises the imminent prospect of a mass, indeed universal, move to
fascism, since the argument for the masochism of all human sexuality is
also reiterated in *Homos*. To this Bersani offers no solution except S/M's

own (masochistic) flaunting of its social unacceptability, and thus the future possibility of its abolition in the name of anti-fascism. How seriously we are to entertain either of these possibilities is not revealed. Instead, in an attempt to retain the fantasy within history, Bersani returns to his *Ur*-history of ancient Greece, and its isomorphism of gender roles and social status, this time quoting the Foucauldian classicist David Halperin's description of Athenian sexual norms:

> 'Active' and 'passive' sexual roles are therefore necessarily isomorphic with superordinate and subordinate social status.[88]

Again, the classical convention is said to have feminized those men who accepted phallic penetration, and again, their position is compared to that of the bottom in the contemporary sadomasochistic scene. And if every (implicitly masochistic) gay man finds an erotic appeal in fascism, so must every (implicitly heterosexual) woman, since the two groups are yet again argued to be effectively identical.

> In a sense, the Greeks were so open about their revulsion to what they understood as female sexuality, and so untroubled in their thinking about the relation between power and phallic penetration, that they didn't need to pretend, as nineteenth-century sexologists did, that men who went to bed with other men were all secretly women. Only half of them were women, and that judgment had enormous social implications; the adult male citizen who allowed himself to be penetrated, like inferior women and slaves, was politically disgraced. *The persistence of this judgment throughout the centuries and in various cultures is well documented.*[89]

Fortuitously, *Homos* presents this account of the transhistorical subordination of the sexually penetrated subject in a chapter titled 'The Gay Daddy'. I say fortuitously because its argument so insistently summons to mind Sylvia Plath's 'Daddy' and its famous lines:

> Every woman adores a fascist,
> The boot in the face, the brute
> Brute heart of a brute like you.

Are we returned to Bersani's wilderness, where women (and womanish men) repine in masochistic thrall to the brute beast of masculine sexuality?

One reading of 'Daddy', as a work which questions rather than produces identifications, argues otherwise. Reflecting on the vicissitudes of identification manifested in the analyses of Holocaust survivors, Jacqueline Rose cites numerous cases of patients 'in fantasy occupying either side of the victim/aggressor divide',[90] a fantasy which, she also argues, structures Plath's poem. To feminists, the masochism in that divided fantasy is bad enough. But 'most awkward',[91] writes Rose, is the poem's sadism, not the defensible revenge of Plath the spurned wife and abandoned daughter, but that of a possible identification with the fascist permitted by the unspecified agency putting the boot in. For if absolute authority can elicit desire, it can also, as we have seen, command identification – here, the identification of the fatherless daughter with the German Daddy she calls 'bastard'. The boot may be on the other's foot.

However we interpret Plath's poem, Rose's reading concludes with an argument that should be addressed to any isomorphic account of social and sexual subordination. As she observes, it is *in absentia* that the dead patriarch of 'Daddy' rules most powerfully. The poem is therefore indeed a matter of fantasy, as well as the 'concrete history' of Nazism. Those who collapse the two risk losing fantasy and history both, Rose warns, 'for fascism must surely be distinguished from patriarchy, even if in some sense it can be seen as its effect'. To refuse this distinction, to assimilate each to the other, effectively suspends patriarchy in an 'eternal sameness'[92] of historical invariability.

I read this as a caveat against the identification of fascism with any erotic practice, as well as the hypostatised historiography which would explain contemporary homophobia in terms of a protocol some 2,500 years old. But although *Homos* restates the Foucauldian account, it seems less comfortable in its analytic straitjacket than the *October* article of eight years before. Bersani may retain his history of a prohibition which persists in feminizing gay men 'throughout the centuries', but his discussion of what that femininity might consist of is now subject to question:

> To be a woman in a man's body is certainly an imprisoning
> definition, but at least it leaves open the possibility to wonder,
> as Freud did, about the various desiring positions a woman
> might take. She might awaken in the male body the wish to be
> phallically penetrated, but she might also lead him to love himself
> actively through a boy (as, according to Freud, Leonardo
> sought to relive his mother's love for him as a child by
> becoming attached to younger men); or she might awaken in
> him a complex scenario of orality in which his homosexuality
> would, strangely enough, be best satisfied with a lesbian.[93]

Strange indeed, to contemplate the erotization of a lesbian in Bersani's writing. Or 'lesbianism', I should say, since his subsequent citation of Proust makes it clear that this is the aestheticized appropriation of an elegant erotic *chiasma* rather than the awkward recognition of a subject who might confound his theory. Still, if male homosexuality continues to be conjugated in terms of the 'desiring positions a woman might take', shouldn't this belated discovery of their variety feed back to the women who might take them?

This may be the logic of Bersani's evocation of the 'hypothetically endless crisscross of sexual identities',[94] but it is not one *Homos* pursues. Instead the focus remains resolutely on the fellas, albeit now in a more open prison. Where 'Is the Rectum a Grave?' offered only one possible position for their imputed femininity (the bottom), *Homos'* attempt to posit a gay identity without essence loosens this identification into 'several positions' of desire. Insofar as they make a cross-sex identification, Bersani argues, gay men are spared the defensive adoption of a paternal ego ideal. Instead, they take up an 'indeterminate identity',[95] that of the self which desires its own sex through disidentification with that sex. Not only is the misogyny caused by equating femininity with castration thereby escaped, so is the antagonism to the father created by his identification with the Law. This process is illustrated in a re-reading of a famous account of an infant boy's identification with his mother's pleasure in penetration, and his erotic attitude towards his father. But unlike Freud, who argues that the boy's subsequent repression of that feminine passivity resulted in the replacement of his desire for his father with a fear of his castrating powers eventually manifested in an animal phobia, Bersani stresses the 'compassion' in the Wolf Man's later recollection of the (real or imagined) event:

> during the copulation in the primal scene he had observed the penis disappear . . . he had felt compassion for his father on that account, and had rejoiced in the reappearance of what he thought had been lost.[96]

As Bersani points out, this is not the only evidence of filial tenderness in this case. Not only does the patient remember his pity when visiting his sick father in a sanitorium at the age of six, he also recalls elaborate religious fantasies structured around the father–son relation. For the leading lover of *Homos*, latest in the works of the pre-eminent critic of the culture of redemption, is a little boy with a Christ complex.

Born on Christmas Day and instructed in the tenets of Russian Orthodoxy by his nurse, the Wolf Man recounts to Freud a childhood of obsessive religiosity and an eventual identification with the Redeemer himself. The identification is interpreted to provide the active masculinity necessary to repudiate the boy's passive homosexual attachment to his father. But Freud himself admits that this attempt to sever the attachment is a failure: 'If he was Christ, then his father was God. But the God which religion forced upon him was not a true substitute for the father whom he loved and whom he did not want to have stolen from him.'[97] To redeem humanity, God the Father must sacrifice his Son. To redeem his father, the pious son must sacrifice God. Rejecting the patriarchal cruelty of the Gospels, the boy turns against religion. In order to save his father from becoming the merciless executor of the Law, he forswears the sublimation of paternity into divinity, and his own identification with God's Son.

Bersani concludes the penultimate chapter to *Homos* with a celebration of that child's compassion, for the father almost lost to religion and the phallus (paternal, filial, both) almost lost to the analyst's insistence on the castrating bar between father and son. In his account, the case of the Wolf Man 'unintentionally provides us with one genealogy of gay love'. It does so, I would stipulate, not in spite of 'the redemptive' and 'the salvational', but precisely through those means. Not only is the Wolf Man the Redeemer redeemed, the Christ whose compassion saves his would-be crucifier from his murderous destiny, but his mission is the resurrection of the body – in Bersani's terms, the restoration of the 'oblated' (sacrificed) organ. His chapter on 'The Gay Daddy' closes with a re-writing of the scene of homosexual penetration (now called 'lovemaking'), one which awards the power of phallic representation to the bottom, whose visible penis makes good the temporary loss of his penetrator's:

> We might imagine that a man being fucked is generously
> offering the sight of his own penis as a gift or even a
> replacement for what is temporarily being 'lost' inside him – an
> offering not made in order to calm his partner's fears of
> castration but rather as the gratuitous and therefore even
> lovelier protectiveness that all human beings need when they
> take the risk of merging with another, of risking their own
> boundaries for the sake of self-dissolving extensions.[98]

Earlier in this chapter, I described this fantasy of recovered potency as one of narcissism. So does Freud, observing that his patient's youthful compassion for others (beggars, cripples, the old, as well as his sick father) involved a large measure of uncomfortable identification, which he fended off by ritual exhalations echoing his father's heavy breathing during sex.

At the end of the passage on the Wolf Man's anxiety at the disappearance of his father's penis in the primal scene he notes: 'the narcissistic origin of compassion (which is confirmed by the word itself) is here quite unmistakably revealed'. A footnote on the German for 'compassion' ('Mitleid' / 'suffering with') confirms the etymological association of pity and identification.

If we read this compassion back into an article whose point of departure is a lethal epidemic devastating the author's own community, its savagery takes on a different hue. For surely the *October* essay's projection of redemption onto the feminine and the feminist belies its own rhetorical investments in precisely that process? 'Gay men's "obsession" with sex, far from being denied, should be celebrated,' Bersani writes at its conclusion, 'because it never stops re-presenting the internalized phallic male as an infinitely loved object of sacrifice.'[99] Here sacrifice is commended and the denigrated language of redemption is itself redeemed. But if the phallic male is the object of the sacrifice, on whose behalf is it made? The answer, of course, is also the phallic male, who (Bersani tells us endlessly) the gay man is and is not. Without performing the same obeisance to that idol, I am moved to say that this narcissistic association of the phallus and the (gay) man[100] enables, if only by its gruff disguise, the author's expression of love for those he *suffers with*, the victims of the epidemic, the dead he would have rise again. Beyond the high-flown rhetoric of a fatal eros, one can discern another love and a wish (pastoral, redemptive and selfish as it undoubtedly is): a wish for life.

How might the gendered opposition of wild and tame, savagery and domesticity, be thought otherwise? Three very different cultural initiatives offer a postscript to this problem. In 1989, the American artist Millie Wilson mounted a 'retrospective' of an imaginary early twentieth-century painter entitled *Fauve Semblant: Peter (A Young English Girl)*.[101] Loosely based on the lesbian painters Gluck and Romaine Brooks, Wilson's artist is both an actual and aesthetic cross-dresser, who wears men's clothes and seeks recognition in an art world closed to women. Denied admission to the school of Matisse and Derain on grounds of sex, Peter is a triumph of imagination over interdiction, a defiant artist who is herself a work of art by the lesbian artist Wilson, who poses for a photograph of Peter in drag, bow-tied at her easel, a counterfeit of the already *faux* Fauve. And so *en abyme*. Wilson's participation in the retrospective recalls critical attention to the continued male domination of contemporary art, as well as the sexual apartheid of those celebrated French painters whose 'wild' colourism was proclaimed as freedom.

My second example follows the original Fauves to North Africa, and a discussion of feminist politics and Francophone literature in post-colonial

Algeria. In *Transfigurations of the Maghreb*, Winifred Woodhull exam-
ines the traditional figure of *la femme sauvage*, the ogress of folktale
whose 'wild femininity [is] by turns fertile and sterile, nourishing and
devouring, domesticated and untame, economically productive and ruin-
ous'.[102] Like the wildfire to which she is compared, this savage woman
may rekindle the hearth or burn down the house. In the literature of the
Algerian War and its aftermath, she becomes an agent of revolution, maker
and unmaker of identities, an implacable force for cultural as well as
political transformation. Rather than opposing them, Woodhull allies this
wild femininity to the 'wild masculinity' of male homosexuality in the
post-Liberation fiction of the Algerian novelist Rachid Boudjedra, seeing
in both a disclosure of 'the instability of the sexual binary and other social
oppositions intersected by it', that of 'colonizer and colonized' as well as
'men and boys, ruler and ruled, the sane and the insane, and heterosexuality and homosexuality'.[103]

'Domesticated and untame', the savage woman of the Maghreb beckons
me finally to the poem whose title and first stanza preface Kaplan's
meditations on Pleasure/Sexuality/Feminism:

> Wild Nights – Wild Nights!
> Were I with thee
> Wild Nights should be
> Our luxury!

It is interesting to note that nowhere in *Sea Changes*, the volume in
which Kaplan's essay is collected, does the author offer a reading of
Dickinson's poem, except to observe in passing the poet's preference for
'overt statement, as in "Wild Nights"', to 'project sensuous or lascivious
images'.[104] And indeed, the poem's famous first quatrain – its staccato
succession of monosyllables, the erect exclamation points, the repeated
invocation of 'Wild Nights' – does seem 'overt'. But what is being stated
so overtly? Only in the quatrain's final multisyllabic 'luxury' is a disso-
nant note sounded (a dissonance which many readers ward off by recalling
the final word as 'liberty'). For although 'luxury' is rooted in 'lechery' (via
the Latin *luxuria*: 'rankness, excess') its contemporary connotations of
opulence and indulgence jar with those of the wild.

The second stanza offers a possible resolution to this contradiction by
suggesting that the (wild) winds are precisely a luxury, in the sense of a
'futile' or useless propulsion, to 'a Heart in port':

> Done with the Compass –
> Done with the Chart!

Yet, as the third and final stanza makes clear, passion will not be excluded from the pastoral. The poem concludes with the narrator imagining not a turbulent evening on the high seas of a conventional coupling, but an ecstatic passage in paradise.

> Rowing in Eden –
> Ah, the Sea!
> Might I but moor – Tonight –
> In Thee!

Here I am reminded of Wollstonecraft's 'wild wish' in the *Vindication* 'to see the distinction of sex confounded in society, unless where love animates the behaviour'.[105] But in 'Wild Nights' it is love which confounds this distinction and all that it subtends, from the traditional sexing of the sailor and the harbour to the commensurate division of land and sea. The final stanza vindicates the poem's appropriation to Kaplan's defence of female desire by triumphantly defying that gendered division of civility and savagery which our sexual politics must continue to resist.

Notes

1   Douglas Crimp, 'AIDS: Cultural Analysis / Cultural Activism', *October* 43, Winter 1987, p. 15.

2   Jan Zita Grover, 'AIDS: Keywords', *October* 43, p. 19; emphasis in original.

3   Suki Ports, 'Needed (For Women and Children), *October* 43, pp. 169–76.

4   Simon Watney, *Policing Desire: Pornography, AIDS, and the Media* (Minneapolis: University of Minnesota Press, 1987), p. 12.

5   Watney, *Policing Desire*, p. 126.

6   Ibid., p. 28.

7   Leo Bersani, 'Is the Rectum a Grave?', *October* 43, p. 206.

8   Ibid., p. 222.

9   Jean Laplanche, *Life and Death in Psychoanalysis*, trans. Jeffrey Mehlman (Baltimore and London: Johns Hopkins University Press, 1985) p. 87. Laplanche is commenting on Freud's theory of the 'propping' of the sexual drive on a nonsexual function in the *Three Essays on the Theory of Sexuality* (1905).

10   Laplanche, *Life and Death in Psychoanalysis*, p. 97.

11   Leo Bersani, *The Freudian Body* (New York: Columbia University Press, 1986), pp. 62–3; emphasis in original.

12 Georges Bataille, *Erotism: Death and Sensuality*, trans. Mary Dalwood (San Francisco: City Lights Books, 1986), p. 17.

13 Bataille, *Erotism*, p. 17.

14 Bersani, 'Is the Rectum a Grave?', p. 218, footnote 25.

15 Bersani, *The Freudian Body*, p. 114.

16 Bataille, *Erotism*, p. 18.

17 Michel Foucault, *The Use of Pleasure* (New York: Vintage Books, 1986), pp. 72–7.

18 Cited by Bernard-Henri Levy, 'Foucault: Non au sexe roi', *Le Nouvel Observateur*, 12 March 1977, p. 98, trans. David M. Halperin, *Saint Foucault* (New York and Oxford: Oxford University Press, 1995), p. 78.

19 James Miller, *The Passion of Michel Foucault* (New York: Simon & Schuster, 1993).

20 Aiskhines, *Prosecution of Timarkhos*, cited by K. J. Dover, *Greek Homosexuality* (London: Duckworth, 1978), p. 20.

21 Dover, *Greek Homosexuality*, p. 106.

22 Ibid., p. 104.

23 Foucault, *The Use of Pleasure*, p. 215

24 Bersani, 'Is the Rectum a Grave?', p. 211; emphasis in original.

25 Ibid., p. 212.

26 Leo Bersani, *Homos* (Cambridge, Mass. and London: Harvard University Press, 1995), p. 164; my emphasis added.

27 In *The Use of Pleasure* Foucault notes Plato's reluctance to describe proscribed sexual acts, instead offering euphemisms such as 'to grant one's favors' or 'to do the thing', and claims that 'the Greeks would have found it improper that someone would call by name, in a set speech, things that were only vaguely alluded to even in polemics and law court addresses', p. 209. Conversely, Dover cites a wealth of ceramic illustrations and inscriptions representing homosexual acts, as well as literary examples such as Theocritus's lines in which the goatherd Kamatos recalls to the shepherd Lakon, 'Don't you remember when I got stuck into you and you grinned and moved your tail to and fro very nicely and held on to that oak-tree?' – *Greek Homosexuality*, p. 104.

28 Dover moves out of the Greek to observe that 'Vulgar idiom in many languages uses "buggered" or "fucked" in the sense "defeated", "worsted"', *Greek Homosexuality*, p. 105. And describing the political philosophy of Catharine MacKinnon, Drucilla Cornell writes 'The female condition is the condition of subordination, what is manifested within it carries the taint of our violation. The "base" is that we are fucked; the superstructure, the ideology that we like

it.' *Beyond Accommodation* (New York and London: Routledge, 1991) p. 126.

29 Bersani, 'Is the Rectum a Grave?', pp. 212–13.

30 Catharine A. MacKinnon, *Feminism Unmodified: Discourses on Life and Law* (Cambridge, Mass. and London: Harvard University Press, 1987), p. 3 and p. 172, cited in 'Is the Rectum a Grave?', p. 213.

31 Bersani, 'Is the Rectum a Grave?', p. 215. See, for example, Andrea Dworkin, *Intercourse* (London: Secker & Warburg, 1987); emphasis in original.

32 Bersani, 'Is the Rectum a Grave?', p. 215.

33 Leo Bersani, *The Culture of Redemption* (Cambridge, Mass. and London: Harvard University Press, 1990), p. 174.

34 Bersani, 'Is the Rectum a Grave?', p. 219.

35 Ibid., p. 221.

36 Jonathan Dollimore, 'Sex and Death', *Textual Practice* 9.1, 1995, p. 31.

37 The reference is not to Oscar, but to the term used in media discussions of the notorious 1988 attack on a woman jogger in New York's Central Park by a 'pack' of teenage boys. The term's linking of primitivism, violence and misogyny is discussed by Mark Seltzer in *Bodies and Machines* (New York and London: Routledge, 1992), p. 217, footnote 8.

38 Bersani, *The Freudian Body*, p. 24 and p. 42.

39 Bersani, *The Culture of Redemption*, p. 30.

40 Biddy Martin, 'Extraordinary Homosexuals and the Fear of Being Ordinary', in *Femininity Played Straight* (New York and London: Routledge, 1996), p. 46. The association of femininity with domesticity has, of course, its (ostensible) obverse, in which women are seen as closer to nature than men. For an account of the complexities of this presumption, see Sherry B. Ortner's famous article, 'Is Female to Male as Nature Is to Culture?' in Michelle Zimbalist Rosaldo and Louise Lamphere (eds), *Woman, Culture, and Society* (Stanford: Stanford University Press), 1974, pp. 67–87.

41 I am indebted to Naomi Segal for this observation. See also Carole-Anne Tyler, 'Boys Will Be Girls: The Politics of Gay Drag', in Diana Fuss (ed.), *Inside/Out* (New York and London: Routledge, 1991), p. 40: 'Gay men [in "Is the Rectum a Grave?"] are the better women, represented as better equipped to undo identity.'

42 Bersani, 'Is the Rectum a Grave?', p. 208.

43 Jonathan Dollimore, 'Desire Is Death', in M. de Grazia (ed.), *Material Culture in the Early Modern Period* (Cambridge: Cambridge University Press, 1996). p. 369.

44   Jonathan Dollimore, 'Sex and Death', *Textual Practice* 9:1, 1995, p. 27.

45   Ibid., p. 35.

46   Ibid., p. 48.

47   Ibid., p. 33.

48   Oscar Moore, *A Matter of Life and Sex* (first published in 1991 under the pseudonym Alec F. Moran by Paper Drum; subsequently London: Penguin Books, 1992). Moore's posthumous article, 'Rites of Fatality' (*Guardian* Weekend, 21 September 1996, pp. 16–23) is a virtual compendium of the themes under criticism here: gay men knowingly courting death through sex; fatality as the inevitable concomitant of pleasure; promiscuity as the cause of AIDS. In the typical style of the *memento mori*, it is illustrated with 'before' and 'after' pictures of the stricken author.

49   Rupert Haselden, 'Gay Abandon', *Guardian*, 7 September 1991, pp. 14–15.

50   Douglas Crimp, 'How to Have Promiscuity in an Epidemic', *October* 43, 1987, p. 253, footnote 17 in Dollimore, 'Sex and Death', pp. 50–1.

51   John Rechy, *The Sexual Outlaw* (London: W. H. Allen, 1978) p. 301, cited in Dollimore, 'Sex and Death', p. 31.

52   Dollimore, 'Sex and Death', p. 36.

53   Jeff Nunokawa, ' "All the Sad Young Men": AIDS and the Work of Mourning', in Diana Fuss (ed.), *Inside/Out* (New York and London, Routledge, 1991), p. 316.

54   Dollimore, 'Sex and Death', p. 27.

55   Ibid., p. 31.

56   Ibid., p. 32, citing Michael Rumaker, *A Day and Night at the Baths* (California: Grey Fox Press, 1979).

57   Dollimore, 'Sex and Death', p. 49.

58   The reference is to Paula A. Treichler, 'AIDS, Homophobia and Biomedical Discourse: An Epidemic of Signification', *October* 43, pp. 31–70.

59   Cyril Collard, *Savage Nights* (trans. William Rodarmor, London: Quartet Books, 1993), p. 8. The French original is *Les nuits fauves* (Paris, Flammarion, 1989).

60   Ibid., p. 12.

61   Ibid., p. 15.

62   Ibid., p. 53. See also p. 27: 'my savages are short, solid and muscular. They lean against walls, one leg bent, one foot flat against the cement, their slightly turned heads bowed, eyes looking up. Or, more rarely, they're girls, always in movement.' As this passage

suggests, 'girls' can be found on the wild side of this novel, so long as they're as exotic, juvenile and persecutory as Laura, with her endless scenes and answerphone threats, proves to be.

63   Ibid., p. 84.

64   Ibid., p. 8.

65   Ibid., p. 147.

66   On the correlation of male masochism and political dominance, see Kaja Silverman, 'White Skin, Brown Masks: The Double Mimesis, or with Lawrence in Arabia', in *Male Subjectivity at the Margins* (New York and London: Routledge, 1992).

67   Mandy Rose, quoted in Melissa Benn, 'Adventures in the Soho Skin Trade', *New Statesman*, 11 December 1987, p. 23; emphasis in original.

68   Cornell, *Beyond Accommodation*, p. 152.

69   Ibid., p. 153.

70   MacKinnon, *Feminism Unmodified*, p. 39, cited in Cornell, *Beyond Accommodation*, p. 154.

71   Wendy Brown, *States of Injury: Power and Freedom in Late Modernity* (Princeton: Princeton University Press, 1995), pp. 90–1.

72   Bersani, *Homos*, p. 64.

73   Bersani, 'Is the Rectum a Grave?', p. 218.

74   Carole-Anne Tyler, 'Boys Will Be Girls', p. 40, argues that in 'Is the Rectum a Grave?' 'promiscuous anal sex has exactly a phallicizing function, swelling the ego of the theoretical impersonator (as "feminine masochist") at the expense of women.' Kaja Silverman, in *Male Subjectivity at the Margins*, p. 350, claims that 'for Bersani . . . the defining feature of the gay man is that he narcissistically loves the phallic attributes of other m ale bodies.' Finally, in 'The Psychoanalysis of AIDS', *October* 63, Winter 1993, p. 114, Tim Dean maintains that 'Is the Rectum a Grave?' paradoxically re-enshrines 'the gay ego as an agent of mastery' . . . '[A]ny appeal to the ego, even an appeal for it to solicit its own shattering, must count as a nonpsychoanalytic solution, for in seeking to eliminate the significance of the unconscious, Bersani's recommendation implicitly advocates a redemption of subjectivity – if not selfhood – as such.'

75   Guy Hocquenghem, *Homosexual Desire* (London: Allison & Busby, 1978), p. 89. See also Eve Kosofsky Sedgwick, 'A Poem Is Being Written', *Tendencies* (London: Routledge, 1994), p. 204 (emphasis in original): 'Although there is no reason to suppose that women experience, in some imaginary quantitative sense "less" anal eroticism than men do, it can as far as I can determine almost be said

as a flat fact that, since classical times, *there has been no important and sustained Western discourse in which women's anal eroticism means*. Means anything.'

76 Bersani, 'Is the Rectum a Grave?', p. 211; emphasis in original.
77 Cora Kaplan, 'Wild Nights: Pleasure, Sexuality, Feminism', *Sea Changes: Culture and Feminism* (London: Verso, 1986), p. 34.
78 Mary Wollstonecraft, in Carol H. Poston (ed.), *A Vindication of the Rights of Women* (New York and London: W. W. Norton, second edition, 1988), p. 11.
79 Compare MacKinnon's *Toward a Feminist Theory of the State*, p. 130: 'So many distinctive features of women's status as second-class – the restriction and constraint and contortion, the servility and the display, the self-mutilation and requisite presentation of self as a beautiful thing, the enforced passivity, the humiliation – are made into the content of sex for women. Being a thing for sexual use is fundamental to it. This approach identifies not just a sexuality that is shaped under conditions of gender inequality but reveals this sexuality itself to be the dynamic of the inequality of the sexes.' With Mary Wollstonecraft, *A Vindication of the Rights of Women*, p. 117:. 'Every thing that they see or hear serves to fix impressions, call forth emotions, and associate ideas, that give a sexual character to the mind. False notions of beauty and delicacy stop the growth of their limbs and produce a sickly soreness, rather than delicacy of organs. . . . This cruel association of ideas, which every thing conspires to twist into all their habits of thinking, or, to speak with more precision, of feeling, receives new force when they begin to act a little for themselves; for they then perceive that it is only through their address to excite emotions in men that pleasure and power are to be obtained.'
80 Kaplan, 'Wild Nights', p. 56.
81 Ibid., p. 32.
82 See also Cora Kaplan, 'Pandora's Box: Subjectivity, Class and Sexuality in Socialist Feminist Criticism', *Sea Changes*, pp. 147–76.
83 Kaplan, 'Wild Nights', p. 55.
84 Bersani, *Homos*, p. 87.
85 Ibid., p. 90.
86 Ibid., p. 88.
87 Ibid., p. 89.
88 Ibid., p. 105, citing David M. Halperin, *One Hundred Years of Homosexuality and Other Essays on Greek Love* (New York: Routledge, 1990), p. 30.
89 Ibid., p. 106 (my italics). With the publication of Simon Goldhill,

Foucault's Virginity: Ancient Erotic Fiction and the History of Sexuality (Cambridge: Cambridge University Press, 1995), the absolutism of this ancient ordinance has been challenged. See James Davidson's review of Goldhill, 'Cures for Impotence', *London Review of Books*, 19 October 1995, p. 22, on Foucault's debt to Dover's citation of homosexually submissive positions in primate power relations: 'Even Foucault, who would not normally allow a monkey within a hundred miles of his philosophy, is quite happy to refer to Dover's bestiary as evidence for ancient attitudes to penetration. His followers have tended to follow suit, producing a curious blend of primatology and psychoanalysis, treating the penis as a transcendental signifier and reading the meanings of making love without reference to cultural conventions. A theory which claims to challenge universalising notions of sexuality depends on universalising interpretations of sex.' See, further, letters in response in the 2 November 1995, 30 November 1995, 14 December 1995, and 4 January 1996 issues of the *London Review of Books*.

90   Jacqueline Rose, *The Haunting of Sylvia Plath* (London: Virago, 1991). p. 209.

91   Ibid., p. 235.

92   Ibid., p. 235.

93   Bersani, *Homos*, pp. 106–7.

94   Ibid., p. 140.

95   Ibid., p. 59.

96   Sigmund Freud, 'From the History of an Infantile Neurosis' (1918), in *Case Histories II: The Pelican Freud Library, Volume 9* (Harmondsworth: Penguin Books, 1984), p. 327.

97   Freud, 'From the History of an Infantile Neurosis', p. 301.

98   Bersani, *Homos*, p. 112.

99   Bersani, 'Is the Rectum a Grave?', p. 222.

100 Any association of the phallus with an actual man risks the naturalization of male privilege which both Bersani and MacKinnon so constantly contest and concede.

101 For a discussion of Wilson's work, see Cherry Smyth, *Damn Fine Art* (London and New York: Cassell, 1996), pp. 109–13.

102 Winifred Woodhull, *Transfigurations of the Maghreb: Feminism, Decolonization and Literatures* (Minneapolis and London: University of Minnesota Press, 1993), p. 57.

103 Woodhull, *Transfigurations of the Maghreb*, p. 75.

104 Kaplan, 'The Indefinite Disclosed: Christina Rossetti and Emily Dickinson', *Sea Changes* (London: Verso, 1986), p. 112.

105 Wollstonecraft, *Vindication of the Rights of Woman*, p. 57.

Chapter 9

Coming Out of the Real: Knots and Queries

Elizabeth Wright

Just because we are subjects of language, why should it be 'somehow necessary to have a masculine and feminine', asks Gayle Rubin in the course of being interviewed by Judith Butler (p. 42 in this book). Well, if it is a question of aeons it is not necessary, but if a millennium, maybe it is. This chapter is an attempt to whittle away at the question of the binary division necessitated by the symbolic in its work on the real. The question raised will be to what degree distinctions upon which identities are founded in the present social field can be reoccupied. The theoretical approach adopted here inevitably has repercussions on the issues raised in this book about the historical relations among feminism, lesbian and gay studies, and queer theory. The articulations of desire within the actions of the subject always take place at the juncture of symbolic and real; without an analysis of this juncture no political position can be adequately accounted for.

The Real

The real is at once the curse and glory of any system, since it is both the possibility of holding such systems in place and of changing them. So much, both philosophy and psychoanalysis would agree on. In the academic discourse the real often emerges as conflated with 'reality' – the mundane world – whereas the 'real' is the ground from which reality and its objects are selected, 'out' of which they 'come'. Hence Lacan will distinguish what *exists* (mundane reality) from what *ex-sists*, 'stands outside' (the real). Lacan borrows and adapts two terms from Aristotle: *automaton* as 'the insistence of the signs', the dominance of the symbolic; *tuché* as 'the encounter with the real', that which undermines the existence of signs (Lacan, 1977b [1964], pp. 53–4). For Lacan the real is beyond and behind the *automaton*, the ontic, the mundane, the taken-for-granted, while *tuché* is the ontological, which may save us because it undoes the fixity of the sign. For the philosopher, in the wake of Heraclitus, the real is the continuum, the river which is not identical with itself and hence in which you never step twice. For the psychoanalyst the relation of repetition to the real is not inspirational in the same way, and certainly not as exhilarating. The relation of repetition to the real can be seen in the psychoanalytical transference: 'what is repeated, in fact, is always something that occurs – the expression [occurs] tells us quite a lot about its relation to the *tuché – as if by chance* (ibid., p. 54). Lacan here speaks of a 'missed encounter', an oxymoron which brings together, on one side, the underlying being of experience (the 'encounter') and, on the other, the fact that it is not understood. It is not recognized because it is unrepresentable, unassimilable, and yet it is precisely this which triggers the repetitions. 'Is it not remarkable,' asks Lacan, 'that, at the origin of the analytic experience, the real should have presented itself in the form of that which is unassimilable in it – in the form of the trauma determining all that follows, and imposing on it an apparently accidental origin?' (p. 55). It is the task of analysis to discover how the real gets caught up in the machinic repetitions, geared as they are to the Other's expectations.

The real is only ever experienced. It is what concepts, percepts, words apply to, not in any way what they are. Therefore any separation produced by the symbolic (*a fortiori* in the earliest moments) will break into the chaotic experience of the infant and produce shock. To 'miss' the encounter is to fail to grasp the brute experience. Because the symbolic is unable to secure it, it seems to present itself as '*Nothing, perhaps? – not perhaps nothing*' but *not nothing*' (p. 64), which is as much as to say, the experience in itself must be regarded as a part of being and therefore as a positive. The symbolic works upon the real by means of repetition, but never turns into it: 'reality is in abeyance there, awaiting attention [*en souffrance*]' (p. 56). Mundane reality awaits construction out of the real, at the behest of pleasure and pain. However, the construction is not something that can be wholly altered at the whim of a subject; the historicity of the symbolic itself has a brute aspect. Although the symbolic inevitably founders on the rock of the real, there is also a sense in which, contingently, the symbolic is itself a rock.

Sexual Difference

In the Freudian universe of discourse sexual difference is neither reduced to a biological given nor wholly constituted by social practices. A great conceptual difficulty for psychoanalysis, but also a central part of its theoretical importance for feminism, is its tenet, now reduced to a cliché, that anatomy alone does not determine sexual identity, since the latter is a matter of identifications. Neither can sexual difference be reduced to the social alone even though the child's identification with one or the other sex is both variable and subject to social convention. So, if male/female sexualities are not essential categories and masculine/feminine not just historical constructs, what creates sexual difference?

For Freud it was the meaning ascribed to anatomical differences, of male and female sexual organs, when interpreted in terms of presence and absence. As a consequence neither sex is complete: males suffer from castration anxiety, females from penis envy. This part of the Freudian doctrine has produced much incredulity and offence because it invited and still invites so literal an interpretation. Lacan, by considering psychoanalysis as a sexuation process, takes psychoanalysis a step further. But his theory of sexuation, the origin and development of sexual difference within the field of language, has really not fared much better. Initially hailed for its decisive turn from biology-as-destiny to the constitution of the subject in language, his theory all too soon lost its popularity with feminists of all kinds as his various statements on Woman and the emphasis on the phallus as signifier of difference in his earlier work became as contentious as Freud's several treatises on femininity and his pronouncements on penis envy. Until recently not a great deal of Lacan's work has been available in translation, and hence critical comment in the Anglophone world was largely restricted to the essays from the fifties in the *Écrits*, particularly his essay, 'The Signification of the Phallus' (Lacan, 1977a [1958]; see, for instance, Silverman, 1992).

Crucial to a proper understanding of Lacan's revision of Freud on sexuality are the sexuation formulas (Lacan 1975 [1972–3], chapters 6 and 7, translated in Mitchell and Rose, 1982, as chapter 6). When Lacan is upbraided for privileging the phallic signifier (e.g., Grosz, 1990; Silverman, 1992; Butler, 1993), these formulas of the later Lacan are rarely taken up by his detractors, yet without them it is hard to counter the almost universal accusations of phallocentrism that are levelled against him. In his first theory of sexuality in the 1950s, Lacan, taking his cue from Freud, did centre on the function of the phallus as distinguishing between the sexes, seeing the man as wanting *to have* the phallus, the woman as wanting *to be* the phallus, which does not imply at all that the two sexes can be seen as complementary since masculinity and femininity, as will be seen, rely on completely different dynamics. Although the being/having dichotomy gives two clear types of sexual position, this indicates no more than two imaginary modes of identification by means of which each sex wards off castration. 'Waiving the phallus' (Adams, 1992), rather than waving it, is the fate of man and woman alike.

The Aporias of Sexuality

The formulas show each side as embodying an existential and a universal proposition which are in a contradictory relation to each other. In each case there is a failure of the symbolic, but it is a different failure for each sex; the failure is a question of the degree to which *jouissance*, the satisfaction of drive, is accommodated for each sex within a given symbolic system. Lacan uses symbols from a modified form of the predicate calculus as he is dealing with the application of binary definitions to a hitherto disorganized part of existence, the distinguishing of entities in sets being common to language, mathematics and sexual difference, to all three of which the Laws of Thought (the guarantee of binaries in speech) apply. The logic of sexuation divides the field of speaking beings in two (figure 9.1): in the top half of the formula there are four propositions, two existential ($\exists$) and two universal ($\forall$).

The male existential ($\exists x\ \overline{\phi x}$) can be rendered as 'there is an entity x that says "no" to the phallic function'; the male universal ($\forall x\ \phi x$) as 'all x's are subject to the phallic function'.

On the female side there are two contrasting propositions: the female existential ($\overline{\exists x\ \phi x}$), 'there is no entity x that says "no" to the phallic function'; the female universal ($\overline{\forall x}\ \phi x$) 'not all of x are subject to the phallic function'.

The phallic function (ϕ) is the castration performed by the symbolic. As a product of this procedure the (imaginary) phallus comes to signify the prohibited *jouissance* – the greater part of drive satisfaction that is forbidden to all subjects. This is the sacrifice demanded of men and women alike for entry into the symbolic, for the very assumption of subjecthood.

On the male side there is an attempt to identify with the phallus, that is, to imagine oneself as the master who issues the prohibitions, but the universal proposition states that all men fall under the phallic function, that is, must submit to symbolic castration. However, this rule is guaranteed by virtue of an exception, namely the existential proposition, that there is one man who is exempt. For Lacan, this exception to the rule is linked to the primal father in Freud's *Totem and Taboo*, who had made no sacrifice of his *jouissance*. We can take this to represent the illusion upon which the symbolic works, namely that in the last analysis *jouissance* will

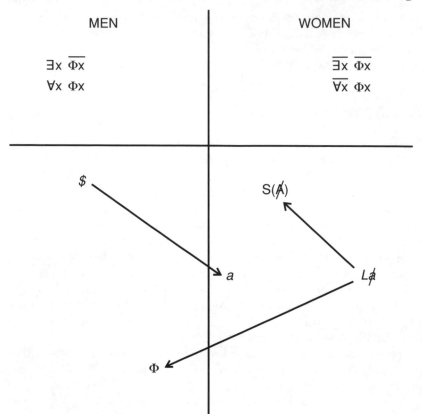

be returned in full. This position is one that all subjects could briefly,
transiently occupy, in that everyone has the opportunity *to be before the
law*, in the sense of Kafka's 'man from the country' (Kafka, 1970 [1935],
pp. 131–2) who might have gone through the door that was demarcated
for him, or, as in Kant's categorical imperative, the position is that the
universal law might be promulgated by the subject alone (Kant, 1966
[1797], p. 94).

The universal proposition on the female side is to be read as 'not all of
woman is subject to the phallic function', i.e. falls under the law of the
signifier. This does not mean she is 'not at all' in the symbolic, but that
there is no universal affirmation possible on the side of women. The
existential proposition states that every woman is at least partially defined
by the phallic function and this implies that there is some part of the
existence of woman which escapes the symbolic, 'a *jouissance* proper to
her and of which she herself may know nothing, except that she experi-

ences it – that much she does know' (Lacan, in Mitchell and Rose, 1982, p. 145). This gives woman a possibility in addition to the pursuit of the phallus, as is shown in the lower half of the sexuation formulas. The other option is S(Å), which, according to Lacan, 'designates nothing other than the *jouissance* of the woman' (ibid., p. 154). 'S' stands for 'signifier'; (Å) for the barred Other, the gap or lack in the Other: together, S(Å), they mean that 'there is a signifier of the very impossibility of signifying' (Leader and Groves, 1995, p. 118), in other words, woman has a direct relation to what lies as unsignifiable outside the symbolic. L̸a (Th̸e) is crossed through because 'it is by being constituted as not all that they are placed within the phallic function' (Lacan, in Mitchell and Rose, 1982, p. 144); that is to say, that the only way the symbolic can encompass them is by admitting its failure to capture them. From this erasure Lacan moves to his aphorism, 'There is no such thing as *The* woman' (ibid.). She is radically Other, though not acknowledged as such, because she cannot signify this part of herself in the symbolic. Not all of woman comes under the law of the signifier.

The Aporias of Reason

In her ground-breaking essay, 'Sex and the Euthanasia of Reason', Joan Copjec (1994) undertakes a defence of Lacan against those feminists who see in the sexuation formulas proof that the phallus (as symbolic index) determines both sexes, and that all difference is reduced to the possession or non-possession of it. What they fail to see is that there is a mismatch between the two sides: the phallic function (the process of castration) does not produce complementarity between the two sexes, they do not have a complementary relation, which, in Lacan's views, is an imaginary one.

Copjec uses Lacan's sexuation formulas and Kant's distinction in *The Critique of Pure Reason* (Kant, 1964 [1781]) between the mathematical and the dynamical antinomies of reason to argue that 'Kant was the first to theorize, by means of this distinction, the difference that founds psychoanalysis's division of all subjects into two mutually exclusive classes: male and female' (p. 213). What arises from this is that in both Kant and Lacan she discerns the aporia that bedevils the attempt to use at the same time totalizing and particularizing terms.

The fact that reason has various modes of failure arises from the attempt to bring the real, which lies outside ideal law, under such an ideal law. It is significant that the two antinomies that Copjec selects from Kant are precisely those in which there is an attempt to bring continua, which have nothing discrete, nothing countable about them, under a system which requires the counting of separate units, a placing of limits or boundaries which can be marked by a binary division, a yes/no, a positive/negative. This attempt to count from a continuum is the reason why Kant calls this antinomy 'mathematical'.

In the mathematical antinomy, the continua Kant takes up are those of time and space. The first antinomy arises by reason's attempt to assert that these two propositions are both true: 1. the world has no beginning in time and no limit in space, i.e., they are both infinite; 2. the world has a beginning in time and a limit in space, i.e. they are both finite. Each of these propositions can be developed to prove the falsity of the other, but their own truth cannot be proved. According to Kant this shows that the two propositions are not contradictories exclusively dividing up all that is the case, but that there is a third possibility, that the continua they refer to are neither finite nor infinite, but *non-existent*, that is, they cannot be thought of as things-in-themselves simultaneously at the level of a totality and as an endless series. In Lacanian terms, this is as much as to say that the real cannot be confined to the binary divisions of the symbolic, or that language is unable to capture being.

In common with Slavoj Žižek (1993), Copjec aligns the mathematical antinomy with the female side of Lacan's sexuation formula and the dynamical to the male.

In the case of the female/mathematical, the application of symbolic language to sexuality in the case of woman has precisely the same logical pattern as Kant's rival propositions. In both Lacan's and Kant's analyses, 1. there does not exist an entity which does not fall under the predicate [$\overline{\exists x}$ $\overline{\phi x}$]; and 2. not all entities fall under the predicate [$\forall x\ \phi x$].

For Kant this is to say 1. the world has a beginning in time and is limited in space; 2. the world has no beginning in time and has no limits in space.

For Lacan 1. there is no entity x that does not fall under the phallic law; 2. not all of woman is subjected to the phallic function.

In both, reason is failing in exactly the same way in its attempt to impose a binary on what is metaphysically resistant to it – for Kant intuition (or phenomena), for Lacan the real.

In the case of the male/dynamical antinomy Copjec draws a similar parallel between Kant and Lacan. This concerns much more immediately the process of identification in a subject because it deals with the apparent contradiction between a pure freedom on the one hand and a strict determinism on the other. Kant calls this the 'dynamical' antinomy because it deals with moral action in the world. In Kant's terms the two propositions are that there must be a causality of freedom outside the laws of nature and that there is no such thing as freedom since everything happens according to the laws of nature. Again it is a question of something resistant to language: namely, a decision which reorders or adjusts the laws being apparently subjected to those very laws. As before, this appears to be a contradiction, but Kant claims that his analysis of moral action shows that there is a third possibility, as was the case with the mathematical antinomy. In this case it is that the subject, in making a moral choice, applies what Kant calls a transcendental law of practical reason, thereby initiating a new law, one applying to all other subjects. This is his categorical imperative, an act of good will. The parallel with Lacan here is, paradoxically, that an ethical act must be one which takes account of 'not having given ground relative to one's desire' (Lacan, 1992 [1959–60], p. 319).

As with the female/mathematical parallel Copjec reveals the same logical structure between the male side of Lacan's formula and Kant's dynamical antinomy. In both Kant's and Lacan's analyses 1. there is an entity x to which the predicate does not apply [$\exists x \overline{\Phi x}$]; 2. all entities fall under the predicate ($\forall x\ \Phi x$].

For Kant 1. a causality of freedom is operative which does not fall under the laws of nature; 2. everything in the world happens according to the laws of nature.

For Lacan 1. there is an entity x that says 'no' to the phallic function; 2. all x's are subject to the phallic function.

In both cases, the application of a law is circumvented by the ability to promulgate the law oneself.

A further point to be made here is that it is significant that, *from reason's point of view*, the dynamical antinomy which deals centrally with how the law comes to be promulgated is logically associated with the male side of the formula; whereas the mathematical antinomy which deals with the attempt simultaneously to limit being and to extend it infinitely is logically associated with the female side, looked upon as a continuum subject to male definition. Lacan's point is, as was Kant's, that these two efforts of reason at definition fail in different ways. The two 'third possibilities' found in both the mathematical/female and dynamical/male antinomies coincide, because each signally indicates the irruption of the real of the subject within the symbolic.

For Copjec and psychoanalysis, sex lies at the point of contradiction that arises in reason itself. The symbolic operates by presupposing a logical totality and then working in such a way as to deny it in yielding new meanings to new desires. Sex is not something to be thought of 'complete' or 'incomplete', but rather empty of such categorizations: 'sexual difference . . . is a real and not a symbolic difference' (p. 207). This is not a return to the biological. Speaking of 'sex' here is a way of acknowledging the historically sedimented structure of male and female out of which subjects come into being and which has to deal with recalcitrant drives that keep the subject inside and outside this binary structure. One cannot get out of it, nor does one need to, since cultural discourses are perpetually changing and the subject is bound to participate in them as a potentially subversive element, and this includes subjects of all sexual orientations. It is at this point I cannot align myself with that aspect of feminist and queer theory in which this opportunity appears not to be recognised.

The structuralist view was that the sum total of signifiers determined the meaning of any one of them through its differential effects: *la langue* has to be presupposed as complete, since, unless there is a systematic totality of signifiers, there can be no determination of meaning. The post-structuralist enterprise emphasizes, on the other hand, the inevitability of diachronic movement through *la parole*. As signifiers shift so will the boundaries of the signified. Linguists criticizing Saussure have pointed out that every new use of a signifier will change its meaning, even infini-tesimally. Nevertheless, it is obvious that there are categories which, though their boundaries may blur, have an historically established ground which is resistant to fundamental change, this being the contingently brute aspect of the symbolic (Lacan's *automaton*).

It is on this point that Joan Copjec takes issue with Judith Butler. She argues that Butler deduces from the instability of the terms of sexual difference the instability of sex. According to Copjec, language, as soon as it is applied to sex, falls immediately into contradiction, because sex is itself 'the impossibility of completing meaning' (p. 206). By this she means that sex is linked to those conflicts of reason which she has demonstrated as common to Lacan's sexuation formulas and Kant's antinomies. To the extent that sex is bound up in the primary constitution of the subject (at the level of primary repression) it has a different function from other binary signifiers, such as race and class (which are inescapable at the level of secondary repression; for another antinomy see the present debate about hate speech, Salecl, 1996 and Butler, 1997). Copjec argues that Butler, in ignoring this crucial function, has placed a lop-sided emphasis on the diachronic movement of the signifier and has assumed that sex is discursively or culturally constructed (pp. 203–4). She acknowledges that Butler neither wants to make the subject entirely determined nor does she want to take up a purely voluntarist position in which the subject is entirely free to choose its own identity: nevertheless, Butler does not bring into her theory the contradictions inherent in every discursive practice. This amounts to a disregard of the real, for, unless the real is given a place within the theory, there can be no explanation of a subject's agency located 'on the same level as language' neither 'below', wholly determined, nor 'above', wholly choosing (Butler, 1990, p. 145, cited by Copjec), a good general metaphor for what goes on in the social field.

Although within the sexuation formulas one may change one's sexual position, one cannot change the positions of the formulas. Copjec's conclusion is that 'from the standpoint of culture *sex does not budge*' (p. 210), in that a contemporary cultural agency can have no purchase on such a foundational element in the construction of the subject as sex, this being the brute contingency of the symbolic. Freud, Copjec points out, insisted that sex had to be apprehended in the terrain of the drives (produced out of the polymorphous state of the infant by the workings of the symbolic on the body) and not that of culture, even though sex does not exist outside it.

Knots

More recently Butler (1993) has returned to the knot of determinism-versus-voluntarism by grappling with the relation between performativity and the materiality of the body. No freely choosing Cartesian ego, securely sexed, is performing its gender in the Austinian mode; nor is it the case that the hegemony of culture has produced a passive agent. We can only agree that 'construction not only takes place *in* time, but is itself a temporal process which operates through the reiteration of norms; sex is both produced and destabilized in the course of this reiteration' (1993, p. 10).

The knot here lies in producing a theory that, on the one hand, explains how a reiteration can be destabilized and, on the other, how it is avoiding the accusation of voluntarism. Too constructivist an approach neglects 'the body that matters': a too voluntarist one ignores the symbolic system that is required to inscribe a subject in the first place, this being the structure Copjec noted as common to the sexuation formulas and Kant's dynamical antinomy.

Performativity under the Austinian reading places an ideal fixity upon what is performed: Austin uses the metaphor 'felicity' of an appropriate performance without either questioning the pure legality of the act or realizing that his use of 'felicity' indirectly acknowledges the part played by a subject's desire in the establishment of a norm. In the case of an established performative (such as the 'I do' of the marriage service) he only considers the criteria as already laid down by the norms that govern the act: the act is 'infelicitous' if those public criteria are being ignored (for example, in the Austinian view, as uttered by a lesbian?). Butler goes beyond Austin for she wants her performativity to allow for novel interpretations to intrude upon and recategorize the norm being enacted. Her intent in this is to allow the renewal of the criteria of sexual difference to take place without a prior delimitation by the existing patriarchal system, even to the questioning of the binary division of two given sexes. She is right to claim that a radical view of democracy must make salient the possibility of altering the criteria of application of a binary, that, in particular, women must refuse the ideal descriptions that a rigid notion of the existing symbolic would impose; and, further, that identity itself must be open to continual redefinition. These are indeed the sites of political and ethical contest.

Butler turns to Derrida (1991, [1972] p. 80) for the notion of 'citationality'. In considering performativity, Derrida points out that, when a subject performs an act that derives its constitutive character from that very performance, two elements come into play, the derived will of the first legislator and the actual will of the subject performing. He uses the metaphor of *citing* because, when someone cites another, the thought comes in a new context via a new speaker who adds a new connotation that shifts denotation. Hence a real element in the present alters meaning even though the letter of the law has been scrupulously adhered to. Citation will thus fit the performance of a norm, be it a question of language or sexuality. Yet although Butler has correctly characterized the dual nature of a norm's performance, this metaphor of citation, on which she wholly relies, does not undo the knot of the determinist/voluntarist problem. Moreover, even though she addresses the circumstances in which the real appears, she fails to recognize a direction that can be found in Lacan, namely, that the realignment of the symbolic comes out of the real.

With many feminists she declares war on the phallus as master-signifier, because, even though they may well recognise that 'phallus' is here used figuratively instead of literally (the penis), they still find objectionable the use of the figure derived from that bit of a man's body. Although there are good historical reasons for the use of the term 'phallus' inasmuch as the phallus has played the role of penis in the cultural fantasies and imagination of the West, from, for example, the Dionysian mysteries to the fantasies revealed in early psychoanalytical case-histories, the algebraic signs of the sexuation formulas cannot be given a signified which can be culturally monopolized. In these formulas it becomes evident that the phallic function applies in different ways to both sexes, that neither sex can have or be everything. In each case there is a failure with respect to the symbolic: woman's failure is with the signifier and man's failure is with the object. The man, posturing as the one who lacks nothing, pursues a fantasy by which means he attempts to totalize the woman as the absolute Other; the woman is tempted into a 'masquerade', a performative act in which she tries to become the fantasy for the man. Both attempts are a denial of lack and both fail because of the invasion of the real into the symbolic. The real also makes its presence known within the sexuation formulas in providing women with a supplementary jouissance that the historical male symbolic does not recognise. Thus, the logic of sexuation produces two kinds of speaking being that are not in a complementary relation to each other. The two pursuits are incompatible, 'one does not make up for what is lacking in the other' (Copjec, 1994, p. 234). Each sex is lacking but it is not a penis they lack, even though it is used as a metaphor, 'stands' for the phallic function, that which enjoins the separation that constitutes a subject.

Queries

Copjec's linking of Kant's antinomies with Lacan's formulas has been seen as undermining queer theorists' attempts and those of some feminists to deconstruct social norms and to historicize sexual difference by positing 'a formal law guaranteed by (sexually differentiated) limits to pure reason' (Martin, 1991, p. 21), a logical argument against queer theory. However, Copjec has produced a philosophical argument, based on the materiality of the real, on the very failure of a formal law; the discourse of sexuality and gender cannot escape the relation of word to world, concept to being.

In her essay 'Critically Queer' Judith Butler (1993) considers how a term 'that signalled degradation has been turned – "refunctioned in the Brechtian sense" – to signify a set of new and affirmative meanings' (p. 223). Butler's 'citationality' here becomes 'creative' in resisting terms of identity that constrain and pathologize. But what is the source of creative citation if not the real? The Lacanian real is much nearer to Butler's own 'materiality' base than she would have it. If the real is indeed that within which subjects carry out the performances that the symbolic has provided, then, as Lacan and Kant have shown, it will cross the binary unexpectedly within these constitutive reiterations. What is not alterable, from Lacan's point of view, is the structure that is currently existing. This makes the symbolic something of a Kantian regulatory idea in that it is a necessary guide rather than a necessary enforcement. This is the burden of Copjec's dictum 'Sex will not budge', which does not imply that a homosexuality cannot be positioned within the sexuation formulas. The formulas do not plot which sexual position a subject may take up; they are not hetero-sexuation formulas. What the formulas reveal are the historical limits of the possibility of change, not a particular subject's object-choice. Over aeons a hermaphroditic society may arise (Rubin, p. 43 of this book), but to be capable of speech it will still use a binary of some kind on which to base the emergence of identity, perhaps making its key distinction pre-pubertal and post-pubertal, allowing for Lacanian 'pubertation' formulas. A pre-pubertal could chiasmically inscribe itself as post-pubertal without displacing the symbolic relations of the formula.

Butler fights on the feminist objection to the phallus as the structuring principle of the symbolic by wittily figuring it as detached from the body, as 'the lesbian phallus' (Butler, 1993, pp. 57–91). She praises it for its mobility, for having a 'plastic transferable property', believing this to destabilize the distinction between being and having the phallus' (p. 63). But this mobility can only produce effects if there is a firm ground over which it can move. An overflow of the real cannot be detected if there is no line over which it can flow. This implies that 'the straight lines of all the binaries' (Introduction, p. 4, in this book), if mobility is to invest them, have to be performatively maintained as if they cannot be 'unravelled'. A radical democracy is concerned with the subversion rather than the uprooting of laws. Although sexuality is one law which is embodied in speaking beings, it is nevertheless possible to query it.

The sexuation formulas offer the basis for a complete re-shaping of traditional standard notions of homo- and heterosexuality. For Lacan these formulas are concerned with how a speaking being experiences sexuality on the level of the psyche. They have nothing to do with biological sex, neither with the love of a man for a woman, nor that of a man for a man, nor that of a woman for a woman. This implies that a biological male can function according to the female side and a biological female according to the male. Following this line of reasoning a Lacanian feminism would imply a fundamental recognition of the singularity of the feminine element: in this sense you could have a grouping across the categories of feminine/masculine/lesbian/gay/queer which might be politically active for whatever changes it wishes to promulgate. One of these might well be to allow for the emergence of a new 'master-signifier' to stand for the limitation of *jouissance*. It is as well to remember though, that any kind of categorization is in danger of lending itself to a new form of hierarchical totalization.

Acknowledgements

I would like to thank the following for their helpful and constructive critical comments: Wayne Barron, Russell Grigg, Dany Nobus, Juliet Flower MacCannell, Ken Reinhart, Emma Wilson and Edmond Wright.

References

Adams, Parveen 1992: Waiving the phallus. *differences*, 4:1, 78–83.
Butler, Judith 1990: *Gender Trouble: Feminism and the Subversion of Identity*. New York and London: Routledge.

——1993: *Bodies that Matter: On the Discursive Limits of "Sex"*. New York and London: Routledge.

——1997: */Excitable Speech/ A Politics of the Performative*. New York and London: Routledge.

Copjec, Joan 1994: Sex and the euthanasia of reason. In Joan Copjec, *Read my Desire: Lacan against the Historicists*. Cambridge, Mass.: MIT Press, 201–36.

Derrida, Jacques 1991 [1972]: Signature Event Context. In Peggy Kamuf (ed.), *A Derrida Reader: Between the Blinds*. New York and London: Harvester-Wheatsheaf, 80–111.

Grosz, Elizabeth 1990: *Jacques Lacan: A Feminist Introduction*. New York and London: Routledge.

Kafka, Franz 1970 [1935]: 'Vor dem Gesetz'. In *Sämtliche Erzählungen*, Frankfurt-am-Main: Fischer Verlag, pp. 131–2.

Kant, Immanuel 1964 [1781]: *The Critique of Pure Reason*. Trans. and ed. Norman Kemp Smith. London and New York: Macmillan.

—— 1966 [1797]: *The Moval Law: Kant's Groundwork of the Metaphysic of Morals*. Ed. H. J. Paton. London: Hutchinson.

Lacan, Jacques 1975: *Encore: Le séminaire XX, 1972–73*. Paris: Seuil.

——1977a [1958]: The signification of the phallus. In Jacques Lacan, *Écrits: A Selection*, trans. Alan Sheridan. London: Tavistock Publications, 281–91.

——1977b [1964]: *Tuché* and *Automaton*. In Jacques Lacan, *The Four Fundamental Concepts of Psycho-Analysis*, Jacques-Alain Miller (ed.), trans. Alan Sheridan. London: The Hogarth Press and The Institute of Psycho-Analysis, 53–64.

——1992: *The Ethics of Psychoanalysis, 1959–1960: The Seminar of Jacques Lacan*, Jacques-Alain Miller (ed.), trans. Dennis Porter. London: Tavistock and Routledge.

Leader, Darian and Groves, Judy 1995: *Lacan for Beginners*. Cambridge: Icon Books.

Martin, Biddy (1997): *Femininity Played Straight: The Significance of Being Lesbian*. London and New York: Routledge.

Mitchell, Juliet and Rose, Jacqueline 1982: *Jacques Lacan and the école freudienne: Feminine Sexuality*. London and Basingstoke: Macmillan.

Salecl, Renata 1996: See no evil, speak no evil: Hate speech and human rights. In Joan Copjec (ed.), *Radical Evil*. London and New York: Verso, 150–68.

Silverman, Kaja 1992: The Lacanian phallus. *differences*, 4:1, 84–115.

Žižek, Slavoj 1993: *Cogito* and the sexual difference. In Slavoj Žižek, *Tarrying with the Negative: Kant, Hegel and the Critique of Ideology*. Durham, North Carolina: Duke University Press, 45–80.

Index